On Judging Books

On
Judging Books

IN GENERAL
AND IN PARTICULAR

Francis Hackett

Essay Index Reprint Series

BOOKS FOR LIBRARIES PRESS
FREEPORT, NEW YORK

INTERNATIONAL STANDARD BOOK NUMBER:
0-8369-2400-2

LIBRARY OF CONGRESS CATALOG CARD NUMBER:
79-156657

PRINTED IN THE UNITED STATES OF AMERICA

To
Pearl and Dick

Acknowledgments

I wish to thank Mr. Harrison Smith for kind permission to reprint "The Monkey and the Sun," "In Search of an Idiom," and a review of *The Great Conspiracy*. These appeared in the *Saturday Review of Literature*. I owe thanks to Mr. Henry Goddard Leach of the *American-Scandinavian Review* for the Blicher review, and to Mr. Arthur Hays Sulzberger, publisher of the *New York Times*, for permission to reprint all of the rest, with the exception of the Introduction, and the articles on James Thurber, James Joyce, and Nietzsche.

Contents

In General

Introduction

I

CLIFTON FADIMAN has put my theme in one straight affirmation: "A literary critic is a whole man exercizing his wholeness through the accidental medium of books and authors."

It is inseparable from the understanding of book criticism that we take it as part of the whole activity. To judge a book, no matter how, is to belong to the humanist group, and out of this group stem a craft and a profession. The book critic may be as casual as a fly, but his particular attitude has little bearing on the craft itself. Fundamentally the man who judges books is a man of letters, essential to a society like our own. Our civilization cannot possibly be sound without men of letters, and to judge books pertains strictly to its self-direction and its sane continued existence.

Does anyone who thinks of Europe's dead cities today need to be reminded how its mind was first perverted? Modern society could not be perverted so long as there was political freedom, and political freedom cannot operate without the printing press. Before the war a Nazi official led a friend of mine into a room with filing cabinets and said, "In these files we have the dossiers of every newspaperman in Germany. It doesn't matter how young he is, or how obscure his paper is. The minute he writes the least article or editorial, signed or unsigned, we find out who he is, and if he shows any promise we take him in hand. We call him to Berlin, discover what training he needs, send him abroad, and see that he studies. In that way!" In that way, naturally, there would be nothing to fear from him.

Revolutions do not start in bomb factories. They start in inkpots. The government that looks into the minds of its writers, as Germany did and as Russia does, deliberately calculates the ferment of criticism, and by politically directing, controlling, or destroying its men of letters the roots of freedom are killed. Every country is aware of this. In New York there are powerful publishers who kill books for political reasons, and it is open to any student to learn from newspaper files how the early writings of revolutionaries were belittled or boycotted. Democratic societies have a collection of epithets for the gadflies that torment them—troublemakers, soreheads, reds, pinks, reactionaries, bolshies—but when a dictatorship comes to grips with the tradition of freedom, it doesn't feint, it exterminates the independent men of letters. From this single fact we can measure their root importance. Little or much as we may think of them individually, they have to be recognized as the one group indispensable to what can roughly be called our humanist civilization. That they frequently abuse their authority is beside the point. The corrective is provided by free criticism. But author and critic must not be seen as separate. What is basic is the whole man out of whose assertion of judgment grows the humanism essential to our civilization. And when you look into it, the author-critic is to be seen as a familiar unit. Edgar Allan Poe, Walt Whitman, Henry James; Tolstoy and Dostoevsky; Baudelaire and Gide; Oscar Wilde, Shaw, Wells, Bennett, Chesterton; the list of literary men who have orientated as well as created, from Ben Jonson and Dryden and Goethe and Wordsworth down to Masefield and Yeats, Huxley and Eliot, is a list that reinforces the amphibian character of all letters. Specialists there are, and the more a critic refines, the more he judges, as does an expert at a dog show. Yet if he is a whole literary man, he is not a mere specialist. He is at one with the creative. He pursues freedom. Even from underground presses he has asserted it, during war and tyranny, because free art interweaves with free politics.

2

Having said this, I wish now to turn to the world we are living in, the world of literary guys, literary blokes, in all their urgent humanity. Lots of very queer people are in this writing business, and many of them crash down on the least suggestion that, for the most part, we do much more than earn a living.

In years gone by, when I ran across a highhanded author like George Moore, I was at once struck by the native barbarity of the man himself, in spite of his skill as a man of letters. It was Gerald O'Donovan, the gentle author of *Father Ralph*, who suggested in London that we should meet George Moore. O'Donovan telephoned Moore and then told us when to call at Ebury Street. My wife and I were naturally eager to greet the author of *Hail and Farewell*, who had really said farewell to Ireland when Moore Hall was burned down by a gang of partisans.

Moore himself opened the door and led us up narrow stairs to a charming, rather foppish sitting room. And at once he began, like a cat dipping its paw into the cream, "So you are an American publisher?"

His unction was evident, but what was I to say? I had fancied, poor fool, that we were meeting him because of things I had written. You never know. And here he was kindly granting me a business interview, into which I had introduced my loving family. That accounted for his having told the maid at the foot of the stairs, "They are to call for me in twenty minutes." So I said, "I'm not a publisher. My brother is a publisher."

"But you should be in business with your brother," he observed genially.

"Mr. Moore," I responded brightly, "that's strange from one who has written about a brother as you have."

Though he had baited Colonel Maurice Moore so publicly and mercilessly in *Hail and Farewell*, he did not visibly enjoy a reference to it. "If you are not a publisher," he inquired, "then what are you?"

"I'm a critic," I said.

"A critic?" he snapped. "There are no critics in America." That made me laugh. "It'll be news to Mencken," I said. "But if we are not critics, what are we?"

"Reviewers," he replied contemptuously. "Anybody can be a reviewer in six months."

3

This scorn for book reviewers, as against book critics, is a widespread feeling that has to be looked into, if, as I contend, the independent writer is really so indispensable for our civilization. Are we to say that criticism is part of a whole literary activity if book reviewing can be picked up in six months? And, if it is actually picked up in that time, can we give it weight? Or must we qualify our attitude toward wholeness?

Any clear look at American journalism in 1947 will leave no doubt about the mental squalor of book reviewers. They boom, they blurb, they boost, and nothing satisfies them but the superlative. "Epoch-making," "terrific," "another wonder book," "a triumph of art," "headlong power," "superbly written," "a major contribution," "should be in the hands of every student," "not since Tom Paine has there been such a clarion call," and so on, the gushers and the geysers.

Well, isn't it a local idiom? Isn't it wrong to be literal about it? When a leading reviewer in the Middle West said, "Frances Winwar is one of the truly great biographers of our time," he didn't seriously mean "a great biographer." "Truly great" weakens the simpler statement, as if one said "entirely sober" instead of "sober." "Of our time" waters the phrase, as does "one of the." But even dilution leaves it powerful strong. Evidently this reviewer meant to pin a medal on Miss Winwar, one of the truly great medals of our time. Well, what then? Isn't opinion free? Who is to keep us from proclaiming masterpieces?

The weary retort is to ask, "Is it feasible to stop it? It's publicity. Book reviewing is a racket." Or, in the politer words of Clifton Fadiman, "a device for earning a living."

Mr. Fadiman states the fact. Most book reviewing in all countries is oriented to bookselling, not literature. It parts company with literary considerations to become an adjunct of sales promotion, publicity, and money-making. This helps it to be a new device for earning a living.

Mr. Fadiman does not say a base device. He thinks that book reviewing serves the public as a sieve—"a generally honest, usually uninspired, and mildly useful sieve."

But are there not holes in this sieve, holes no bigger than a man's hand, through which the epoch-making and terrific books come tumbling? These holes allow judges, "usually uninspired," to pronounce verdicts, "generally honest," in a fashion that is "mildly useful." Apply the description to your dentist. Your teeth are important? How is your mind? Mr. Fadiman thinks reviewing can be left to "the corner druggist."

He thinks so because he argues that today the book reviewer is a professional. "A reviewer is not a whole man," he admits. "A reviewer is not in the self-expression business. He knows that he cannot afford to any extent the luxury of indulging his own prejudices." Why not? If he did, "he would run the risk of becoming an artist." That would hurt him in his job. It might turn him into a writer.

For a reviewer, Mr. Fadiman argues, is a type to whom the job is a job. "A reviewer reads the books he reviews, exactly as an accountant examines his costs sheets, with the same routine conscientiousness. It's his job, that's all." "Today book reviewing is staider, duller, but unquestionably juster and more serious. It has a professional touch. It is growing up." And so the expert at it, "many of his human qualities vestigial, others hypertrophied," arrives at the accountant's summing up: to wit, that Frances Winwar is one of the truly great biographers of our time, and that other books of a spring season are clarion calls, wonder books, terrific, and epoch-making. That is so like the language of accountancy.

Grown up? Take the advertisement pages of the *Atlantic Monthly*, May 1946, to go forward a little bit. Judge how much it has grown up in two months. "A truly great book," the Scientific Book Club discovers. "A work of transcendent importance," says the *Chicago Sun*. "It should be read and re-read by our 140,000,000 Americans." "Surely one of the most beautiful books," says the New York *Sun*. "A stalwart and beautiful contribution to the literature of our time," says the *New York Times*. "A triumph, a superb novel," says the *Philadelphia Record*. "Magnificent and inspiring. A brilliant novel," says the *Chicago Sun*. And around these staid, dull, just, and serious judgments Mr. Fadiman would like to build up the prestige of accountancy, the familiar build-up of the closed corporation. Very humble before any work of creative scholarship, he himself claims merely to be a technician, able to dispose of an "average" historical novel at the rate of two hundred pages an hour, an "average" novel at one hundred pages an hour, and yet ready to give "two weeks, about five hours a day, to read Thomas Mann's *Joseph in Egypt*." But how can the daily book technician spend the necessary two weeks on a book? He must cheat. He does cheat. And how can "we professionals" bespatter the publishers' pages with adjectives if "we" are not in the "self-expression business"? At the root of this unhealth, masquerading as strict accountancy, there seems to be a rottenness unsuspected by the corner druggist. Other professionals, doctors and dentists and clergymen, dare not be so shameless about their "device for earning a living." They must believe or ape a belief in the "ethics." But literary practitioners are not merely relaxed about ethics. They become aggressive, as when Miss Amy Loveman, in the *Saturday Review of Literature*, delivers admonition to the intellectuals. Where Mr. Fadiman at least separates book reviewing from literary criticism, saying that "literary criticism is an art, like the writing of tragedies or the making of love, and, similarly, does not pay," Miss Loveman attacks wholeness in the interest of a charlatan called Dr. Frank Crane, whom the "sophisticates" used to make fun of.

You independent writers, says Miss Loveman in effect, you intellectuals, you "sophisticates," you think yourselves so smart, but who gives American democracy its eternal verities, "*the truisms, the reiterated wisdom and ethical precepts of the world"?* It is the Frank Cranes. America may look educated and informed, but "there is a deceptive surface which conceals superficiality of thought and knowledge. Under the outer layer of American literacy frequently lies confusion and ignorance. The American is quick, perceptive, ingenious, but he is more given to doing than to reflecting," and in any battle to rouse public opinion it is the Frank Cranes who can use pressure. "The Frank Cranes have as real a part to play as Capitol Hill." Which may mean Demos.

From accepting the separation of book reviewer and critic, followed by separating intellectual and public, it is a short step to the base conclusion that the independent writer must close this disastrous separation on the terms of Miss Loveman's ignorant, confused, shallow, parochial America that "can be easily inflamed to interest." The masses, in short, as defined and bamboozled by Hitler, are to be played on. "The Dr. Cranes of the world will often bring them to life where more subtle preaching proves sterile."

And Orville Prescott echoes the same imploring cry that the mass-produced reader has the right to be considered and catered to. "Why, why, Sean O'Casey," he wails, "do you who can write so well take such delight in writing so badly? That is the question provoked by hundreds of pages of this book. It may give you private pleasure, but it cuts you off from communication with thousands of readers who would otherwise enjoy your great gifts and your stimulating mind." The consumer, in short, wants the goods in a handy package. Why doesn't Sean O'Casey oblige?

Of course, this is in good faith, as Miss Loveman's plea for the Dr. Cranes is in good faith. But by uncritical subservience like Miss Loveman's, Mr. Prescott's, and Mr. Fadiman's, the triumph of Demos is made uncontrollable, and its triumph comes bellowing from the commercial jungle. The "intellectuals" are attacked by the radio hucksters as "trying to impose their own tastes" to the exclusion of majority preference. So Jack Gould perceptively relates in the *New York Times*, May 12, 1946. And he quotes a spokesman for soap. "We want to attract the biggest audience we can. The way to do that is to find out what the public want to hear and give it to them. That, I submit, is the essence of democratic radio." This squalid sentiment is entirely to the liking of innumerable newspaper and magazine editors. What the public wants, says the copy desk. What the public wants, says the advertising department. What the public wants, says Hollywood. And then they wonder why they are called prostitutes by Russia, which does the same thing in quite a different way.

If the reviewer is not a whole man, then his echoing of "verities" is merely music for the cow. Because there is so much money in a canned population, in the mass production of their "verities" such as Dr. Frank Crane practiced, the democrat as consumer, flat on his back, becomes a victim of the market place. Once the duty of understanding a writer was put on the reader. He was told to make an effort, and to try, try again. Now, without shame or apology, he asks for sliced bread, ready-to-serve breakfast food, laxatives, antacids, sleeping pills, tabloids, digests, omnibooks, and books by enema. He lives on them and dies of them. Even then, as authors are forced to observe, the mere effort of consuming a book is felt by most people to be almost insurmountable. Every day forty million newspapers are sold in the U.S.A.; it takes three months to sell as many Pocket Books. Every week over a hundred million will buy tickets for the movies. As many as half that number will listen to a single broadcast. In competition with radio, movie, and daily paper, the sale of books is miserably small. None can be sold to the ten million illiterate adults, and if twice that number have wobbly or defective minds it may be assumed they are relatively impenetrable. But beyond that, beyond losing to shopping and motoring, to games and gossip columns, books have to be crowded into a mental rush.

This rush is now increasing by the square of the distance covered by press, movie, and radio. The prostrate consumer is having One World funneled into him from everywhere. You can see it in his haggard face. Tramp, tramp, tramp, the boys are marching, and the high-school girls, the old men, and the old ladies. Even at the point of death the faithful struggle to keep up with the march, to inform themselves, to take what else is coming, from atom to universe, from science, art, religion.

The brain totters. But even as it begs for news in extracts and capsules, it has the harder struggle for emotional attunement. The effort to keep abreast is put on the Puritan conscience, but the ability to feel cannot be delegated, and as the world rolls its eyes at burdened recipients, they can only murmur, "What am I to think? What am I to feel?" And they simply can't "keep up with" all the nine thousand literary Joneses who are published every year in the U.S.A. alone.

But neither can they convert into life stuff the adroit approximation of their mass sentiment that is fed to them by the bucket. Literature is in irreconcilable conflict with this profitable muck. It demands the alienation from mediocrity which it brings about by candor. And every time a popular reviewer says that a book is "dull," "gloomy," "disappointing," "bitter," or "decadent," the chances are it is good. At least it breaks with the requirements of mass production, so well understood by commerce.

4

Yet why isn't it legitimate, in literature as in everything else, to give the public what it wants? When we observe how the public can be led by the nose, how it can be seduced by flatterers, bamboozled by medicine men, turned swinish by warmongers and panic-mongers, is there any hope for it? Is there any other name for it than the ugly one coined by H. L. Mencken? Isn't the People a boobocracy? And, if a boobocracy, why not play on it for profit? What else is it for?

The liberal critic is not blind to popular folly. He simply differs from Mencken in refusing to make democratic a synonym for popular. Give the democracy what it wants, yes, because he attaches a real meaning to the word. He does not identify Demos with it.

It is hard for him not to. Good critics, we must admit, are frequently at odds with the world they live in. God, after all, gave the precedent for a total break with an infuriating public when he tried the little experiment of the Deluge. The most generous of natures as well as sheer maniacs are driven at times to feel contempt for the tyranny of averages, and to say, "Drown the lot of them. Wipe out the breed, except for Noah, the kangaroo, and the elephant." The little creators, like the Creator Himself, would like to delouse the planet.

The free critic shares this divine fury because the mediocre are inevitably antipathetic to him if he has to coddle them, gratify their egoism, and pet their prejudices. Hall Caine, if you remember that top best-seller, covered his donkeys with lion's skin, as Elinor Glyn lent a tigerskin to a lounge lizard. By means of a lot of noise, noise about sacrifice, cruelty, lust, heroism, disaster, the bells of St. Mary's, the stars in their courses, the song of Bernadette, popular authors manage to excite without disturbing, and to mush without moving. When an author means business, however, the tendency of the mediocre is to fight shy of him. The literary conflict with the tyranny of averages is a revolt against substitutes—substitute of herd for individual, of folk mind for mind in evolution, of standard specifications for the self-knowing, self-searching person.

Fame, power, and money are to be gained by authors who work out standard specifications. The same goes for editors and publishers who gather together, and gather in, the millions. They are not policed, as Russians are, but they stock prevailing prejudices, which vary from sheet to sheet and city to city, and a critic who "goes outside his province" or doesn't keep step will be invited to the publisher's office. He knows that the name of democracy is being wrapped around a deft manipulation, an appeal to Demos, the mob, the mass, the herd.

That appeal is not always bourgeois. It may be very good and very big business to cater to the proletariat. A managing editor may not have to yield to a theater or a bank or a dry-goods store, but he may have to heed a communist group. There is an amount of pressure that no newspaper can resist, since it must pull in subscribers.

They can be pulled in by a brawl. A critic who never voices an opinion without shouting, a columnist who brags and roars and bullies, may be so independent of a newspaper that he can go as far as he likes, drunk with money, words, and false prophecy. America is no different from Britain in bloating up these monsters, who parade opinion for its color or off-color, its bombast and extravagance. "I predict that the war will be over September 15." "My two dollars are on Knockdown." They'll predict anything, tip anything, endorse anything, damn anything, and the mob swallows it hot and strong, salty and saucy. Free of an immediate boss, these grotesques work for the boss's boss. They serve dope to Demos, and accept the tyranny of the average love of dogfights. The objection to their brawls, their harsh and insensitive judgments, is by no means an objection to candor. It is a revolt against corruption of manners in which civilized candor is impossible. No critic is privileged to butcher, since the art of criticism excludes virulence. Otherwise a whole age becomes shameless, braggart, and brazen.

But neither is the answer to exalt the impotent and timid. If you can't assert that the popular appeal is good, neither can you say the antipopular is good. It may be very bad. There is no virtue in the bare fact of antipopularity. The free critic rejects those, like Frank Crane, who boldly promised salvation through love, as do revivalists. Love in and by itself is love without wisdom, even a debauchery of the heart. Fraud on the hungry heart is a major industry. But to despise democracy on that account, to confuse the victim of debauchery with its originator, is wholly uncritical. The public needs the artist who no more repudiates it than he seduces it.

Lincoln did not abnegate either literary or moral elevation when he spoke at Gettysburg, nor yet did he give up the widest appeal. He sought to reach the heart of a nation in a few words. But, unlike the peddler of "eternal verities," he lifted his hearers to a genuine emotion, first laboring to elicit his own feeling, which was sensitive and refined, and then affirming strongly and sedately its bond with humanity. He did not profane it, but neither did he shrink from a banal, heterogeneous multitude. He had the magnet by which to draw them into sympathy, the emotion bigger than self, which found in multitude the very reason for compassion. Great literature had its part in attuning him, but Lincoln's were honest words tolled over a pitiless battlefield, and unfolding a consequent purpose to living Americans. This was not to say to the public it should have what it wants. It was to say that men had died at Gettysburg for a reason. The reason was not soap-selling. The reason was not Dr. Crane's soft lather. The reason was not "entertainment." The literature that had enabled Lincoln to speak deep, noble words was not written for entertainment. It was not cakes and ale to him, but communion with death, and the bread he gave America was dipped in blood, for America's compassion and commiseration. They were then humble in affliction and he gave them pity and beauty.

The populace of 1863 was not widely impressed by the great Gettysburg address. Immediate interests distracted them. Only later did clearer critical judgment help democracy to discern it.

5

What's wrong with immediate interests? Why should "community interests" be separated from them?

. The market, for its own sake, for the stimulus and adventure in it, for the immense irrational satisfaction of success in it, occupies and fascinates most active men. It has its own tempo, and its excitement is life itself to Jew and Gentile. Black market and white, men trade for the love of it, love a bargain, love a deal, gleam with the fun of it. Trade gives luster to eyes in the bazaar, but is the Arab unique? Englishmen love it, Frenchmen, Germans, Russians, Italians, Yankees. The man who sells postcards is more shamelessly trading in sex than the advertising manager of the *Times*, but nudity is an appetizer in the movie ads, and the *Times* sells all the sex that's fit to print in its kiss-and-kill advertisements. It isn't for the money, of course, it's for the power, which depends on mass-consumption, big numbers.

In the market that concerns book criticism the person to be lined up, the person to be hooked into the bazaar, the person who makes big business possible, is undoubtedly the general reader. But most book publishers, periodical publishers, and newspaper publishers no longer think in simple terms of selling books. They think in terms of selling soap. Is it experienced book buyers who give a newspaper its revenue from book advertisements, say a thousand dollars on a good day? The revenue doesn't depend on the book criticism, which probably costs 3 or 4 per cent of the intake. It depends on the ways of the bazaar. The passer-by has to be hooked into literature. And the publishers look for books that have hooks in them. Hence bookstores tend to disappear. The dry-goods stores, the drugstores, and the chain stores make little pretense of literary feeling. They may invoke authors to book fairs or drag them in to sign autographs, but this is merchandising. They distribute books as merchandise. This is a great game with its own crazy attraction, apart from literature, and its own tangible reward and dominion.

Books *are* merchandise. Neither authors nor critics can live, in the long run, if a busy world shuts down on consumption. Publishers even "create" a market by their ingenuities of promotion, and no one, not even the Pope, disdains publicity. Churches, museums, colleges, orchestras, research institutes, and most welfare institutes as well are compelled to scramble for whatever endowment they can tickle out of society. Otherwise the state provides endowment, installs bureaucrats, and assumes mastery.

What is the answer? If the radio advertisers make their principal killing by appeals to "the ailing, credulous, and neurotics of social inferiority," as Dixon Wector said in his *Saturday Review* article "Public Domain of the Air" (May 18, 1946), then a liberal critic, concurring with Mr. Wector, is in conflict with such an appeal. He has to qualify the cynical notion of books as merchandise. He has to urge responsibility, and to turn from a public made drunk on publicity to a democracy critical and sober.

Who will pay him for that? Clifton Fadiman says frankly that literary criticism has no market value. It doesn't pay. Critics have to be "kept," like pretty ladies, yachts, and race horses.

6

We cannot accept this conclusion, or what Mr. Wector wisely deplored as "the unproductive deadlock between high-brow and lowbrow."

Mr. Fadiman is right that the grand intellectual approach to literature which engages scholars (who are paid considerably more than newspaper critics) has no place in a book column. Literature proceeds in a great movement rather like the voyage of the earth around the sun, and to place any man's work in such a prodigious cycle is to judge it on permanent lines, for which journalism in the main has little use commercially. It doesn't work. The author of *American Renaissance* sets out to encompass an epoch, to establish a constellation as well as the stars, not confining himself to single books or single authors, but revealing the immediate and remote influences to which literature itself is subject. It is sometimes half a century before a significant forerunner of potent character emerges, and no reviewer in nine hundred or a thousand words can do more than hint at such sidereal movement. His business is to catch new books as they appear on a rotating earth, and as the morning light falls on them. They come up like fresh bread, and stir our appetite because fresh. We reach for them instinctively, since a new book is like nothing else in the world. Little islands of type on great sheets of paper are folded and gathered and put between boards. Once a name is stamped on the cover they are baptized, and the life in them is special and unpredictable. Though a machine prints a book, and a machine may sell it, no machine wrote it. A manuscript, done by hand, is as unique as a thumbprint. A book may be a botch or a fraud or a crime, but it is always a spiritual event, and the critic who inspects it is no factory inspector. He is not required to place it for all time, even were he able to. He must ticket it for immediate consideration and make it locally intelligible. That is the compromise he has to make, a social one. It doesn't permit him to go deep into literary origins or preoccupations. It requires him to relate permanent standards to those under the press of immediate interests.

Many deep writers cannot make this compromise. You may, if you like, divide the literary as the Church does the religious. Some orders exist for contemplation, others for teaching, and others to have a commerce with vulgar humanity that would not be possible for the contemplative. The mystic clearly apprehends realities that are lost on the earthbound, and without the mystic these apprehendings would be lost for everyone. The great question for the intermediary is how far he can compromise without impairing the truth itself. When Demos says, "This is too highbrow for me," it may be that help is possible. But it can also happen that help is impossible, unless Demos comes to heel and is literally brought to book.

Take a mechanical problem, that of boarding trains at a great central station. It would be delightful for the lazy if a long train could be emptied onto a platform that had cabs across the way. Suburban stations have this convenience. But the best brains have not yet devised a way of deft unloading in a crowded space and time. The longer the train, the more hopeless the problem. The public can't have long trains and short walks. It must leg it or be wheeled away, calling for effort or escalator. The conveyance can't land you in a taxi. You yourself have to put in the hyphen, even if you have to walk.

So with literature. Authors can do a great deal without impairing it, can lessen resistance, heighten interest, cut, clip, jab, perk. But while miracles may be attempted, not dissimilar to the teaching of Chinese in three months, there is a limit to concession. Twilight sleep, yes, but not a baby in three months. There are some things that nobody can do for a craven public, no matter how eager it is to absorb culture.

7

But if a populace yields to inertia, and so offers a Hitler or a Mussolini the chance to debauch society, the proper response of a liberal critic is not to turn antipopular, highbrow, and disdainful. That, curiously enough, goes in the same direction.

Criticism, as has been said, is part of a whole. It is not an "assignment" by a fatigued managing editor who cannot understand how anyone *wants* to do book reviews. It is not a "job," or a way of syndicating snippets, an attempt to make books into spot news, or a tie-in with the advertising department. It pertains to these secondary activities, but only because such are contemporary working conditions. The idealist who despairs of "the whole thing," and looks to a little review, a little theater, a little colony, as better for himself and his art than having commerce with the Great Public, may agreeably avoid the banal, fraternal, heterogeneous multitude, but he also gives up wholeness as a citizen. And if aristocracy has a meaning it does not reside in withdrawing from the inferior mass. It lies in the virtue of superior natures to appeal on their own level to those who are under the press of circumstance. Aristocracy cannot cheapen itself. Neither can it abdicate. To shrink from the world is to wither the heart.

Rebellion against Demos may be poisonous and withering egoism. The false exactions, the usury, of society should be a spur to a rebel's sincerity. He has a right to revolt against being harnessed for the milk run until he has won at least the local Derby. But divorce from contemporary life does not prosper even a great poet. He is not a gazelle or a unicorn, to seek the wild, nor an armorer, a lamplighter, a waterman on the Thames, to yearn for the archaic. In the eighteenth century, among those who fitted themselves into the aristocratic conventions, certain authors who clambered out of Grub Street may have had all that author, authority, authoritative imply. If a writer looked promising through an aristocrat's lorgnette, he had the advantage of noble approval, and any class that emphasizes privacy, decorum, and refinement can enhance a poet's dignity and lap his nerves. Such readers do not loll in his company. They defer, and in their deference he unfolds. Even into the Victorian period a system of tutorship and privilege and subscription protected the favored author. Young as Oscar Wilde's father was, for example, when he eagerly compiled his two-volume account of his grand tour, 1,250 copies could be sold at twenty-eight shillings each, giving the author 15 per cent. It was a small success, but the age conferred successes on those who could impress and please a select list. Then there was an élite to save literature on aristocratic terms. Now literature must seek a patron who, on other terms, can defer, discriminate, revere, and define.

Our commonplace world looks crass and mercenary to the sensitive man who is also timid. To give himself, and to give himself away, he desires protected intimacy, forgetting how an apothecary's boy was refused it, even though he was Keats. Any poet brought up in "an aristocratic traditional society, contemptuous of commerce, oblivious of industry or science," as the Irish poet W. B. Yeats was, and wishing life to be the theater of great character and heroic gesture, or else peopled by folk still simple and instinctive, while himself being drawn to beauty in women, in language, in nature, and in the dramatic spark of conflict, can scarcely, whatever his fund of heart, embrace the clock-punching, gum-chewing, wordchopping, jam-packing world. A few country houses remain, a few clubs where valets hold the ends of your trousers as you insert your legs in them, and sprinkle you with hyssop if requested. That antiquarian concept, personal service, hangs on in odd places. But for W. B. Yeats, aloof and prone to "verbalizing" (there's a word for you), agoraphobia and claustrophobia might easily have been the only solutions, had he not been indomitable.

Still, he could not buck the century of Balzac and Ibsen, according to F. O. Matthiessen, "the world of the expanding middle class," and out of his romanticizations of oligarchy he was brought "close to a sympathy with fascism." The antipopular led many writing men to this ultimate disdain. But the highbrows who followed Yeats as devoted critics climbed him as if he were Mont Blanc inverted. "The poet and the reductive scientist," to quote John Crowe Ransom, "have their respective ontological prejudices to look out for. Synecdoche is a way of indicating the irreducibility of the object as a whole by citing some perfectly intractable part, while scientific reduction is a way of indicating the docility or gen-

erality of the object by attending only to its commonplace."
That rates a Purple Heart. How much easier is Kenneth Burke.
"Were I thus to speculate beyond the readily available facts on
the page, I should suggest that the lunar white of Yeat's imagery is related to the seminal, and the solar gold related to
the excremental." It may indeed be, and if, as we are told,
"ultimate reality is a phaseless sphere that but becomes phasal
in our thoughts," the phasier and phasier it grows, the worse
the jargon.

At the same time, even if we approach this verbalizing in the
spirit of jargon-loving boys and are ready to call Kenneth
Burke and John Crowe Ransom the lunar white hopes of criticism, it does seem that they put the price of initiation pretty
high. To cater complacently to an inert multitude is, admittedly, Godforsaken. But equally sterile is to pulverize a
poet, however engrossing the analysis. It becomes a game of
hide-and-seek, with Yeats more and more lunar or lunatic in it.
A phaseless sphere of ultimate reality.

There is a considerable school of American highbrow criticism, but literature is not used by it to embody the whole man.
Where violence in popular criticism denies the mood of
candor by emphasizing sweeping hostility, crude assertion, and
pugnacity, the tendency in this antipopular criticism is all the
other way. So far so good. But it refines on ideas to the exclusion of any partnership with the reader of that candid kind
which is the highest form of intimate pleasure. It is the ivory
tower at zero, with Yeats's cadaver on the slab. It does not
offer the deep offense of demagogic method in criticism. It
offers the face mask and the rubber glove. What did Yeats do
to deserve it? He was not abstracted from time and place. His
power over words sprang from a wealth within, and with this
affluence he entwined his particularity of origin and accent.
Withdrawn in youth from common things and people, he had
to admit his inescapable connection before he died. Thin-
skinned and touchy, he became avid for the fruit of knowledge, asserting passion and insight. He disputed the claims of
common sense, but only to expose the brand of tragedy in his
mortal flesh. He is literary in the true sense, not a colossus but

a princeling, and a whole man, with as many phases as any moon.

8

The withdrawal into metaphysics would not matter if fertile thought came out of it, but the present unhappy state of criticism shows few signs of it. It needs men who can write candidly and intelligibly to end the book review racket, the filthy commercial taint that corrupts the name "democratic."

Newspaper publishers look blank when they hear of a taint. It is astonishing how confounded they are by any hint that the situation is infected. They can't imagine it. And indeed James Bryant Conant, president of Harvard, softens the blow for them. "We have no reason to be unduly apprehensive," says this educator, on the proposition that "the health of our universities depends on keeping a balance between the advancement of knowledge, professional education, general education, and the demands of student life." "We have no reason to be unduly apprehensive." (Who on earth ever had a reason to be "unduly" apprehensive?) "The public," he goes on, "has come to understand both the function of the universities and the necessary conditions of their health." (Which public?) "Therefore I view the future of our institutions with the greatest confidence. I see the American universities as leading the way in the development of a unified, coherent culture, the expression of a true democracy in a scientific age."

So far from echoing Dr. Conant, the boy wonder of 1893, we hear the direct contrary from the president of Chicago University, Robert Maynard Hutchins, born in 1899.

"If we want to save the world within the next few years," says Dr. Hutchins, "we must attend to the education of adults, for only they will have the influence within that period to affect the course of events." "The death of civilization" is the alternative. Civilization can be saved only by a moral, intellectual, and spiritual revolution to match the present scientific age which leaves Dr. Conant more than satisfied.

Dwell on the Conant proposition that "the public" has come

to understand the necessary conditions for the health of education. Were that true, how could Dr. Hutchins lay such stress on adult ignorance? And if adults were educated, or even a very modest proportion of them, would Mr. Luce's journals be a success? In the ranks of decent journalism, rosy with sweet reasonableness, you meet the most moderate, air-cushioned, air-conditioned, calm, and kind exponents of the eternal verities, ready to praise any irregular fellow so long as he is dead. But what goes on in literature? What are the best-sellers? With ten million adult illiterates in the most prosperous nation on earth, and twice that number put down as mental cases, Dr. Conant has the placidity of milk toast.

How can John Crowe Ransom entangle himself with a synecdoche, or Kenneth Burke with a phaseless sphere, when the house is burning?

9

Houses are always burning, and perhaps neither of these men can do better than theorize. But if to judge books is to judge something of human quality, if the relationship between critic and author is ultimately personal, then the sooner we emphasize humanism the better.

Literature is not a neat term. A boy without compass or chart may take a power boat out to sea and if he is in luck he may make port and reach home again. But rough weather or a thick fog will prove how little he came with. Every summer the Coast Guard picks them up. The sea of literature is navigable by all and sundry, but to exercise judgment takes not only aptitude but equipment, and the theorists and academicians have equipment as their charge.

Yet the native quality of aptitude comes first. The number who have it is inestimable, but though wars may do nothing else they disclose how, under pressure, human cultivation can startlingly advance. Unsatisfied, and quite unsuspected, aptitude exists everywhere. Even so disdainful a man as Yeats found his best actors for the Abbey Theater among Dublin clerks and shop assistants and members of that dreadful group, "the expanding middle class." The art of equipping it, shaping it, giving it compass and chart took many a long day. But soundness of judgment is substantiated by exercise. It cannot be documented into existence. It is more emotional than mental. And that marriage of heart and brain, of aptitude and equipment, must be consummated and fertile.

It must, that is to say, bring forth sensitive imagination. The essence is there. A man may be as conversant with whole literatures as George Saintsbury, and yet hard of heart, hard because positive and prejudiced. The word empathy covers "the power of projecting one's personality into, and fully understanding, the object of contemplation." Without it, in spite of omnivorous reading and investigation, no lightning flashes. Saintsbury rushed vigorously from his doghouse at every new object of contemplation, but the chain of his Englishness pulled him up short, and he barked at Frenchmen for not being English. They were never English and he continually barked.

The essence does not reside in projecting personality alone. The object has to be fully understood in its surrounding world. A man who cannot project into the object is a pedant, a heavy-duty truck that fails to be amphibian. A man who is able to project but not fully understand is still at sea and not up to the landing operation. Pedantry is no equivalent of aptitude, but aptitude must add power to grace. It does well to be humble, for this reason, and the apt are frequently remiss. They hate to work.

Have they not a right to judge books? They have. Everyone has. The right of private judgment in literature can be asserted by everyone, initiate or uninitiate. As George Moore said to the Dublin policeman, the day his cook fled into the street to escape his reproaches about an omelet, "What are you going to do? You can't make me eat it." That was before the Irish government, having censored hundreds and hundreds of new books, began to consider the feasibility of a literature "passed by the censor."

The right of judgment inheres in a free man. It is perhaps

the best thing in life, so vital is it to man's exercise and development, rounding him for any excursion. Those who are assured of it, and use independent judgment as of right, catch imagination. Children have notorious affinity for them, even for "bad men" who seem so "free." And this right of judgment is an admission ticket to literature, the one inexhaustible resource and instrument for emancipation, the most perfect the mind has devised. Religions have wiped out books. States have burned them. The right of private judgment is obviously a passkey out of prison. Without it men are dependents, whether happy or unhappy, and dependents end as slaves.

Slaves to others. But if the right of judgment is used idiotically, slaves to themselves. Private judgment opens the bar but doesn't shut out alcoholism. Only criticism can do that, if it comes from the inside. Criticism can never be prescribed for "people." It is an aspect of self-government. It refuses self-intoxication. A great many young men and women are so afraid of being conscripted by the society they live in that they seem supercilious and self-intoxicated. But these so-called intellectuals, printing weedy, sleazy weeklies and monthlies all over the world, reducing the public's partnership to a vanishing point, are in reality in the first stages of achieving independence. Their revolt against average existence stirs the banal moralist, but even when the angry enmity of the middle class calls them "decadent," contemning their refusal to "adjust," it misplaces emphasis. "Decadence" is a very pre-Freudian word, generally meaning a poodle's odd haircut. Many do set out to be regularly irregular, opening their beaks for worms, swallowing anything from cocktails to scholarships, arriving pregnant at confirmation and dirty at a dance, bundling so hard for Britain that 40 per cent have babies, and taking with poker faces the other fellow's ration points. So mongrels behave, male and female, whelp and bitch. But in an age when dogmatic boneheads step into the shoes of God, ruling as government agencies, as psychiatrists, as editors who rewrite, as cartels or social workers, the one viciousness promotes the other, and rebellion wears vine leaves.

The first question Bernard Shaw asked us, twenty-five years

ago, was "How is Frank Harris?" He was eagle-eyed about
Frank Harris, but scoundrels in the ruling class were so trans-
parent to those eagle eyes that he shot up his eyebrows at irate
mediocrity. In a Britain of voracious empire Shaw did not ride
herd for the great congeries of conventional English whose
impenetrable self-deception went with the deception of others.
He did not have to go to Africa to hunt pachyderms. Shaw
was the most zealous big-game hunter of his time, and he was
not quarreling with Frank Harris, to whom England was a
jungle, with its trumpet calls and water holes.

But while Harris was a cheat (he diddled me), the nonsense
of correlating loose conduct with art, of confusing the man's
misbehavior with his power of empathy, could not excite a
police instinct in Shaw. Why not? Partly because he puts
crimes in perspective, and also because literature, art, music,
can be a function of pure play and display, no more disheveled
by the moralist than the waves are, or the clouds. Poetry lends
itself to the inhabitation of feeling for its own sake and in
accord with its own laws, leaving the social proponent out of
it as the serpent before the Fall. To recapture Eden is the aim
of this spontaneity. Mozart had hard work staying on earth,
and so had Shelley. Up they go, larks enraptured but obeying
the tact of their art. They have no accountability to anything
but delight and the ascendancy of their mood. They do not
rebel; they elate. For them the tree of knowledge is still in bud
so they lead us not into temptation. This is to be pure of heart,
and the key to such elation is to have a taste for it. Yet it is
among the very masters of this elation that critics find "de-
cadents."

Much better is a feeling for coherence and consistence. Is
Finnegans Wake a new language or a schizophrenic document
of fascinating license? You cannot deny that new resources
dethrone the classic, those "points of repose" of which Donald
Francis Tovey speaks. Again and again there are no recognizable principles for the control of new material. But "the task
of organizing new resources into a consistent language" is the
artist's, and "if experiments are to revolutionize art it is necessary that their novelty shall already embody some artistic

principle of coherence," which is inherent. "In art, as elsewhere, new thought eventually shows itself as an addition, not
a substitute for, the wisdom of the ages." Yet out of chaos and
old night the begetter is merely one who sees a fire and
ravishes it.

10

The danger from prigs, dogmatists, and snobs, from hauteur
and superciliousness, is never absent from critical cliques. The
love of power is strong in intellectuals. Books are centers of
force, whorls of a creative activity, and aspects of ideas. The
critic can seldom leave ideas out of it. All kinds of single-
minded people, discoverers of the true truth, inevitably propa-
gate ideology in books. For four hundred years, ever since
books have been set from movable type, men of letters have
not only fought for specific ideas, but more valuably fought
for the play as such, and for literary judgment as a prompt,
personal, intuitional verdict on what is good and bad. It is a
great tradition, that of literary criticism. It cannot be best exercised by a man in a cult until the cult merges with culture.
And it has to be a verdict of time and place if we are social.
Who would want Fragonard after the guillotine was red-
edged? Who would have wanted Danton in a painting by
Fragonard? Literature is many-sided, prehensile, eclectic. It
should not be crushed into a theory. Excessive guidance by
theorists has for its excuse a revelation, and this revelation will
be from on high. But this is to exaggerate the guidance of
education.

Somewhere on the mountain a wanderer came on nine
nymphs. His condition was miserable. He wasn't shaved, for
one thing, he had been out all night, lost on the mountain, and
frightened. As he spied on them in the sacred grove, each of
the muses absorbed in her own art and unable to resist her joy
in it, he probably thought them decadent. But as they beheld
the intruder, who ran for his life, they instantly ran after him,
their veils fluttering and arching in the wind. He was bewildered, grimy, his face smeared with wild berries, but as

the eternal spirits caught him and brought him back, something crept into him of their mystery. They were grouped around their spring, the one with the lyre, the one with the little lyre, all of them, and as he parted his lashes and gazed with lost eyes, the spring no purer than their natural ecstasy, they smiled on him and yearned to solace the unfortunate. In that enchanted dawn, after a helpless night, his heart swelled with pure beauty, and a critic was born, the first critic.

But as he went down the mountainside, to a world made forever alien, he naturally began to think. He saw a red rose tree in blossom on the slope, for instance, lifting its crowned head in perfection, and he said to himself, "I am dreaming this tree. It is not in perfection. It is the semblance of an imagined perfect one. The real tree is nothing." He saw a countryman and said to him, "You have a pretty rose tree. Quite a decent one." The countryman had himself grown this rose tree. Being a nurseryman by instinct, he had done a good job with an old thorn stump and a bit of grafting. Out of new material, new resources, he had begotten this unimagined tree. The eternal pattern of it was not even in his head. It had come out that way. "I made that tree," he said to the smudgy dreamer. But the dreamer went down the hill, laughing. He had been the man of vision, the man of eternal pattern. He believed there were nine muses, like nine justices of the Supreme Court, all working on an eternal body of law, nine old ladies and a constitution.

Pedants like the idea. And it does make for coherence and consistence.

II

But the temper of criticism is better if one does not possess eternal patterns. In the course of my life I have met a few people who seemed to me great, and each of them, whether American, Norwegian, Hindu, had a unique quality, a quality that belonged neither to the male nor the female exclusively but seemed to mingle the nature of both. It was a scrupulous discernment in them, satisfying the demand of one's critical sense and at the same time releasing their immense fund of sympathy. But it was not dissolute. It was administered. Flame as it was, and kindling as it was, it united with an impersonal passion for justice, not because they would refuse themselves but because they refused chaos. They had no fierceness of preoccupation with a self that goes from anxious childhood to anxious second childhood. The self, as in Lincoln, gained identity by losing its aggressiveness. They did not grant assent lightly or hold it back rigidly. They did not chastise society for its incompetence by prescribing the hard heart and the hard head. They had misericordia. It should be at the core of criticism, as Anatole France conceived, and, like the light high on a miner's head, should sport a point of irony.

Odd Man Out

I

IT'S EASY enough to insist on the commercial aspect of literature in America. In a chapter that occupies only half a page de Tocqueville summed it up over a hundred years ago, putting the gist of it in a single sentence—"Democratic literature is always infested with a tribe of writers who look upon letters as a mere trade." He already blamed this on "the ever increasing crowd of readers and their continual craving for something new."

The arbitrary rejection of this crowd of readers, however, he was far from commending. An aristocracy had its own virtues, but "every aristocracy that keeps itself entirely aloof from the people becomes impotent, a fact which is as true in literature as it is in politics."

What then of any honest man of letters who, adhering to the people, still holds to his private, not to say his secret life? What of the man who must live by writing and yet refuses to "look upon letters as a mere trade"? In proportion as he is drawn to be an artist and at the same time obliged, as the saying is, "to appeal to the public," he is driven toward a contradiction that he usually evades by comedy. Over and again comedy or tragicomedy has been the refuge of subtle authors who, by their very nature, cannot produce those works that de Tocqueville held to be inevitable in America—works primarily sensational and extravagant. Tocqueville foretold the best-sellers of our era when he said that our public "prefer books which can easily be procured, quickly read, and which require no learned researches to be understood. They ask for beauties self-proffered and easily enjoyed; above all, they must have what is unexpected and new. Accustomed to the struggle, the crosses,

29

and the monotony of practical life, they require strong and rapid emotions, startling passages, truth or errors brilliant enough to rouse them up or plunge them at once, as if by violence, into the midst of the subject." It is really a definition that fits soap opera. But authors who seek to please rather than astonish, who want less to stir the passions than "charm the taste," are in a special case. That, for the critic, is the acute predicament in which the sensitive generally find themselves, those who appreciate "the minor shades," "the more delicate beauties," and yet wish above all to escape "the natural perils of literature among the aristocracies." (It is in de Tocqueville's second volume of *Democracy in America,* the new Knopf edition, that he gives his analysis of these tendencies in American literature, pages 58-61 in particular.)

Whether all sensitive Americans find a journal like the *New Yorker* entirely happy in its bold line of comedy is a question by itself, but no one may doubt that everyone connected with the *New Yorker* was very happy in 1944 about *The Thurber Carnival.* James Thurber was fifty years old that year, and into one volume, as the announcement said, had been gathered the cream of his work and eighty of his "immortal drawings." This became the occasion of a triumph with Mr. Thurber garlanded and looking rather stricken and bewildered. Clifton Fadiman, for years with the *New Yorker,* compared the *Carnival* to the best of wine, to love itself, and to good bread. The Book-of-the-Month Club chose the volume for its great public's pabulum. Not outdone in appreciativeness, Mr. Thurber responded by dedicating the *Carnival* to Harold Ross, the editor of the *New Yorker,* which he did with "increasing admiration, wonder and affection." It was ring around the roses, for I am right and you are right and all is right as right can be. What could be more in order, considering that Mr. Thurber made his name in the *New Yorker* and helped the *New Yorker* to make its name? But no matter how warm, cosy, and convivial a charmed circle is, or how big the appreciative crowd that gathers, attracted by the celebration and its celebrities, the fundamental interest in these pages lies in James Thurber's use of humor in a peculiar defensive role.

2

Mr. Thurber's talent, oddly enough, does not bear the bright hallmark of the *New Yorker*. That periodical has invented and patented a distinct slick type, a man about town. His exterior is perhaps unfairly inferred from the *New Yorker* advertisements. Whatever this smart creature does for a living, he goes to the right places after working hours, an inveterate gadabout with a sharp eye for what misses fire in urban entertainment, and an even sharper eye for the hits. Satirizing a world that makes much of the unimportant, the *New Yorker* engrosses itself in the unimportant. Its Profiles, aggregations of gossip and spite, use the method that Lytton Strachey applied to Queen Victoria, but with a meaner sting than a gadfly's. When the Profiles are admiring they are insolently familiar. When they search out weaknesses, they exhibit them with malicious glee. Under the chamois glove there is a pointed nail. The *New Yorker* is amusing, mincing, supercilious. It has little place for tragedy. In general it makes small points. It tears passion to titters.

About Mr. Thurber, on the contrary, there is nothing hard and fast and supercilious. Where most New Yorkers fear to be known as "jay" or "hick," Mr. Thurber tells the world. He was born at 147 Parsons Avenue, Columbus, Ohio. He trails Ohio with him. This alone marks him off from the provincial once-removed who are intimidated today as they were in the days of Congreve and Wycherley—for the *New Yorker*, after all, sprang to life in a postwar period, and its line of harsh Restoration comedy is nothing new under the sun.

Not that Mr. Thurber is the less disillusioned, but his disillusion is within, and genuinely preoccupying for himself. He was born in 1894, in a cooling-off period. In early Ohio, there was a high romantic light, and its glow touched even Andrew Carnegie of the libraries and Andrew Mellon of the National Gallery. Anyone who glances at a map of that great mid state may see for himself the memorials of its early high-mindedness. Long preceding Walt Whitman in their cosmic elation, the schoolmasters and clergymen who baptized Ohio communities

had no feeling that the landscape around them could ever be
a deflated one. For nomenclature they turned to revered Old
World—to Canton, to Toledo, to the Cincinnati, to Antioch, to
Akron, to Columbus, to Jerusalem, to Ravenna and Illyria, even
to Euclid. By the time that Mr. Thurber was growing up this
light had begun to fade. Heavy industry smudged the Ohio
sky. The Black Belt had as its oases the fair grounds and the
country clubs, but Dante was no longer in the public mind,
the schoolmasters were no longer baptizing new communities
or bestowing names like Marcus Alonzo on any babies except
colored ones. Ohio had come through an epoch; the old epoch
was now a joke. And the new epoch was dollar-marked.

As you glance through the line drawings at the end of Mr.
Thurber's *Carnival*, you find that he isn't bowling along on
Springfield or Akron tires into a satisfyingly prosperous era.
He is pulled over on the soft shoulder, away from the proces-
sion, and he is inspecting a "flat."

But that puncture, that deflation, divides him not merely
from rugged Ohio males. It cuts him off from the romantic
elation that has still persisted in America's women. The "culture" of Ohio, like the culture of the whole Middle West, had
not really been placed to any degree until Sinclair Lewis wrote
his epoch-marking *Main Street* and *Babbitt*. Mr. Thurber was
at that time groping for his particular attitude, since on account
of an eye injury he had not gone with the procession to the
first world war nor was he going along with it on the high-
road to business. He was still a regular guy, but becoming that
American anomaly, a man on the side lines, a side dish. He was
a man who worked at home, thus observant of a woman-made
environment, and for himself, as for Clarence Day, the anomaly
had a comedy in it.

Some of his first commentaries are grouped under the title
Men, Women and Dogs. The *morgue* of this title is evident.
On the title page we see a chinless man, a faithful bloodhound
pup, and a purposeful female all in vain pursuit of a star. This
isn't the knife-sharp "gal" whom Clare Boothe Luce exhibited
in *Women*, the New Yorker streamlined for action and cleav-
ing into publicity like a destroyer. It is for the feminine, soulful

grandchild of the Ohio Illyrians that Mr. Thurber reserves his
attention. She is not a siren. She is a frump. She hasn't the suspicion of a Profile. What he sees in her is her blithe domes-
ticity, her comic afflatus, her bookishness, her sub-urbanity.
Under her dominion is a faithful spouse. She is a worm-tamer.
He is a worm.

Observe her in her elated moment, reading a romance after
she has done the dishes. To her subjugated spouse she carols
from her easy chair, looking up from her best seller: "It's Our
Own Story *Exactly!* He Bold as a Hawk, She Soft as the
Dawn." The line itself might still make a covert appearance in
any of the bitter-sweet moderns who bootleg romance into
short stories, because Illyria has only gone underground and
the lovers of verbal magic persist. But Mr. Thurber is gunning
for the subjugated husband and the possessive matriarch. One
of these ladies bursts into a suburban living room, brandishing
a fern, her basket plumped from the wild woods. "I Come
From Haunts of Coot and Hern!" she exclaims. And the sour
Marquand family group looks at her, as if saying, "The devil
you do!" Another of her species grubs in the garden. Her
mother purrs, "She Has the True Emily Dickinson Spirit Except That She Gets Fed Up Occasionally." The joke is not a
little on Emily Dickinson.

But if the matriarch, with all the ineffableness that is never
missing from "My Day," is Mr. Thurber's target, he does not
limit himself to those who aspire to the Higher Good. The sex
itself is his objective. To a war on woman he devotes a separate
little volume. The juxtaposition of two sexes that gird against
one another goes beyond any mere conflict with the matriarch.
It sees the unfortunate male as a spider who is to be devoured,
an apprehensive, ineffectual pip-squeak, almost an object of
pity. Mr. Polly and Mr. Britling and Sentimental Tommy had
something of this, as well as Caspar Milquetoast and The Kid
and Mr. Pipp. In this figure is objectified the humor of lovely
woman's obdurate romance at the expense of the provider.
That there should be matrimonial bickering is bad enough, but
it is her incredible moral pretentiousness that is the worst.
"Well," the Middle-Aged Man yaps at his spouse, "Who Made

the Magic Go Out of Our Marriage—You or Me?" This is the deflation that has humor for Mr. Thurber. Bald as a coot, his Middle-Aged Man leans not from a balcony but from a sofa to plead to a remote lump of undifferentiated female frumpishness, "What Do You Want to Be Inscrutable *For*, Marcia?" Marcia glowers. In a situation like this, so frequent in grand opera, the imp in Caruso used to make him wink at the audience when, as a plump Samson, he had to wrap his pudgy arms around a bulging Delilah. Mr. Thurber bitterly dwells on the irony of solid flesh. He loves the irony of romance physically prostrated. Prone at a lady's feet, the sozzled lover protests, "This is Not the Real Me You're Seeing, Mrs. Clisbie." And when he sits sozzled in the bosom of his family, the proprietor of that bosom gathers her diminished offspring to her. "Well, I'm Disenchanted Too. We're *All* Disenchanted," which makes it unanimous. But she'll revive. With the little fellow once more sober and subjugated, she breaks in on the neighbors. "Yoo-hoo, It's Me and the Ape Man."

The cream of the *Carnival*, here and elsewhere, is to bring the historic repository of American uplift down to earth, and to show her mate as almost crushed under the burden, hampered and disconsolate. This is one mainspring of Mr. Thurber's comedy. But while the subjugation of the male is much on his mind, quite another subjugation and one that says nothing of Mother's Day reveals itself in a different line that should also be referred back to Ohio.

3

This second subjugation is, roughly speaking, to the mass mind, and he meets it, not by rejecting the mass, but by affirming its preposterousness. A lot of American humor is, in reality, the assertion of common sense in terms of herd instinct. The object is not to get off the earth because you may get hurt if you take a toss. Hence endless good-natured kidding, the caricature of his own genius by a man like John Barrymore, the fear of being a sissy, an irregular guy, a "highbrow." Conformity is a card of introduction, a proof of good will among strangers, a kind of reassurance and nose-rubbing, and if we think of the Flying Trapeze as the symbol of individual withdrawal and secret fantasy, Mr. Thurber is highly conscious that the Trapeze may throw the Don Quixote. Hence one of his mocking titles, *The Middle-Aged Man on the Flying Trapeze.*

Here the imaginative man turns his comedy against himself. It is not as an *"imaginatif,"* an Ariel, that Mr. Thurber began at Parsons Avenue, Columbus. Some of his most ingratiating pieces exhibit shy ineptitude, such as his own experiences with the Draft Board in 1917. He did not come in naked as did Lytton Strachey in England, carrying a round red rubber pillow, which he proceeded to inflate with exasperating slowness and then seat himself carefully, with a polite "Well, gentlemen?" Mr. Thurber's comedy is to contrast gentle, feeble flights of fantasy with, first of all, his acknowledged timidity and commonplaceness. This is naturally in play, but not entirely, and in his earlier work it is on pretty regular lines, the person who breaks away romantically being the incredible one.

Several times, he tells us with the familiar touch of college humor, he had "some thought of spending the rest of my days wandering aimlessly around the South Seas, like a character out of Conrad, silent and inscrutable. But the necessity of frequent visits to my oculist and dentist had prevented this. You can't be running back from Singapore every few months to get your lenses changed and still retain the proper mood of wandering. Furthermore my horn-rimmed glasses and my Ohio accent betray me, even when I sit on the terrasses of little tropical cafes, wearing a pith helmet, staring straight ahead, and twitching a muscle in my jaw." The daydream is from Kipling and Richard Harding Davis. It is romance in terms of the extravert Middle West. But only bead salesmen and native women with postcards tag after our Columbus escapist. "Under these circumstances it is impossible to be inscrutable and a wanderer who isn't inscrutable might just as well be back at Broad and High Streets in Columbus sitting in the Baltimore Dairy Lunch.

Nobody from Columbus has ever made a first rate wanderer in the Conradean tradition."

Here, under the joke, is a mocking deference to the Columbus norm. Had Mr. Thurber been born in the Dublin of W. B. Yeats it would have been simpler to be deliberately cut off. Though his eyeglasses would have been from Prescott's in Merrion Row, he would have dangled a black ribbon from them, as Yeats did. And, with the help of a flowing tie, he would visibly have been a long-haired artist. Yeats began on the marge of shadowy waters, "alone and palely loitering." Dublin afforded facilities for loitering. Democratic Columbus didn't even imagine them. Or, rather, the facilities were not admitted. The deflated epoch with its debunking humor, its sex acridity, its hardboiled realism and what-not, could not see that at the Baltimore Dairy Lunch at Broad and High in Columbus the most typical figure of all might be an Ernie Pyle. Ernie Pyle could fail Richard Harding Davis on every sartorial point, he could have horn-rimmed glasses and an Ohio accent, but this daring young Pyle could ingenuously follow to their last frontiers any number of Dairy Lunch Galahads. For that matter, Winesburg was in Ohio, and Sherwood Anderson, who still felt the glamour of the Civil War, had kept his own romantic elation. After futile years of conformity, that Ohioan no longer struggled with the fact that he was an artist. Anderson was poor but he differentiated himself. He had to. Herd instinct was against him, as it is against all irregulars. But nonconformity was not yet laugh-proof.

One evening at Clarence Day's, perhaps a quarter of a century ago, I heard Paul de Kruif tell of his youth in Michigan. Paul de Kruif loved the piano, knew how to play it, and was to make his debut in Holland, Mich. Being a regular guy, as strong as a tug, he was a jovial mixer with all the high school gang and they came in force to the concert and filled the front row, in order to make faces at him. He turned away from them as he sat at the piano but watched them out of the tail of his eye. For a time Beethoven dominated them, but as one of them made a crack, catching de Kruif off guard, he guffawed, and it was the end of that recital and all subsequent ones.

For this tale of clipped wings he could not have had a better listener than Clarence Day, who took it in without a move or sound. Lying by his Riverside Drive window, high on his hospital bed, with no curtains on plate glass that left exposed the whole of the midnight Hudson, not even scratching his bald head with the scratching stick from Chinatown, Clarence Day gave his full, ravenous attention to de Kruif's story. "Oh, God! Oh, *God!*" He laughed till it hurt, and because it hurt. Paul de Kruif, seeing it as funny, had no *morgue* but Clarence Day saw it, saw into it, around it, behind it, his eyes luminous and aggrieved, and those blue lips of his laughing.

His own conventionality had been clipped by invalidism, and that made him a writer. The strong pull for Clarence Day was toward the conformities of American life. Bedridden though he was, he became director of a glove factory, to be financially reputable. Plenty of sympathetic women were only too ready to be matriarchs to him, and he was unable to run away from them. He was tied down, marked off. But like Father he could roar, "God damn it," and have none of it. He would be anything but, damn it, not feminized. And yet, for all the humor with which he saw himself refusing to be different, he was not always in the crow's nest. It was gradually, though his wings were clipped, that he learned to become articulate.

In the same way, leaning more and more to autobiography, Mr. Thurber has gradually come to terms with the exigent artist in him. The simple emotions, in fact "the strong and rapid emotions," for which an Ernie Pyle had the common touch, are too uncritical for the subtlety and deviousness in Mr. Thurber. In his life with Grandfather the Civil War is taken as broadly humorous. Barbara Frietchie and Gettysburg and Appomattox—the things ennobled for an Oliver Wendell Holmes because he had lived them—become the subject for crude skits on schoolbooks, as does the poem "Excelsior." Perhaps this is a timidity at bottom. Few pieces of virtuosity surpass his account of Columbus in panic, "The Day the Dam Broke," and the cream of the jest is that the dam didn't break, thus adding ridicule to the panic. This is vengeance on a sensationalism that has to be deflated; yet to be inflated, to be enchanted, to admit magic, to be carried away, is still native in him, and comes to him in blasts of fantasy that are touched with nightmare and fear and horror. He does not want to be differentiated lest he be too much so. He may be from Columbus, but he may also be brother to Salvador Dali under his skin.

4

Mr. Thurber is at his highest point of perception when he comes closest to objectifying a comic insubordination. At an early stage, as in several of the pieces in *My Life and Hard Times*, he prefers the crude farce in fantasy, as in "The Night the Ghost Got In." "The Night the Bed Fell" is clowning, of a sort that English practitioners might be capable of. But in "The Secret Life of Walter Mitty," in "The Lady on 142," and in "The Remarkable Case of Mr. Bruhl," as well as others, he checks his power of fantasy against his sense of reality and enjoys an increasing mastery of this particular battledore and shuttlecock. And in "The Topaz Cufflinks Mystery" he extracts from a small matrimonial tiff, no great situation in itself and rather flat in "A Couple of Hamburgers," a wholly new and delightfully funny crux. A real motorcycle cop comes along at night to find the Middle-Aged Man crawling in the tall grass on the edge of the road while a lady in the car toward which he crawls giggles helplessly at her husband's plight as he searches for the cufflinks. This is a glimpse, not of an inept man who cannot get the better of reality, but of a spontaneous mutt, a little bit odd, who by his own nature brings himself into a grotesque situation. The humor is intrinsic. Mr. Thurber gives it substance by ringing the hard idiom of the cop against our resonant knowledge of Walter Mitty, or whatever he calls him—the *"imaginatif"* brought into an inimitable predicament by his own stubborn, singular, perverse but completely plausible pursuit of his own harmless idiosyncrasy. He is the same man, once again, at whom the orthodox garage man glares with hate when he sees him holding the umbrella over the poodle.

Much as Mr. Thurber has deflated the Illyrians, little as he wished to fit himself into the mold of the moldy romantics, he has finally revolved on himself until modern city-dwelling New York life and its nonconformities take on a meaning and a quiet amplitude. He began with "light middles," a literary form that usually twitters somewhere in the void, not abstract enough to be philosophy, not projected enough to be fiction. Addison and Steele began it, in those evergreens that make classes in English literature like a damp walk in the cemetery between the cypress and the yew. Out of this arid form Mr. Thurber has made a kind of imaginary confession, a creative soliloquy, personal, intimate, and with the inconsequence of drawings that betray no effort. Even when he writes regular short stories, they have the same confidential and insouciant touch. In "The Cane in the Corridor," the Man, the Woman, and the Faithful Dog of a friend all proceed to become sozzled, and it is certainly "perceptious" as a glimpse of the American social scene. The woman defends her man against the old friend who was neglected when in hospital, and she is almost like a cat taking a helpless kitten in her mouth in her protectiveness. The friend, drinking out of his empty glass, mumbles a reproach. "He wasn't so goddam sensitive when we were both with the Cleveland Telephone Company. He wasn't so goddam sensitive then. No, he was practically a regular guy." To which the deadlier of the species responds, "It is just quite possible, perhaps, that you were not quite perceptious at that time." That is the offensive-defensive to a regular guy.

It is a good answer, since we identify Mr. Thurber with the goddam sensitive, who grows more perceptious. His friends now proclaim he is a very great man. Perhaps it is enough that, in a path where pioneers trod whimsically before him, he now pursues his similar adventure in a perfect medium, a worm but a glowworm, lighting up the thickets of easy assumption and idiotic handicap, of midnight and bats in the belfry, and doing it in recognizable Connecticut and Manhattan with fertile fantasy and the magic of humor.

Enthusiasts who surrender to him unconditionally have a way of insisting, "Love me, love my humorist." They create a vogue, feeling their enjoyment trebled if they can be part of a crowd. But, while he has done nothing to shock them, while in a sense he placates and insinuates—America is very large, he is very small—it is along lines of a loneliness bred by equality (so acutely defined by de Tocqueville) that Thurber links himself to universal vagary. The essential in him is something that occasionally lets him behold the unicorn in the garden. The essential is the secret life. It is something achieved without breaking with the tribe.

The Misfit as Superman

THE delight of James Thurber's comedy, and Clarence Day's for that matter, derives partly from seeing how a deadly respectable environment can be encountered. Thurber poses a feeble and ineffectual victim, a squirrel in a cage, but his amused perception of the cage is constant. He gives no heroic or romantic accent to his rebel. American experience provides the environment in which this rebel is a slight misfit, and Thurber lets his rebel's fancy roam, with sozzling as a relief, while others prefer to show him taking a walk, choosing the Left Bank or Bloomsbury.

What was called sugariness in *Life with Father* by certain European critics, still bitterly serious after years of occupation, was, in essence, an American tolerance highly developed in Clarence Day. For a growing boy, not to speak of a growing man, every environment is likely to be misfit, which drove many patriarch Americans to be pioneers and adventurers, even revolutionaries. But the quandary selected by Clarence Day is a domestication in which the goal was to disestablish Father without renouncing him. To move away, to gang up on the parent that oppressed his family, was not the solution that suggested itself. Connive at a better arrangement, yes, but go on with the misfit. That was the play of Clarence Day's social instinct, exhausting all possibilities of change before rebellion. The general run of family experience, come day, go day, God send Sunday, afforded plenty of opportunity for his comic spirit. Had he been sugary, he would have hidden the male egoist so rampant in Father Day. The enormous vogue of the comedy, in America at any rate, owes as much to the unsparing perception as to acknowledged piety. The piety has to be taken not as a sugariness but as a tenacity, a feeling for continuity. It doesn't presuppose that the son knuckled under. He exercises perception yet retains membership in the family. To be a patricide would offend the comic spirit!

This patience so marked in Clarence Day goes back, I suppose, to the peculiar temper of the Revolution. Lewis Gannett, wishing to soften asperity against Soviet Communism, recently said that Soviet Communism, "like the American Revolution, has its roots in Voltaire and Rousseau." That might be a hard thesis to defend, though some of the Fathers did learn from Rousseau to equate democracy and individualism. Pope Pius XII, who once lived in Washington, D.C., was nearer the mark when he reminded American journalists early in 1947 that George Washington held "religion and morality" to be the indispensable support of political prosperity. Insubordination inside the family could be carried far, but insubordination carried desperately beyond fraternity to any secret society against fraternity, to any co-conspiracy, a Bund, a Klan, would be a violation of the American compact, a repudiation of the accepted environment. The one fundamental claim of America is to provide for change without requiring any sane misfit to gang up on the majority.

How, then, about the gentleman who is known as Nit-shee in Brooklyn? A year or two ago a Brooklyn student was so stirred by Nietzsche's words on the beautiful terribleness of murder that he nerved himself to go into a park and kill a comrade. This is a small increment from Nietzsche's piquant genius. The grand legacy was made visible in its works during the trial at Nuremberg.

It is unnecessary to re-hash war charges to bring out what Raymond Daniell reported observing in the Nuremberg public at that period. He termed it an "ethical lacuna." It wasn't that the Germans had waged war. Hitler had endlessly pointed out that other nations had from time to time waged aggressive war, even though pledging peace and asserting international morality. The "lacuna" came from an experiment with guilt which owed much to a philosophy expressly "beyond good and evil," a philosophy inculcating ethical lacuna. And that was Nietzsche's big contribution.

Not that he was Nazi before Nazism. He didn't preach Blood and Soil. He wasn't in politics. He wasn't tainted with anti-Semitism. He repudiated Bismarck's German Empire, and on a score of Nazi policies and procedures he would have been hostile, especially as a Swiss subject. But Nietzsche's dictum, "I am morality itself and nothing else is morality," was of deeper encouragement to Hitler than any specific endorsement of policy or program. Nietzsche did not have to be a Nazi. It was enough that he justified a course of national conduct beyond good and evil. That was all the Nazis asked of a great teacher. It was a legacy they could build on.

The fastidious Nietzsche could not personally have endured a raucous soapbox, or rather pillbox, orator of Hitler's stripe. Hitler sanctified Nazis who murdered political opponents. His gangs bludgeoned dissidents at Nazi rallies, and Nazis who became dissident were privately disposed of. All this kind of thing, with the Gestapo to back it up, might impress knaves like Laval or fantasts like Quisling, but Nietzsche was also "goddam sensitive." The difference in spiritual degree between himself and Adolf Hitler may be put down as immeasurable.

Was there a difference in kind? No. During the dozen years in which Nietzsche's intellect was unclouded, he concentrated extraordinary brilliance against the enemy of his dictum that "I am morality itself and nothing else is morality." That enemy was the democratic tradition. He quite rightly proclaimed that the democratic movement was an inheritance from the Christian movement, and he scorned both. He particularly denounced both for seeking to provide the bases of international morality.

His credo, in this respect, was the credo of the Gestapo. "We believe that severity, violence, slavery, danger in the street and in the heart, secrecy, stoicism, tempter's art and devilry of every kind—that everything wicked, terrible, tyrannical, predatory, and serpentine in man, serves as well for the elevation of the human species as the opposite." Piquant? Of course, but too Dachau, too Belsen.

Thus spake the precursor of the Nazi Messiah. Democrats, Nietzsche said, may "glorify public spirit, kindness, deference, industry, temperance, modesty, indulgence, sympathy by virtue of which he is gentle, endurable, and useful to the herd." But morality in Europe at present is "herd-animal," all right for the "socialist fools and shallow-pates" but not for the Superman. Democracy is "not only a degenerating form of political organization, but is equivalent to a degenerating, a waning type of man." It had to be met by men with a new "mission," to whom murder was beautiful, cruelty commendable, and beasts of prey the healthiest of growths. The Nazis concurred in this.

And the *führer* principle was demanded by Nietzsche as the proper means of counteracting democracy. "What a blessing, what a deliverance from a weight becoming unendurable, is the appearance of an absolute ruler in Europe." Nietzsche said this half a century in advance of Hitler. He wanted Napoleons, "those marvelously incomprehensible, and inexplicable beings, those enigmatical men, predestined for conquering and circumventing others."

Had intellectual democracy rejected Nietzsche, the "ethical lacuna" in Germany might not have resulted. But the Superman, supernally brave, proud, and masterful, the Byronic hero, was a blazing success. From Nietzsche's torch such Americans as Jack London, Theodore Dreiser, and H. L. Mencken caught fire. In 1908 Mencken said, "He reigns as king in German universities." "No one in our time," Georg Brandes testified, "has experienced anything like it—this prodigiously rapid attainment of the most absolute and world-wide renown." In 1909 Brandes said, "He holds undisputed sway over German minds." Already there were over 1,000 entries under his name in the British Museum library, and Jack London's Superman worship was not to be confined to his own country. It was to leap from America to Red Russia.

Nietzsche's influence on American intellectuals was a radical reversal of their simplicities, considering that he urged men to be criminal, to be hard and strong and dangerous, to be remorseless, to love cruelty, to take the whip to women, to stand alone. "Fear is the mother of morals." And democracy the mother of international code.

Nor was this without a political inspiration. Georg Brandes maintained Nietzsche's relation with "the all-dominating militarism of the new German empire." On principle, he said, Nietzsche is opposed to Bismarck "who has piled up for the Germans a new Tower of Babel, a monster in extent of territory and power and for that reason called great." At the same time, Nietzsche "dwells on the necessity of the struggle for power and on the supposed value of war to culture." "As regards the question of war, the only difference between them [the philosopher Hartmann and Nietzsche] is that Nietzsche does not desire war for the sake of a fantastic redemption of the world, but in order that manliness may not become extinct. In his contempt for women and his abuse of her efforts for emancipation Nietzsche again agrees with Hartmann," who on many points, according to Brandes, shared the German snobbish national feeling.

The bare facts of Nietzsche's life show how indisputably he shared German national feeling. He was never in the least opposed to militarism, however much he defined himself as a "good European." And he imbibed his national faith in correct Prussian fashion.

Nietzsche was born in a parsonage. On both sides he was descended from long lines of Lutheran pastors. His grandmother Krause had a brother who was a doctor of divinity, and his Nietzsche grandfather was also a doctor of divinity. There could scarcely be a more refined or respectable background. His father tutored four daughters of the ducal Altenburgs, and Nietzsche, happening to be born on King Friedrich Wilhelm IV's birthday, October 15, 1844, was named after the King, his father's patron.

Fritz, according to his faithful sister, was a perfect little model of a child. He was modest, pious, serious and grateful— grateful to God, to his forebears, his teachers, and to Germany.

From the first he was brilliant. By the age of ten he was taking a passionate interest in the science of war. The fall of Sevastopol to the Turks in 1854 made him exceedingly angry with the Russians, who forfeited his respect for their lack of military science. To be a Prussian grenadier was the height of his ambition.

War was in the air. The Prussian theorist von Clausewitz had laid it down that "war is nothing but the continuation of state policy with other means." "Force is the means; to impose our will upon the enemy is the object." Here was the serpent in the parsonage. When he began to read about *The Origin of the Species* and Schopenhauer's Will to Life, he threw off the old faith and had a new one. But he was a good boy. He would not discuss the irreligious Schopenhauer with his sister because dear Aunt Rosalie had left him a little legacy on that condition.

He had poor eyesight. He could not become a Prussian grenadier because of this, but a doctor who examined his eyeglasses instead of his eyes passed him for the horse artillery. He had to content himself with that.

His adoring sister thought it was horribly humiliating to have poor Fritz currying a horse, but he was a good recruit, deep in his studies of Greek language. He wanted to be a philologist. One day, misjudging his leap on to the back of a restive army horse, he cracked his breastbone and for five months had great pain. He used the time for study and went to a chair at Basel university, becoming a Swiss subject.

This young fire-eater shrank from "beer materialism" and swilling German students. While agreeing that "war is nothing but a duel on a larger scale," he sought for a genteel combatant. "You are a man after my own heart," he said one day to a new acquaintance. "Could we not have a duel together?" Music, poetry, and friendship were his joys. Across the lake from Basel lived the Wagners. Nietzsche was accepted as a worshiping young visitor and campaigned loyally for Wagner's Bayreuth. But in the end Wagner's Christianity disgusted him.

Basel made Nietzsche promise at the outbreak of the Franco-Prussian War to serve with the Red Cross as a Swiss subject. Cholera was prevalent and Nietzsche's heart was full of pity for the victims. One episode, however, released the volcanic romanticist in him. He saw the Germans go into action—a magnificent cavalry regiment, his own artillery dashing forward, and then the flaming infantry contingents. "Then I felt for the first time, dear sister, that the strongest and highest will to life does not find expression in a miserable struggle for existence but in a Will to War, a Will to Power, a Will to Overpower."

His health impaired by war, his eyesight said to be ruined by close work in philological research, his nerves shattered by illness, Nietzsche was a lame duck at thirty-two, pensioned by Basel so that he had about $1,000 a year to live on. He went seeking a benign climate from Rome to Turin, from the Alps to Nice, forced to take chloral because of pain, changing restlessly from one boardinghouse to another. His Gospel announcing a Superman was issued from exile. He urged "the moral honor" of being dangerous. "A conscience should be steeled and a heart transformed into brass." It was a release from current hypocrisies, and radicals adored him for it.

With the wind-up of the Nazi chapter at Nuremberg, it may be supposed that an ethical lacuna was opening up for a democratic feeling. But if the lacuna has to be filled by Americans who themselves have lacunae, the prospect is not entirely clear. Nietzsche's repudiation of "abstract moral principles" was extremely succinct. Shaw's epigram, "the golden rule is that there are no golden rules" weakened the superb German dueling challenge, "I am morality itself and nothing else is morality." But Shaw's derivation from Nietzsche was no accident. The very words "religion and morality," quoted by the Pope from George Washington, sound hollow in 1947. They bring to mind the officiousness of priests who turn up in the wake of the midwife or the undertaker, or else astoundingly prove themselves to be as good as any soldier in their role as padres and chaplains.

The aridity of conventional religion in America hasn't been the sole cause of ethical lacunae. The evangelists' strongest critics have insisted on attacking morality itself. No one supposes that John Dewey has a Will to Overpower like Nietzsche's, yet he has recently reiterated our "subjection to abstract moral principles" as though their only advocates were bores and hypocrites. With the troglodytes in mind, men who resist change by democratic process, he identifies "evil" with the sort of things that they call evil—the aspirations of the common man. John Dewey has long scorned the whole vocabulary of evangelism.

But it isn't fundamentalists who cry "Wolf, wolf," when Nietzsche urges men to be "tyrannical, predatory and serpentine." John Dewey himself is in arms against the predatory who create the disenfranchised, the dispossessed, and the disprivileged. How, without "abstract moral principles," without a notion of good and evil, can we think of the categories of dispossessed and disprivileged? When rigid "authority" lays down crushing rules in the name of "good and evil," it is natural to move beyond to new ground in order to combat such authority. But the lacuna thus created leaves no place for moral reproach. There can only be force against force, precisely the situation that Nietzsche exulted in. The only moral life "beyond good and evil" is the intrepidity of a Superman lording over victims disprivileged forever.

Against such intrepidity no democrat has a valid argument, since a Will to Power or to Overpower transfers all conflict to the plane of will. On that plane there can only be admiration for the intrepid, and young Americans in Germany are often won by its exponents. The feasible alternative, as a critic has to remind himself in this epoch, is to assert humanism again—that humanism from which Nietzsche was an apostate though saying black masses for it. In order to dislodge Germans from the Will to Power or Overpower, Americans themselves have to recover the democratic ethic, which inevitably implies a conception of values. The leverage for those values in Germany has to be found in anti-Nazi Germans.

When Abraham Lincoln was alive he had a difficult moral situation with certain Southerners. Like the pro-democrat Germans, these pro-Union Southerners wanted at once to work with the North and yet not conflict with the intrepid South. They wanted leniency to be shown to them because the secessionists were so intrepid.

Lincoln did not spare Unionists who wanted it both ways. "Why did they not assert themselves? Why stand passive and allow themselves to be trodden down by a minority? Why did they not hold popular meetings and have a convention of their own to express and enforce the true sentiment of the State? If preorganization was against them then, why not do this now that the United States Army is present to protect them? The paralysis—the dead palsy—of the government in this whole struggle is, that this class of men will do nothing for the government, nothing for themselves, except demanding that the government shall not strike its open enemies lest they be struck by accident."

Lincoln did not evade good and evil. He had no "ethical lacuna." He did not seek to find a common principle between Master Men and himself. He knew that they had to be downed, whether in Louisiana or elsewhere. And he recommended democratic process to those who protested their good will. That was their way to use it and prove it.

To revivify democratic morality, as liberal journals have tried in America, is hard and ungrateful work. When a phalanx of mummies gathers around pious American tradition, the struggle is not only with the predatory but with the academic. Revulsion is so strong on this account that until people learn George Washington had false teeth they can hardly feel he was bearable. But ours, for better or worse, is Life with the Fathers. They were not "marvellously incomprehensible, and inexplicable beings, those enigmatical men, predestined for conquering and circumventing others." Unfortunately such beings, magnificent in themselves, are too big for the planet. Our "sniveling petty-bourgeois democrats," as Russian graciousness and in some measure Charles Beard's analysis depicts them, did at least humanely provide a triumphant liberal principle, a method for amending the governmental prescription. Our aim, therefore, is not to fit a man to the planet, or a Superman either, but a morality in a situation otherwise anarchic. It is a morality, not of predestination or race, but of method inside humanism, a morality of "globaloney"—not a religion of J. P. Morgan slipping cheques under bishops' plates or a pervert commercial creed vitiating human decency but a general agreement on the insupportability of power and overpower. So long as criticism entertains Nietzsche's fine boast, "I am morality itself and nothing else is morality," the simplest norms of literary judgment are in dispute. If Nietzsche opens the door wide to power, it is the Napoleons of industry who walk up the red carpet, not pagan heroes.

James Joyce

JAMES JOYCE is a special literary case, by far the most difficult of our time. Though *Finnegans Wake* was published in the year the war broke out, it still remains unfinished business for most critics. In 1944 two gifted and devoted students of its text, Joseph Campbell and Henry Morton Robinson, issued a work, *A Skeleton Key to Finnegans Wake*, to unravel Joyce's meaning. To have an elucidation of considerable size, no mean skeleton, published within five years of a work written in English has never to my knowledge happened before. And the emotion that prompted it commands respect. "If Joyce had spent eighteen years in its composition we might profitably spend a few deciphering it." Which makes the critic, with a few days or weeks at his disposal, seem wholly impertinent, especially as Campbell and Robinson place beyond themselves "the unimaginable prize of complete understanding."

They regard *Finnegans Wake* as a masterpiece, a "mighty allegory of the fall and resurrection of mankind," a kind of "terminal moraine in which lie buried all the myths, programs, slogans, hopes, prayers, tools, educational theories, and theological bric-a-brac of the past millennium." It is a "complete and permanent record of our age," in which Joyce "presents, develops, amplifies and recondenses nothing more nor less than the eternal dynamic implicit in birth, conflict, death and resurrection." To call him a mere "genius" after that eulogy seems barely polite.

A casual glance at *Finnegans Wake*, a random reading here and there, cannot confirm one word that Campbell and Robinson have uttered. The text is apparently gibberish. Anyone can guess that if Joyce had come on a phrase like "portal to portal," he would have crossbred it endlessly. It would become potable to potable, portaloo to portugal, porthole to pokeagal, popebull to popecrawl. Dip anywhere into the text and you see him concocting a Mairzy Doats language. "For Portsymasser and Purtsymessus and Pertsymiss and Partsymasters, like a prance of findigos, with a shillto shallto slipny stripny." That fandango leaves you dizzy. Yet the trick of crossbreeding is perfectly intelligible. Some months ago a British Museum porter from Cork, wishing to tell me of a learned man's centenary, called it his "anniversity." That sort of double-jointed word is typically Joycean, and it makes double sense, combining university and anniversary.

But the ultimate consumer, even if convinced that *Finnegans Wake* is not a nonsense book, has to be brought over a hump. Is it worth spending years to decipher? That is the essence of it. As the last installment of James Joyce's ubiquitous self-revelation, is it sufficiently imposing? Art is long and time is fleeting. Must we bow to it and bend the knee?

A sound critic is chary of strictures on any author's choice of style. Trim writers have always been ready to do a better job with Shakespeare than he did with himself. Dryden wrote much better. But the power of any great writer implies magic communicativeness. He doesn't follow a prescription. The breath of life in him prescribes his style. He makes the norms by which we live in him. As our taste changes, he may no longer communicate to us, but if he once won us our recapture is not improbable. We respond as we do to people we both like and discriminate about. The heart is moved, the inner being stimulated, and we experience ourselves on a plane where we are transported and completed, with the assent of our total nature. We don't fend off delight because mentors frown on us. Only our own taste can protect us from ravishment. Our boon is to surrender, in accord with the instinct of our being, to pursue writers who give the acme of delight, "the unimaginable prize of complete understanding," with ourselves having a part in it.

And, in a bitter epoch, harsh and shattering experience may

be the richest. The question comes down to an author's unique quality and his reader's imperative need for it. But a wise reader has to discriminate.

It is a highly personal discrimination in this instance. I wish I had known James Joyce. Once in my life, at a restaurant in Montparnasse in 1923, Janet Scudder said quickly, "That's James Joyce," and I saw an Irishman of fine features that had something of the cleric, something of the lawyer, in them, with sensitiveness in the nose and the jutting chin. He must have observed through his thick lenses that he was being stared at, and his fair skin flushed with a uniform flood of redness, but though Janet Scudder knew him, we did not hold him up. And yet, not only because he was Irish but because I had gone to Clongowes, the same Jesuit school in Ireland that he had attended, and because *Portrait of the Artist* was one of the books I had reviewed with sense of its consummate importance, it was regrettable not to have sound of him, as well as sight. Padraic Colum always spoke of him as a singularly easy and amiable companion.

That he had exiled himself was another bond. His struggle to disengage himself from Mother Church and Mother Ireland was discernible in *Portrait of the Artist*, which H. G. Wells reviewed in the same issue of *The New Republic* as I did, with the same sense of Joyce's inexorable candor. In *Ulysses* Joyce made more explicit the huge process of orientation on which he was embarking, and the final exploration, recognizing the full multiplicity of human impulse, its moral indiscriminateness, its drowning oceans of phantasmagoria, occupied his years from 1922 to 1939, and the 628 big pages of *Finnegans Wake*.

His own words about *Finnegans Wake* may be a help to understanding. It comes slowly "to unfold all marryvoising moodmoulded cyclewheeling history (thereby, he said, reflecting from his own individual person life unlivable, transaccidentated through the slow fires of consciousness into a dividual chaos, perilous, potent, common to allflesh, human only, mortal) but with each word that would not pass away the squidself which he had squirtscreened from the crystalline world waned chagreenold and doriangrayer in its dudhud." It is, as he says, "stardust and sinner's tears," "the whirling dervish, Tumult, son of Thunder, self exiled in his ego a nightlong a shaking betwixttween white and reddr hawrors, noondayter-rorised to skin and bone by an ineluctable phantom (may the Shaper have mercery on him!) writing the mystery of himsel in furniture," which may be Purgatory. He makes few claims for "our low hero" in this penitent need of mercury; and he "cannot behold the brand of scarlet on the brow of her of Babylon and feel not the pink one in his own damned cheek."

Cheek, however, wasn't Stephen Hero's scantity. It took unprecedented cheek to invent his *Finnegans Wake*, and there isn't a page that lacks it.

The form is in itself a monument to audacity. He probably did not count on rational readers of the kind who spent a hundred years unraveling cuneiform writing or the recondite details of the Kabbalah. In Joyce, beyond doubt, there is a scholast, a pedant who says yes to a design for its own sake, who interweaves for diversion, tucking the serpent's tail into its mouth and tracing the Liffey as it loops, much as the artist in the Book of Kells filled a page with intricate initial. But the cipher in which Joyce wrote *Finnegans Wake*, besides forestalling the censor by limiting the text to the initiated, had the advantage of inciting us to a complicity with his mood-moulding. And the child in us that is caught by crossword puzzles, Chinese puzzles, or detective stories can also be arrested by a cipher. Not long ago I saw a small boy, a little Lord Fauntleroy, who insisted on his colored nurse lifting him up to peer through a knothole in a wooden fence on Park Avenue. He ran for it so directly that I was amused by his eagerness. When he had gone on and no one else was in sight, I felt myself wondering, "What *is* behind that fence?", so I stooped to squint. By posing *Finnegans Wake* beyond the knothole of his cipher, Joyce hadn't much to learn from the showman he calls P! T! Barnum! And questionable as his means are, for reasons worth discussing, he does cram into his circus lot a great deal that is appropriate to a knothole.

But the initiated who take the immense trouble to learn the cipher are too quick to call James Joyce a genius, if they mean a genius in the humanist tradition. This is a disputable claim. Certainly he is an inventor of fantastic resource and wide acquaintance with literature. In form as well as in substance he is supremely alive, not to an everyday community in its rational existence, but to the community he can document from James Joyce. The literary tradition in which he has his place is a great tradition of self-revelation by means of confession and myth.

Rabelais began it in our times, and Montaigne continued it in a social idiom. What they experienced, with eyes, nose, tongue, throat, sex organ, hands, skin, liver, gall and the rest, had not only the most vivid reality but enabled them to surmise what subjective experience in general was like. These were the first modern behaviorists. Whatever the Church's theory of the Fall, they considered the monkey in the family tree well worth reporting, and their bold assertion of autonomy was an effect of the Renaissance, though they well knew that the Church understood naturalism, inculcated guilt feelings about the animal in man, and convicted him of sin as a limit to his autonomy. The Puritans shut out Shakespeare as an occasion of sin, and naturalism has never ceased to be reprobated in Puritans. Paul Elmer More was recently browbeating it at Princeton. But humanism has properly regarded any naturalistic work as one aspect of man's struggle to emancipate himself.

Hence the predisposition of liberal critics to welcome Joyce. He, like Rabelais, had everything that the Oxford Dictionary ascribes to a poet—"imaginative power, insight, sensibility, and faculty of expression." Finnegans Wake is no less uninhibited than Rabelais, so far as expression goes, and has its own extravagance and profuseness of invention.

But for autonomy to be earned, there has to be discrimination in social terms. Against the dead weight of the bourgeois community, as James Thurber shows, a post-romantic Ohioan can develop fantasy and inhabit twilight. James Joyce, a post-romantic Irishman, seeks to devise a much more revolutionary procedure. From his earliest text to the seething complexity of Finnegans Wake he has gone his nostalgic way, eternally looking at Ireland over his shoulder. While seeming to be tethered to nothing that can retard autonomy, he has one of those extremely elastic bonds with the past which snap him back to Home and Mother if he ever relaxes vigilance. That the primary impulse of his career was to end infantility is unmistakable, yet as he plunges into the "dividual chaos," feeling that to disintegrate Catholicism in himself is to lose himself though he must blaspheme and profane it, an oscillation begins which escapes the control of reason. This oscillation is part of any attempt at autonomy. A writer is not a cow. But if great wits are allied on one side to madness and on the other to criminality, the oscillation must not become irrational. It cannot, as in the case of Nietzsche, make an ethic of denying ethic. Or, as in the case of Joyce, see woman as the occasion of sin while regarding woman as the supreme symbol of forgiveness. That is also an aspect of infantility. So is the eternal recurrence of a resurrection, which is the doctrine of grace in a sentimental form, asserting that all is for the best in the worst of all possible worlds, and there isn't a damn thing to do about it. Evil is too inevitable, human nature too incorrigible, and its civil war too radical, in this new doctrine of predestination.

At the end of their remarkable book, Campbell and Robinson take up the defense of James Joyce as a true humanist. "If Joyce is sick," they say, "his disease is the neurosis of our age." And then they proceed to incriminate the society we live in.

"Lifting our eyes from his page," they say, "we find in every aspect of society the perversion, the decay, and the disintegration of religion, love, and morality that he has described in *Finnegans Wake*. The hypocrisy of political promises, the prurient preoccupation with sex, the measuring of all values by mercantile standards, the fascination of lurid headlines gossip and its effect on a literate but basically ignorant bourgeoisie— all these are mirrored to the life by this liveliest of observers. Yet there is not a syllable of tirade in *Finnegans Wake*. The lesions of the modern soul, the ulcers of the modern state, are to Joyce but the recurrent fever sores of life in ferment. He is a clinician who knows that although individuals, indeed whole societies, may be desperately ill, there is a principle of health in the human germ-plasm that survives pestilences, wars, and dissolutions. If Joyce's viewpoint is pathologic, then any rosier lens is sentimental."

This is strictly a matter of opinion, but it has to be noted that most artists who feel clinical take the precaution of relating the diseased to one healthy specimen, a man in a white coat. Joyce does not do this in *Finnegans Wake,* and he mirrors the fall of man with a glint of satiric satisfaction that is unusual among moralists. Humpty Dumpty falling from the wall is a figure of fun, and his shame in Phoenix Park is colossal, stupendous and farcical. The atmosphere of the book, with its almost incessant blasphemy and profanity, is in general one of a depraved familiarity with dirt of every description, and if Joyce is free from moral indignation, unlike Swift, it is as if he wished to revenge a divided nature on the poor sentimentalists who think that any human being can be integrated. That his apologists recognize this to be the truth they clearly and sufficiently indicate when they say, "The dynamic of obsessional guilt, personal and racial, animates these pages." Sin, in other words, not evil, is Joyce's obsession, so that sex is an incurable guilt in spite of the cleansing naturalness of "Annah the All-maziful, the Everliving, the Bringer of Plurabilities, haloed be her eve, her singtime sung, her rill be run, unhemmed as it is uneven." He returns to her as to a refuge.

But the emotional chaos in *Finnegans Wake* is not the only sign of Joyce's neurosis, which may or may not be universal in our day as *A Skeleton Key* says it is. Another witness to neurosis is the language. No one may urge that for the sake of quick and wide intelligibility a poet should sacrifice his peculiar appeal to the trained imagination. Some things, as the *Key* says, cannot be simplified. But language is a medium of exchange. An issue of the mind, to be deemed a sound currency, must be redeemable at par. If a style is not securely based, not founded on etymology, safeguarded by grammar, the author has everyone at a disadvantage. His readers may work hard and think themselves initiated, but out of clangs, puns, parodies, associations, onomatopoeia, an illusion of comprehension may give them a false affluence. They may miss the whole point, in spite of years of application. And it shows how dangerous Joyce's method is that essentials in *Finnegans Wake* escape experts who gave years to its analysis.

Possibly the authors of *A Skeleton Key* have had a major interest in Joyce's bits of Danish and Sanskrit, his acquaintance with Vico and Croce, with Schopenhauer and Spengler, his awareness of music, of contemporary politics, the sheer mass of information that he plays with and draws on. Their footnotes reveal his devouring curiosities. But it is the fall and resurrection of national Ireland, not the fall and resurrection of mankind, that, as I see it, led Joyce to begin *Finnegans Wake*. *A Skeleton Key* virtually ignores this acute preoccupation. The authors make intelligible the large frame he has given to his "cyclewheeling history," and they can go back from Phoenix Park to Egypt and the Book of the Dead. But the real Heliopolis in Phoenix Park is Tim Healy. He and his nephew Kevin are slyly identified repeatedly. No one who studies the text with this in mind can fail to be overwhelmed by the evidence. Joyce began when the treaty with Britain at the end of 1921 marked *Finnegans Wake* for him. Phoenix Park with Healy's Chapelizod near by, and Healy in the Vice-regal Lodge near Wellington's Monument, is his theatre of the downfall of an aspiration to independence. Kate, with "a month and one windies" in the house, I take to be Ireland with the thirty-two counties, though the *Key* has an erudite gloss on it. The Peace Treaty, a gorgeous truce to some, becomes "a gorgeups trucefor happinest childers," which gives us Childers with his gorge up, puking the treaty. "The last sigh that came from the hart" of Anglo-Ireland brings in what "bucklied" it, Governor General Buckley, the last of the viceroys. Separation "With Kiss. Kiss Criss. Cross Criss. Kiss Cross. Undo lives 'end. Slain." So, in his excruciating cipher, Joyce shows how the Church once more, as from 432 A.D., played crisscross with Ireland, undoing life's end and slaying it.

Tim Healy, "always a priest's man," as the *Encyclopædia Britannica* dryly says, is the symbol of compromise, and Joyce calls him Jute. Mutt says to him, "Here is the Viceroy's jobgrab." And Jute says, "Wad!" A fat job for the Stone Age money-grabber, and "what a meanderthall-tale to unfurl and with what an end in view of squattor and anntisquattor and postproneauntisquattor! To say too us to be very tim, nick and larry of us."

The story moves to "heegills and collines," O'Higgins and Collins. "Move up, Mick, make room for Dick," scrawled on Dublin walls after Michael Collins was killed, becomes "Stand up, mickos! Make strake for minnas! By order, Nicholas Proud." And so the civil war enters, Shaun fighting Shem, Mutt fighting Jeff, Nick fighting Mick, Brown fighting Nolan. "The voax of the turfur is hurled on our lande," or another chapter in "borderation," with Kevin as the bright young lawyer. "We bright chaps of the brandnew brain trust are briefed here and with maternal sanction compellably empanelled at quarter sessions under the six disqualifications," meaning the "maternal sanction" for the Six Counties by Mother Church— "Our Ireland, Rome and Duty."

Much "soul speech wearing an artful of outer nonsense" is contained in *Finnegans Wake*, and not a few "seeklets of the alcove." But the vital point for criticism is that Joyce's commentators give little or no hint of it. The majority of Joyce's readers may derive pleasure from his flow of words, but they have no real notion of the things he is driving at. They haven't the Key to it. Even his experts haven't.

The "enthusiasm of the faithful few" is an admirable quality in itself and his editors possess it. Yet before *Finnegans Wake* can be taken as a "resilient, all-enjoying, all-animating 'Yes,' the Yes of things yet to come," it would be well to know what the text reveals and conceals. And Joyce has stated at the beginning that "hides and hints and misses in prints" are the essence of his work. "So you need hardly spell me how every word will be bound over to carry three score and ten toptypsical reading throughout the book of Doublends Jined." That Dublin from whose midden heap he drags them all, enough that they have smelled the same Liffey, whose fountain he woos into perpetual flow, and to whose grandeur he defers so mournfully, so proudly.

For a cry of intense loneliness, of division and separation, gives poignancy to the end. Of course life marches on, Ireland

continues from era to era, the Liffey still runs to the sea, Finn-
again will be Finn-again. But though Dev do us part, the plaintive cry is, "try not to part. Be happy, dear ones . . . How
small it's all . . . You're only a bumpkin. I thought you the
great in all things, in guilt and in glory. You're but a puny."
A resilient Yes? And, like a lost bird, a wild goose in a wind,
he says farewell:

> I'm loothing them that's here and all I lothe. Loonly in me
> loneness. For all their faults I'm passing out. O bitter end-
> ing! I'll slip away before they're up. They'll never see.
> Nor know. Nor miss me. And it's old and old it's sad and
> old it's sad and weary I go back to you, my cold father,
> my cold mad feary father, till the near sight of the mere
> size of him, the moyles and moyles of it, moananoaning,
> makes me seasilt saltsick and I rush, my only, into your
> arms.

For an imagination that was exiled from its native soil, lace-
rated and denied, *Finnegans Wake* is the most imposing pyra-
mid. Self-shaming and yet shamming, it presents an incessant intellect that feeds on itself remorselessly, a thwarted will that
hides and hints, a faith that craves a haven. He is basically in
reaction from humanism, but the archaic twist in him has no
hard viciousness such as in Nietzsche. His is a labyrinthine
mind, half-aware of forgotten magic, wholly aware of secrets
lost to multitudes who live on the surface. Yet he is marred by
Dublin education and there is a disease in his divided spirit
His poetry has a sadness that pearls the disease.

The Monkey and the Sun

I T IS astonishing how many writers are using "individual" or "individualist" as a term of reproach. When the rugged individualist was in fashion, it was the other way round. Men gloried in it. Now the mark of the beast is on it. One writer speculates on man's "individualist or competitive habits" as though every individual must be a selfish one. Another writer tells how Americans "were taught to become individualists, rugged individualists, gadgeteers, selfish, pleasure-loving," and, by inference, lone wolves, anti-social and predatory. Since the Russian Revolution, it is probably correct to say, this good old brownstone word inhabits a neighborhood that falls behind the times. Newcomers have to be observant to see that it was once respectable. Now it is shabby on the face of it. Soon it will be shady. Then it may be officially condemned.

Of course it can bear a low interpretation, but is it the only one? When a civilized man says, "My home is my castle," he obviously is no collectivist, but he does not not really mean that he refuses to let the gas-meter be inspected or intends to shoot callers at sight. He is emphasizing that there is a privacy, an independence, that is intensely precious and must not be invaded. The ultimate value of private ownership, in this aspect, is not that it enables him to be aggressive, competitive, but that it secures for him that subtle privilege, the right to be and to consult himself. Gregarious and social he has to be, if the self is not diseased, but society is his means to an honest individual end; he wants above all a social system that has "reverence for the individual human life" at the center of it. The more individuals there are, in this sense of individuated and highly developed persons, the better—the better for society, for life, and for happiness. And who but pronouncedly "anti-social" individuals (saints, artists, and revolutionaries) have striven for the multitude, though themselves to be kicked out, to end on the cross, or to be assassinated? The herd is in fact more the enemy of society than is the individual. The herd betrays itself by not respecting the rights of individuals. The true individual has at once to concern himself with society and endlessly assert himself against it. He has to be no less dissociated than associated.

All of this bears on Virgil Jordan's recent pamphlet *Manifesto for the Atomic Age*. This pamphlet is a sincere, troubled, and instructive attempt, couched in grave terms, to assert the rights of the individual but at the same time to jumble up the individual with free enterprise. In thus playing into the hands of those who say "basically individualist and competitive," Mr. Jordan seems to me to injure the cause he espouses, which is "reverence for the individual." And this line of thought can only be straightened out by asking what we think Americans are driving at and what America exists for.

Our chief danger, as Mr. Jordan sees it, is that mankind, already tending toward what he calls "unlimited" or autocratic government, is now about to cease free enterprise because of applied atomic energy and to attach itself to the state like Romulus and Remus to the wolf. Since he ascribes our strength as individuals to the practice of free enterprise, Mr. Jordan feels like holding tight to it. He dreads a rain of manna from heaven, though he does not deny that it will come. "We can now make anything—materials, machines and energy—out of anything or nothing, anywhere in the world, in any amount, almost without measurable cost." But this will inevitably wipe out "the monetary, financial, or acquisitive incentives to work, thrift, enterprise, saving, investment, and ownership of property." And how then can our home be our castle? Mr. Jordan is frozen by the prospect of goods as free as water, services as free as air, but publicly owned. It is as if he had to spend the rest of his life playing cards in a sanitarium for chips that would have no value.

The odd thing is this, Mr. Jordan values the true individual.

He cites Pico della Mirandola (or J. P. van Mirandola if he prefer), who derived from Plotinus and Plato. And Mr. Jordan seeks in Kant the sense of the unique reality of the individual. America sanctions this ideal. It has personified it in the embracing independence of Abraham Lincoln, in the hair-splitting integrity of Thoreau, in the insurgence of Mark Twain or Walt Whitman. Here are American separatisms sharp as stars in the blue of the flag. But Mr. Jordan intertwines this ideal of the individual with the competitiveness that stems from the machine age and business enterprise, the profit system, and so-called "limited" government.

Mr. Jordan could only reach this confusion by accepting materialist history, a history that ignores the psychological sources of democracy.

To magnify his America of business enterprise, he postulates that up to two hundred years ago this was an unhappy world for the common man, its grimness virtually unrelieved until the Industrial Revolution. Men in general were beasts of burden, dependent on human and animal muscle power—and anyone who has recently had to put chains on his car by himself knows what Mr. Jordan means by animal muscle power. He makes the Past completely beastly—no cartwheels, no waterwheels, no windmills, no sails on ships, no canals, no catapults or pulleys or levers or gunpowder, just blood and sweat and tears, no Royal Societies or Academies of Science, a sort of hydrocephalic Europe that was mechanically imbecile and despicable, with a back curtain of unlimited government and Divine Right, of serfdom and slavery. "Perhaps the only salvation or escape" for the common man was "in some hereafter which their priests or their prophets promised them." Religion as opium.

This is quite a favorite myth at present. It accounts in part for the antipathy that Britain, France, and Italy (not machine-age Germany) promptly excited in hosts of American soldiers. By hook or crook some of our museum directors may want for their galleries the pictures produced in this hell on earth, but Mr. Jordan has to remind us that the beauty was a snare, the plumbing no good, and the service underpaid. Mont St.

Michel whispered disturbingly to Henry Adams but says nothing audible to Mr. Jordan.

His picture of civilization is grotesquely simplified. William of Orange and Oliver Cromwell are not in it. He sees the power and superstition of "unlimited" government as being broken by the Industrial Revolution. He affirms the contrast in order to indicate that with the machine age came a system of cash remuneration for effort, and cash remuneration is assumed to be a real measure of social worth. The Goulds, the Fisks, the Vanderbilts, the Morgans are all seen in glowing light. Business enterprise was thus the true friend of individualism as Pico della Mirandola phrased it. The individual flowered in an economy of scarcity. He grew in "self-reliance, personal integrity, independence, enterprise, competitive effort, and reverence for the individual human life." But now the atomic age, controlled by the state, comes along to atomize the individual.

The retort is obvious. John D. atomized his competitors, being more rugged than they were. All monopolists atomize. Judge Gary, "Divine Right" Baer, George Pullman, were paying fourteen dollars a week more or less for an eighty-hour week. Reverence for the individual human life? If we cast back, not to Gene Debs, but to Bryan skywriting about "the cross of gold," the case cannot be argued. Theodore Roosevelt broke away from Henry Cabot Lodge not because T. R. was a rampant radical or a "traitor to his class" but because he was alive to a mounting threat of world revolution. Lenin stood in the wings. He was to wrench Russia from those who had pulverized labor. That labor was to swap masters and in turn to be pulverized by Lenin was evident to a social democrat. A new book, *Social Democracy versus Communism,* selected from the latest writings of Karl Kautsky (1854-1938), shows clearly the dire tendency to atomize that is latent in Communism as well as in capitalism. But Mr. Jordan shows no awareness of this anti-individual tendency in capitalism.

Nor does he realize that the original emphasis of the American Revolution was primarily on the individual in a free harmonious society that did not predicate the machine age. America started with a galaxy of individuals. They emphasized union among themselves but separatism from the old authority. They believed that the main thing to be said for a democracy was that it would enable people to be individual.

This abides in two germinal phrases, "the pursuit of happiness" and "the consent of the governed." Happiness was an individualist conception. So was consent. The suffrage was inevitably extended to every individual as such, against property prejudice, race prejudice, sex prejudice. It was another means for the individual's fulfilling his real preferences, and presupposes an individual who knows whom and what he likes. The thing you like is the thing that conforms to you, not the thing authoritatively prescribed to you. The "lich" is the form, the shape, the trunk. The "fat and liking soil" of Normandy was the soil that favored growth, the pleasant and congenial soil. Such was the glorious promise that America held out to the individual.

America's long suit, as against traditional royal Europe, was the special facility it gave to those who would work their way. American historians, Charles Beard among them, are quite prone to see Europe as a wicked grandpa only too happy to warm his withered shanks at the American oil-heater, but at the same time that they decry oligarchic Europe the best of them do not remain mute about native oligarchy. The democrat conspicuously renounced feudalism, hereditary titles, and primogeniture, but he did not for a moment renounce business enterprise or the new privilege and the new serfdom to which it inevitably tended.

This point, missed or elided by Virgil Jordan, is inexorably brought home by Joseph Dorfman in his indispensable work, *The Economic Mind in American Civilization, 1606-1865*, and we may be sure that attentive Russian critics of democracy, as Mr. Jordan conceives it, have a lively appreciation of it. The spiritual element that was original in America is put in jeopardy by omnivorous commerce. Modern America that aims at economic justice has had to be tough with commerce and remains in its greatest danger from the unbridled commercial spirit.

American cities, to be sure, were laid out with a rigid rationality that was a concession to commerce by its bleak engineers, but democracy was imbibed in older cities, cities that followed the river beds, the hill contours, and the casual elms. The machine age was a late arrival and its prowess was notoriously abhorrent to Jefferson.

Jefferson thought of all-round and rounded individuals. He did not think moral personality could be subdivided and he did not hail one-piece occupations. "Reverence for the individual human life" was a reality for him. He did not shut his eyes to the regimentation required by machine-tending, with the children of "free enterprise" employed in shifts, canning one thing and another to the limit of their powers and then spending free time eating out of cans, drinking out of cans, listening out of cans, watching canned entertainment, devouring canned jokes or canned political spam or canned columnists, daily canned into subways for transit, born in canneries, housed in canneries, shopping in a chain cannery, taken to a big cannery for an operation and to a private cannery in the end.

Mr. Dorfman's two volumes suggest the crippling of "social justice" by the system that Mr. Jordan takes quite uncritically. "Freedom and individualism," Mr. Dorfman asserts in his conclusion, have been viewed in America not in the light of Pico della Mirandola but "within the specific framework of commerce and finance." The humanist conception has "had a terrific struggle to attain a toehold," and while "here and there through the chinks of commerce flashed the flame of idealism and human passion, and the authentic voice of democracy strained through the hardness of social stratification," its values have never distinguished America.

An illustration of the blind competitiveness inherent in the commercial mind can be found in Mr. Jordan's own pages where he intimates that America "must be prepared to support out of its immense productive resources" the economically inferior peoples, the insolvent collectivisms, and all the other countries that are bankrupt. On this point he is not only in conflict with himself but he asserts democratic superiority on the false ground of capitalistic prowess. If the age of alchemy is here, as he says, America cannot hog it. Mr. Jordan cannot vaunt the advantages of scarcity and at the same time admit that abundance is within reach.

But are we such monkeys that we cannot use abundance in accord with the insights of American democracy? By agreeing on a yardstick for all peoples in the world such as "reverence for the individual human life," we must honestly concede where both our own system and the Russian system fall short.

Scientists are technically capable of reaching into the atom for unfathomable and irrepressible sources of energy, and this may free capitalists and Communists alike from reducing politics to a scuffle about the ways and means by which to subsist. Drudgery can be cut down. Most men have had to dig for their lives since Adam, but this may be avoidable. The hazards of coal mines, with families on the soiled brink of black cavities asking the toll at the "front"—these may be struck out. Power may be tapped as we tap water. We may free the earth from class struggle, from the dwarfing vicissitudes of poverty, from the warping of individuality by mass manipulation, the false and fabulous enmities of politics that mostly have no more basis in them than totem wars or the savageries of swine. The monkey in us has groped upward. He has earned the sun. Now he must secure his achievement through social means.

Democracy can supply the means. It was never a mere device for smoothing mass production. It does not become a side issue when mass production no longer has to be smoothed. If we are in quest of Mr. Jordan's ultimate good life—"that sense of the eternal, absolute, and unique reality of the individual spirit"—we have to keep before us the reasons for not organizing life around either of those two cannibalistic conceptions, commerce or Communism. Each of these, in the hands of oligarchy, will devour the unprotected, the unique reality of the individual. All oligarchies pervert this unique reality.

America knew it, at the beginning. Alexander Hamilton did not close his eyes to the "love of power" behind commerce. He never forgot that "men are ambitious, vindictive, and rapacious"—forever, that is to say, eager to form an oligarchy. And they do it, whether in commerce or in Communism, by holding the purse. "A power over a man's support," said Hamilton once, "is a power over a man's will." That is why the men who love power will inevitably seek to hog atomic energy. By hogging it they can control their kind. If it is freed, the chance of controlling society economically is gone. Men do not kill one another for water so long as the reservoirs are full and the pipes in order.

The state is not, as Mr. Jordan's manifesto puts forward, necessarily an enemy of the individual. Consider this discovery of atomic energy. A statesman who was no business man took an initiative in it that no business enterprise ever took. He spent two billion dollars that no board of directors would ever have sanctioned. He concerted international scientists on a project that only a common conviction could justify. Here the state was an agency for a potential common good.

The point to grasp, surely, is that the state can be an instrument of freedom. But it must be a state in which no oligarchy has the whip hand.

"Society" is not the state. It is another name for the interplay of the herd and the individual. If many an individual is hamstrung in an America that becomes a "pervasive and jealous environment of commerce," or in a Russia that is a pervasive and jealous environment of Communism, the real object of criticism must be the ambitious, vindictive, and rapacious men that Alexander Hamilton saw all about him. What then? The society of which every free writer should be a servant, the one for which he desires to see atomic energy harnessed for mass consumption, has to be referred through thick and thin to a norm outside the state and outside oligarchy, such as reverence for the individual human life, with enough honest regard for the individual to feed him, make a man of him, win his consent, and produce obedience without using the threat of death, or without forcing thwarted individuals to skulk, spy, and threaten revolution. Mr. Jordan upholds this norm, but he entangles it with a system for privilege. The atomic age won't be safe until we limit privilege, oligarchy, and sovereignty. We are no better today than Oswald in *Ghosts*, crying, "Give me the sun!" The world is full of oligarchs, big and little, unfit to be entrusted with the magic key until they adopt a common principle by which to devise law that can contain, rule, and harmonize them. We are doomed if enlightened individuals cannot harness by law the Big Three Oligarchs.

May 11, 1946

In Search of an Idiom

SOME day it may happen. A writer will appear who is as unblemished in spirit as Shakespeare, but who to Shakespeare's benign sanity will add incomparable knowledge of society and all that science has mastered. With the fullest resource of intellect he will have a gift of expression that is matchless. What he writes will not be a book. It will be a new Bible. And this Bible will conquer the world.

A pipe dream? Yes, it was Adolf Hitler's pipe dream. It was Nietzsche's pipe dream when he wrote *Thus Spake Zarathustra*. Nietzsche, wrapped in an old robe from the theological warehouse, a borrowed idiom from the holy books, believed that his was an inspired Word. So, in his self-intoxication, did Hitler. Hitler, moreover, had the will to express an original message in terms more uninhibited than that of civilized human beings. *Mein Kampf* is an effort to give a modern community its supreme text. Uncouth, ignorant, and vicious, the book discarded all that humanism had taught in order to make a new religion for a chosen people and their national state. It was a shrill counterblast to Lenin and Marx, brown against the red.

All my life I have looked for someone, not a smart Mephistopheles like Hitler but a writer with spiritual health and goodness joined to literary genius, who would accomplish the miracle that this age demands. It has demanded it ever since Erasmus and Thomas More ridiculed the stock images at Canterbury. For four hundred years the Western intellect has been divorced from Jehovah. Men have written since then with the magic that a new Bible must possess to move humanity. Tolstoy had it. But Tolstoy, who had a towering intellect, tried to reach his people through the old idiom. He put on a smock and went native, he devised ABC's for rural schools, he went down on his literary hands and knees, and he did it in an agnostic world. He gave simple Russians no spiritual idiom with which to meet the determinism of engineers, of chemists, and of physicists.

Once in London, sitting at Bernard Shaw's table, I had him turn his keen gaze on me. "We may think we write best-sellers," he said, with his short sniff of Irish scorn that was his way of hiding magnanimity, "but we can't hold a candle to our friend here." Our friend had written *By an Unknown Disciple*. How many languages had it gone into? Thirty or thirty-five. But that, too, was in the old idiom, an archaic idiom, a borrowed idiom. And Shaw's own preference in idiom would have been for a gorgeous freedom of expression like that of Lawrence of Arabia. Lawrence vested his English in a flowing glory, a radiant garment in Eastern folds and lines. It was his personal expression, audacious and dramatic, but clothing a restless soul, dazzled by the picturesque and warped by imperial ambitions.

Great writers have striven in France for a new Word that would have flame in it. Michelet caught fire from the Revolution. But the French were habituated to courtly rhetoric, which is emotion after spit and polish have been applied to it. What does a Frenchman think of Shakespeare? He thinks that William lacks spit and polish, which he does. Yet when a Frenchman has true inspiration, as Michelet had, he forsakes the polite method and loses balance. He harangues his assembled audience, while Shakespeare, however public the medium he worked in and however intended his effects, was above all the most private in his tone. He did not ignore multitude, and he was often pompous, but in his best scenes he consummates privacy and sustains his creatures as in a hand.

To do this in our time, but in such a form that the intellect can sanction it, is the necessary preliminary to a new and unified world. How far America can lead in this messianic role is a question, and depends on reconciling the cold idiom of analytic modernity with a full acceptance of spiritual laws which are inexorable and imperishable.

Has America the philosophy? Pragmatism, it seems to me,

is modelled rather closely on the principle of a federal bank. It "values" truth and goodness for what they bring in the market. It extends credit, and it says to the depositor, "You are *good* for this much credit." It even can manage, like Lord Keynes, to give credit or to detain it on rather nebular hypotheses, with new nebulae in the bag. It "works?" Schacht may wonder how well it works, and the late Loewenstein or Krueger may now be pondering it, bug-eyed and blistering, but that was because, pragmatically, they ceased to be "good." The criterion of "good," in short, depends on something that moves in and out like a concertina, so that your pragmatic responsibility is not to go when the Master says so, but go when the going is "good." Thus the pragmatic system has a criterion, science. Ask the scientists when the going is "good." They'll tell you, just as they tell us when it is going to sleet, when it will be safe to come North, and when you ought to sell Tel and Tel. Not that pragmatism is crude or ingenuous about Success. Success, "the bitch goddess," was the rugged individualist's first wife, but pragmatism is the rugged individualist's cautious statistical grandson, married to a low-heeled girl called Scientia. Their child is being analyzed. And this breakdown, as I see it, was inevitable. Were science "sure in prediction," it would be utterly useless to have human preferences and quite pointless to consult our feelings. We feel and choose, however, precisely because the outcome of existence is still something we elect. We elect it through processes that science can revise and educate, but the "human" element is primordial, and all the arts are supremely connected with man's inner power to elect the outcome of existence. They are thus an aspect of religion, and involve loyalty to a state of soul and a concept of the universe. Literature concerns itself with this interior drama, though not unaware that science is busy examining and describing the opera of the universe.

But Scientia seeks to pick a bitter quarrel with the literary. Dr. Lyman Bryson spoke up for her in the *Saturday Review of Literature* not long ago, complaining that "writers of all kinds of literature" are the enemies, active enemies, of social science.

To make good his point, he sallied forth for a safari in the literary suburbs. He potted a rabbit right off, a literary critic who doesn't read papers in biology or physics because he doesn't "know what the authors are talking about." Dr. Bryson peppered Tolstoy, too, a great artist in words but "often notably deficient in the power of abstract thought," abstract thought being presumably thought ready for a Ph.D. Dr. Bryson did better with the store cattle of literature who rub against a trespass sign, resenting the encroachment of science on "part of what the writers think is their job."

But these rumbling, cogitating, ruminating, regurgitating beasts are not "literature." They are its stalled oxen. Dr. Bryson thinks of writers as "self-centered and lyrically gifted," ineffably tender. He defines the artist as "one who conveys emotion by means of design," while the scientist, "who is generally sure in prediction," is seen to be on solid ground, dealing with statistical truths (truths, did you say?), seeking operational definitions and tentative laws, but making no claims to Truth, whereas writers of literature have their "chosen absolutes."

Here we should go to the fountainhead, to the authority of John Dewey. When my friend Dr. Bryson says "social science," we have to be wary. We have Lenin's word for it that Marxism is "the last word in social science." Does any pragmatist think that? John Dewey has called Marxism "the theory which has made the most display and the greatest pretense of having a scientific foundation" but "the one which has violated every principle of scientific method." Hence to be the enemy of *that* social science would not be a cause for reproach.

Yet John Dewey, writing his volume on *Freedom and Culture* in 1939, put his knife into literary persons pretty much as Dr. Bryson does. "Literary persons," he said, "have been chiefly the ones in this country who have fallen for Marxist theory," because "they are the ones who, having the least amount of scientific attitude, swallow most readily the notion that 'science' is a new kind of infallibility."

Writers, to sum up the indictment, don't think well enough of science to understand its attitude, but also think too well of it to criticize it. Their plight is obviously comic. We must be serious about it, however, since this breach between science and literature is the tragedy of our disunited, warring world. My contention is that literature is less at fault than science. Science can say anything it likes about the grand army of parasites that infest literature as if it were a Florida or a Riviera; they are insufficient in science as in everything else. They wind up as soda-jerkers, flippant entertainment being the height of their ambition. An illegitimate ambition? Far from it. But in a sick world it is not literature, it becomes simply the writing business, and you must spy out for literature as you do for a qualified prescription clerk in a modern drugstore. Narrowing down writers to the relatively small band that create a tradition as well as respect one, I say that science has betrayed them in betraying democracy. John Dewey himself puts it in a nutshell when he says, "A culture which permits science to destroy traditional values but which distrusts its power to create new ones is a culture which is destroying itself."

In this drastic statement our culture, American culture, is said to be destroying itself. But the constituents of that culture are democracy and science. The senior is democracy, the junior is science. It is admittedly science that destroyed traditional values, and I hold that science has caused and is causing democracy to distrust its powers.

Why did our fellow-travelers go to Russia in the first place? Science, the science that destroyed traditional democratic values, sent them there in search of other values. Jack Reed, Albert Rhys Williams, Anna Louise Strong, Lincoln Steffens, Emma Goldman, Max Eastman, William Henry Chamberlin, Eugene Lyons—they were all drawn to Communist Russia because their faith in American culture had given way. It began for them, as for many others, with "the dissemination of the results of physics, chemistry, biology, and astronomy." That science was "devoid of moral quality" was axiomatic, and the destruction of traditional democratic values was a consequence. A further consequence, in those evangelical by nature, was the budding of a new faith in the Soviet.

It is an omen ill for democracy, says John Dewey, when scientists regard their activity as "devoid of moral quality."

All civilized values are doomed, he adds, if science is "incapable of developing moral techniques." But we cannot wrap "science" and "civilized" together. Soviet science has not proved incapable of developing what pragmatically for Williams and Miss Strong are "moral techniques."

What is involved in the conflict between democrats and fellow-travelers is the nature of that American faith which science undermined. The elements in democracy that invite faith are a mixed lot, and some of them are manifestly unworthy of it. But while this end of the relation has to be taken pragmatically, and while the shuffling and sifting of the elements can be unending, we cannot be equally shuffling and equally tentative in our consent to the faith as such. Faith is a trust. It is a trust in both senses. It obtains our trust by the very fact that it responds to our preferences, but so long as it does this it obliges us to fulfill wholeheartedly the trust it imposes on us. We are not obliged to blind ourselves about the mixed elements in it. We are, however, under fixed stars, forty-eight to be exact, and committed to the hilt.

It is this entirety of consent and this willingness to abide by faith which cannot be shifty and provisional. Even dogs can have perfect faith. Why not democrats? We rise to a level of fidelity in virtue of the bond being a free one, but we must conquer gravity to keep it on that level. Democracy is not foolproof, nor is the state its goal. The state is its medium, in which free individuals brush against one another to generate its power.

The logical snag for fellow-travelers is to be found in Scientia's double role as mistress and wife. Scientia came as a siren into the home life of Americans who were unhappily married to capitalistic, Puritan democracy. She sang a song and did a dance. She sang of determinism at first, and all being "beyond good and evil." The dance was lively and carefree, whirling away from any burning or binding faith. But after the divorce from traditional values, science in the Soviets brought out the wedding ring and turned on the screws. She resorted to new "moral techniques."

And so it must always be, if these techniques can be devised for given situations and are devoid of essential quality.

It was strange the other evening to hear Bertrand Russell's little crackling voice on the radio, expressing pain that the youth of England is so cynical. Who taught it to be cynical? Every man of my generation has benefited by John Dewey and Bertrand Russell in the fight to knock over institutions that gave us dogma instead of data, cut off evidence and the quest for it, barred the roads to research. Freedom from religious totalities was imperative, and John Dewey was a pioneer in "freedom from." His career is an intellectual emancipation proclamation. But what was he emancipating the slaves into? Into a poverty that proclaimed laissez-faire in ethics, an equivocal condition, a beggarly condition, for which science, mechanistic and brass bound, took no concern.

The result in literature has been chaos. John Dewey is not contemptuous of artists. He doesn't limit art to conveying emotion by design. He says its problem is to unite intelligence with desires. "Art is the name given to all the agencies by which this union is effected." But what if science, regarding all "values" as operational, tentative, statistical, provisional, is asked to tell us how and where intelligence is to get the moral values with which to sway desires? John Dewey says democracy is a "way of personal life and one which provides a moral standard for personal conduct." But a standard is something you measure by. It can't be a concertina. It has to be a "chosen absolute."

In the year that Dr. Bryson published his first book, 1916 (it was a book of verse called *Smoky Roses*), literature was consciously seeking a new idiom for its humanism. It was striving to arrive at the meaning of life. Millions of young men were under fire in 1916, and dying in greater numbers in France than they did in this war. The big topic for humanism was science, then as now. And for science the big topic was atomic energy. Who was writing of it? H. G. Wells as a literary man. Who was "sure in prediction"? H. G. Wells. Who pooh-poohed him? The men of scientific method, not merely the tight-minded social neuters or cold-blooded technocrats, but good scientists. They put "collective mentality," not the autonomy of the individual, in the forefront. They did not say, in the old idiom, A. M. D. G., "to the greater glory of God." Before Moscow's children—just like ours, to the sympathetic—they hang a motto on the school walls that puts the state as the be-all and end-all. "Every student must stubbornly and insistenly apply himself to his education in order to be a real use to the state." Tolstoy foresaw, from the first acts of the red prelude, the moral anarchy that would result from a statism based on science with no place for good or evil in it. In the struggle to give meaning to life, it was not always literature that was tender-minded, with science toughminded, bloody but unbowed. H. G. Wells related atomic energy to *A World Set Free*, when scientists were skeptical, tentative, provisional, and evasive.

But today, is that different? Dr. Bryson does not say a word of Arthur Koestler. Just as H. G. Wells tried to englobe the commissar in *A World Set Free* and the yogi in *God, the Invisible King*, so Koestler, equally devoted to scientific method, writes *The Yogi and the Commissar*. Macmillan let it go out of stock, not having enough paper for *Forever Amber* and all the other important books, but in the last section of this brilliant and remarkable critique we have science related to values in such a manner that even Professor Irwin Edman, who so caricatures *Perennial Philosophy* as a "failure of nerve," should not be able to dismiss it, and Professor Edman seldom fails of nerve.

Without "chosen absolutes," in the end, we are at the mercy of any resolute cynic or any frantic theorist who disputes the democratic acre we stand on. To fence that acre by dogma is no wish of ours, but surrounding dogmas leave us no option. We do actually occupy a perfectly definite and indisputable position.

What weapon had civilization when Hitler set out to exterminate the Jews? It had the weapon of democratic values. These values, John Dewey admits, are to be traced to their source in "Hellenic humanism and in Christian beliefs." In short, to perennial philosophy. Non-democratic and anti-democratic societies like Germany and Russia repudiate these humanist values. The Rights of Man, "chosen absolutes," do not exist for them. Koestler explicitly defines that place in *The Yogi and the Commissar*.

Yet cultural nihilism has now spread so far and wide that democracy swallows it obliviously. The new novels by Evelyn Waugh and Erich Maria Remarque, chosen for our vast public, do a great deal to bring home to us why John Dewey has apprehensions for American culture. Remarque despairs of intelligence in love. Love is blind, women are like that, the French are like that. Into the Paris of Toulouse-Lautrec he brings one sanity, German medical science, and for the rest it is the old picture of democracy patented by Goebbels—feeble, disordered, corrupt, undisciplined. Waugh has the same disdains, disillusions, and distrust, though a monastery provides a mattress grave for his Tory alcoholic.

Arthur Koestler has stood the brunt of war no less than Remarque or Waugh, nor does he disguise the sickening behavior of France toward refugees. But Koestler has not been disintegrated by nihilism. He exhibits scientific method, "freedom of inquiry, toleration of diverse views, freedom of communication." But no matter what collective convenience may demand in the way of civic subordinations—one-way streets, rotaries, green lights, speed limits—he does not confuse this "level of organization" with a higher one. He does not shirk the fact that you must ascend from a lower to a higher level on a ladder of metaphysics. This alone makes the universe intelligible and the autonomy of the individual possible. That autonomy is at the core of America's democratic faith. It is what is meant by speaking of "a moral standard for personal conduct," which presumes such things as order, a universe, and a soul.

But these are precisely the things for which we have no tolerable idiom. When John Dewey went to Russia he was bowled over by the burning faith he found there. It so infected him that he came away predicting world revolution. He was later repelled by Russian ruthlessness, revolted by the treatment of dissenters, and angered by Russia's "refusal to tolerate the existence of incompatible opinions." He regarded this as a denial of our culture.

But our own culture is not a negative one, and there are opinions which, if acted on, are incompatible with it. What still remains to discover is the living idiom by which man's "moral standard for personal conduct" can be made universal. Communism has not found it. Commerce has not found it. Religion has not found it. Science has not found it. And without it we stumble and perish. Yet from faith in social democracy to its ascertainment, and from its ascertainment to further faith, should be no impossible ideal for world citizens.

In Particular

American Esthetic

GERTRUDE STEIN

A WRITER caught in wartime France has ready-made material for a book, and so positive a writer as Gertrude Stein could scarcely have had better. She had been in France most of her life. She loved it. Caught at Culoz, near the Swiss border, she shared the privations of the people. She had to organize a new life, learn to walk six to twelve miles a day with a stick in her hand and a pack on her back, pick up her supplies in new ways, keep a goat and make hay, see the young men taken to labor in Germany or go into the hills as maquis, watch the Germans pass from arrogance to abjectness, and finally share with full heart in the liberation when the American Army arrived.

The experience would have been rich for any person. For a gifted writer, a professional, one accustomed to watch and note her responses, the opportunity was almost overwhelmingly right. It involved danger, but not too much. It enlarged on every side the capacity for receiving impressions. It quickened the heart.

In *Wars I Have Seen* Gertrude Stein has merged this recent awareness with her earlier notions of war, and by doing this she has been able to string it all together. But the string is merely a convenience for autobiography. Her object is to give a narrative of Gertrude Stein under the Nazis and Gertrude Stein liberated. She wishes us to be on the inside, both of the French village and herself.

Anyone who reads it for the story will be rewarded. Miss Stein is a competent witness, and the oppressive presence of

Wars I Have Seen by Gertrude Stein. Random House.

the Germans was like breathing a noxious gas for her. It was not her business to rebel but to endure. With a common sense that never permits heroics but that dwells on the exact details of everyday existence, she lets us reconstruct these years as part of a human history. She foraged well. She had good food from Savoy. She did not suffer bodily. Even cigarettes for Alice Toklas were procurable. She could visit the dentist and have innumerable talks on the trains. Life, in fact, was perpetual communicativeness, varied and exciting. She looked on the Germans as a low form of animal existence. She was able to feel warm and intimate with the French. And for Americans, even if she forgot how many stars were in the flag, she was vibrantly happy. That happiness is the high point of the book.

It is rather strange that so shrewd a woman, one who could get eggs by exchanging dishwater for them, should have felt it necessary to do this book in a style full of mannerism. She is evidently a strong-minded, capable woman, well able to get on with all sorts of people, cheerfully helping them and using them, and quite a power on her own hearth and in the bosom of her cronies and familiars. And yet, curiously enough, she uses elaborate and studied literary artifice. She reiterates her phrases until one labors for firm footing. It is as tiresome as walking through heavy sand.

In a sophisticated society like that of pre-war Paris the arts and tricks of creating illusion were much debated. Customs Officer Rousseau, for example, painted pictures as if he saw the world with a fixed baby stare, and more than one writer tried to do the same thing with words, because of some theory or inhibition.

With Rousseau, it may be supposed, the illusionist was honest. He was himself illuded. He had limited means at the disposal of his powerful imagination when he turned to painting, and this paucity had an astonishing result. Seeing trees as if they were toy trees and horses as if they were toy horses, he could not help making them beautiful. When he painted a tiger in the forest or a lion on the beach or a moon in a sky, Rousseau was so intense and marveling in his round-eyed won-

derment that each frond in the forest was as if known in love
or fear, and the lion was as positive as if remembered from infancy, and the moon held in the sky as if God had hung out a
lantern. Customs Officer Rousseau was a man withdrawn from
adult life, which is so often hackneyed and sensible and rea-
soned; he could look at life with a bird's innocence in a world
of his own. All in him was alive to wonderment. Had Walt
Disney the same visual wonder, he'd have seen on the wing,
not on the hop or the gallop.

Gertrude Stein has an aim in literature not unlike the Doua-
nier's in painting. She goes in for a sort of incantation. She
tries to bathe in impressions, feeling them as a child might feel,
artless and involuntary, and trying to give an almost trancelike
transcript of them. By means of this we are, if we can forget
Miss Stein, inside her soul.

But while her greatest possession in the world is her self-
possession, it is mighty hard for us to take the picture and forget the illusionist. Gertrude Stein may stare at France with a
baby stare. She may sustain it admirably. But who believes
that this strong-minded woman has to prattle? The literary
means at her disposal are not limited by nature. They are
limited by art. Her artlessness is artful. And to have it so sustained is tedious.

She does it in order to be intimate, as if running along to let
us find out what she is musing about. Too much of it,
however, is induced prattle. It is too cute. In reality she is
incorrigibly alert, loves to upset the applecart and say the
unexpected. The Rousseau who returned to nature and the
Customs Officer Rousseau are mixed in her prattling, and the
result is affectation.

Luckily, when her emotions grip her, she throws off the
swaddling clothes, and the faithful reader moves into a full
world that has air in it as well as intimacy. Hers is a powerful
personality, but it needed the American Army to liberate her.

March 8, 1945

PUBLIC BE SAVED

SOME active people open a wide door to the world, a revolving door, so that men and women flock in to them, ideas pour in, a rabble and torrent of schemes and plans jab and excite them; they are right in the midst of things, ringing bells, giving orders, talking into mouthpieces of one kind or another, house telephones, coast-to-coast telephones, dictaphones. Always connected, always disconnected.

Against these bulldozers the literary class lifts its threshold as high as possible and weakly hangs out a sign, "Please do not disturb, out to lunch, gone for the day, the duration." But what is the shrinker to think of Morris L. Ernst? His threshold is almost flush with the ground. "I don't remember," he says, "the last time I was alone for more than a day. Certainly not during thirty years." He cannot "be." He has to do, even when cruising or doing carpentry. And still this doer's new book, *The Best Is Yet . . .* , is warm, high-minded, public-spirited—executive, but tirelessly executive for other people and for society at large. With a ceaseless interest in the world as a mere mechanism, and having no more atmosphere than a moon made of concrete, he still bathes it in beneficence. It is a clear, concrete beneficence.

Morris Ernst would have been high in the higher brackets, just another success, if an "intangible" did not possess him. He says of Russell Leffingwell of Morgan's, "I wish I could be more like Russell, but I can't. It's background, glands—probably many intangibles." The "glands" would have been the explanation some time ago, but the reader of *The Best Is Yet . . .* is now rather more likely to look elsewhere. Morris Ernst's own intangibles have made him what he is, perhaps the most intrepid of local social critics; a home for causes lost, stolen or strayed; a public watchdog with a private conscience. He has plenty of nerve, but the open sesame for him has not been nerve; it has been his goodness.

The Best Is Yet . . . by Morris L. Ernst. Harper & Bros.

Had he cared to stand off from himself, to observe what manner of man he really is, *The Best Is Yet* . . . would have been an autobiography. Good autobiographies do not merely relate events; they give the measure of them. But an outpouring of his public activity swamps the inner Morris Ernst. He accounts for his time but seldom for himself. Even what occupies him with a friend—Heywood Broun, for example—is the money Heywood earned and spent, the causes Heywood fought for, the Newspaper Guild he started. What the dying man had to say, the last words of a frustrated artist, almost pass Morris Ernst by. He is intent on the structure that Broun worked over.

Hence this book relates nearly every one of Ernst's many important friends to the causes that they tilted for. Justice Brandeis was a Zionist, which Mr. Ernst disapproves of, but he was also the social engineer who condemned "too big," and that brings out fascinated comment on chain stores, etc. Dave Dubinsky headed the union that handled the revolution made by women's slacks, and Morris Ernst sees in it a great lesson for other revolutions. If he talks of the insurance business, of the Catholic Church, of censorship, of Cardozo, of birth control, of La Guardia, of John L. Lewis, the specific improvement on which he sets his heart means infinitely more to him than any concept of the whole. He does not relate his experiences to a whole, even when he advises Heywood Broun to become a Catholic.

And yet he is a paradox. For himself the freedom of the individual, "the suicidal effects of personal greed and excess power in industry and government," have a positiveness that he lives by. He could have deepened this "appraisal," as he calls it. He says, "I find my greatest joy in search for odd flashes of cause and effect." But this joy he does not share with the reader, and in its place one often finds recapitulations of anthropology, tags about the North Star, theories of hearing and seeing.

But these excursions of his excitable mind are a minor part of the book. What it gives in the main, and from the heart, is a full, overflowing report of another enlightenment, and a su-

perior one. Morris Ernst's ideas about free speech have been
fighting ideas. His judgment of branch-office communism in
America has been a positive judgment. His love of Roosevelt
has been a devotion put into deeds. "The greatest lawyers of
the land would have shied off the idea," he says of Lend-Lease.
But though himself a lawyer, yet master of his life, unafraid of
chance and change, grateful for his "luck," Ernst makes himself
a missionary and crusader time and again. In this he is frequently intemperate. "With England gone," he says, "the Republican party, close to a majority in Congress, would no
doubt have sat at a friendly table with Hitler and his gang."
It is improbable that "my favorite banker" would have put it
this way, given those glands and "intangibles." But Morris L.
Ernst's "intangibles" enable him to release full convictions.
That's why he counts and why his book has such a true clang.
He is by his very nature a percussion instrument.

April 28, 1945

A MODERN MARRIAGE

IT IS not for restful style that people should look into Henry
Wise Miller's *All Our Lives*. But as he and Alice Duer Miller
were married before the turn of the century, and as he does
his best to account for her, and for himself in relation to her,
and as nearly half a century of New York goes into the me-
lange, his book will fascinate many people. He has a nervous
way of doing business with his reader. His book follows a sort
of egg and dart pattern, a blob of quotation, a dart of narrative, a blob, a dart. But there's meat in the egg and point in
the dart. The book is all Miller, mainly Lighthorse Harry, and
hardly ever wise.

By way of ingratiating himself with reviewers, he enters the

All Our Lives: Alice Duer Miller by Henry Wise Miller. Coward-
McCann.

familiar plea for Alice Miller's work that used to be thought valid for Marie Corelli. She had "real power to appeal to the heart." "Although she was not a critic's author she was an author's author." "She was not angry with life, had no wish to reform it, she created no literary mood and started no literary cult. She wrote of the things that stir men's hearts." Hence, to use his own phrase, "the sacred portals in Hollywood opened easily for her."

No one can force the hand of critics by saying an author was popular, "popular with those who knew what they liked." So was Ella Wheeler Wilcox. Nor does Mr. Miller help matters by saying, "no one knew better than Lorimer, the *Post*'s great editor, how to combine praise and encouragement with editorial guidance. He made Alice his special care and they became life-long friends." "Taking it altogether, I believe, no American author up to that time had ever received, in first payments, so much a word, for a given piece of fiction." "At my earnest request Alice wrote another *Romeo and Juliet* in splendid Shakespearean blank verse, entitled *Juliet and Mercutio*, in which the exquisite Juliet receives a lover worthy of her." "Alice laid rather violent hands on another of Shakespeare's plays. "She wanted nothing from real life but the materials for a story."

All this being the case, the fact that "the accolade of the minority was never hers" had to be expected. But the writer of *Are Women People?* was in fact a brave reformer. She was not a militant, but she was a strong propagandist for suffrage, "a change in our whole way of living and social thinking," and if Mrs. Astor had said of her, "What a pity, that lovely girl going to college," she appears remarkable in this book for one of the most successful transpositions in key that any New Yorker ever straddled.

"Both Alice and I had been brought up in large, affectionate, and closely knit families." "No one represented the late Victorians more happily than she. She was, indeed, one of Meredith's heroines come to life." But with the Duer fortune gone, and with Harry's work as overseer on a Costa Rica plantation the beginning of hard times for them, she was to master the magazine trade out of native grit and independence. And when Harry Miller came back from the first World War, both of them set about doing themselves over. He tells it candidly and lightly. He had a little way of seeming to be all things to all women. She had to rediscover herself. "Victorian principles and prejudices were fast disappearing." "Style in verse did not offend her" but style was going out. She even "disliked" style in prose. New ideas were in full swing, "ushered in by popular songs and slang." Money rolled in then until they became wealthy. "And, rather suddenly, she went completely modern."

Harry Miller still saw Alice as romantic. The breakdown of the old order, the transition to a "large, brilliant, and roisterous gang," a gang that "ranged itself heartily with the new order," while living on the best, is part of the romance. He says a few spiked things about the combative and querulous. "Reformers do not as a rule get much pleasure out of life." "Really civilized well-to-do people make the best innovators, as they salvage much from the old order." This change delighted him. "It was greatly to her new friends' credit that she was accepted instantly as one of themselves," and he adds, "it is hard to say why Alice stood as the pivot and center of the hard-boiled lot of top-notchers that composed our gang."

Perhaps it was that, while writing was a means to an end for her, people, particularly top-notchers, were in themselves an end. She was a strong character whose often tentative manner and shy words and gentleness made her singularly attractive. Harry Miller is dead right when he says, "in some things she knew me better than I knew myself." He, too, was people. People were more her medium than writing, and the 800,000 who bought *The White Cliffs* were, in a sense, her consummate success. The gang she adopted—often a tough gang, by the way, when oppressed by disapproval—appealed to warmth in her that Victorianism had lain on like the softness of snow. She lived in a period of thaw, but the deep part of the book comes with the emergence of strength when she was dying. She was a fighting lady, then, and as stout-hearted as her friend

Clarence Day. The glimpses of the Days are excellent. Much that is sweet and absurd is tumbled into this book, straight out of intimacy, but Mr. Miller hardly thinks of us as present.

June 9, 1945

QUEST OF THE ABSOLUTE

THESE are hard times and they should make for hard thinking. Anybody who wishes to think hard should possess himself of Dr. Harry Slochower's new book, *No Voice is Wholly Lost.* Dr. Slochower, according to his publishers, was born in Austria and came here at 13. He now teaches German and comparative literature at Brooklyn College. Serious reservations must be made about this book, but his worst critic must admit it is brain fodder, definite in philosophy, organized in argument and, within the limits it proposes, a weighty piece of work. It reveals a state of mind that a democrat may well be disturbed about.

When Dr. Slochower says "we moderns" he is thinking of ardent writers who sum up "modern estrangement and agony, as well as the persistent quest for harmony." The period between our great wars he calls a "chaotic period," a period of "alienation." His main object, after describing the stages that made for chaos, is to comb it out and to indicate "the coming victory."

Most of us will agree that Nietzsche started "the surrender of absolutes." Dr. Slochower gives us its modern profile in the work of Arthur Schnitzler, Ignazio Silone, Ernst Toller, Stefan Zweig, Franz Kafka. More rapid profiles are sketches of the earlier Huxley, Hemingway, Richard Wright, Thomas Wolfe, André Gide, John Dos Passos, Louis Ferdinand Céline. By brief extracts and powerful summaries, but treating works of art as raw material for a thesis, the author deepens the "bewildering conflict" of this period.

No Voice Is Wholly Lost by Harry Slochower. Creative Age.

Then he shows efforts at positive faith. Paul Gauguin embraced the absolute on a South Sea island, one of those Bohemians toward whom he is rather severe. D. H. Lawrence and Knut Hamsun sought an absolute in nature. Belloc, Claudel, Maritain, Sigrid Undset are Catholics who returned to "status," in spite of what Dr. Slochower calls the "abolition of the two-world pattern." And under the classical tradition he groups Santayana, Proust, T. S. Eliot, Stefan George, Rainer Maria Rilke.

This is far from his goal. After attacking fascism as "the systematization of confusion," which is to flatter it, he does not spare its stepfather, Oswald Spengler. When he leaves fascism to describe the yearnings of Franz Werfel and Sholem Asch, a real warmth tinges his pages. He feels that in the dredgings of James Joyce, the questings of Eugene O'Neill, the spiral of Clifford Odets, movement begins toward a new dispensation, "the communal personality." Here Bernard Shaw pops in. Arnold Zweig, Feuchtwanger, Heinrich Mann, Anna Seghers, John Steinbeck of *Grapes of Wrath* are allocated their space. And then, with André Malraux and Thomas Mann at the finale, we have Marx and Freud tied in a loose lover's knot, and a thing called "transfiguration by estrangement," if you can grasp it.

Dr. Slochower seeks for doctrine in his authors. He kneads literature into dough for Marx and Freud and their "coming victory." Writing in his own peculiar dialect, he can speak of the chaotic period as "a loneliness only partly bridged by collective immersion." He can say "the critical temper in Marxism postulates the transcendence of social determinants," but he contends that Freud meets Marx, each partial in his truth. "Their perspectives are varied accents of a common set of interests." In short, the vitamin of the "absolute," extracted with great care by early "moderns," is now to be superadded and injected in the name of the "coming victory."

Apart from Dr. Slochower's "shop dialect," and apart from his indifference to art except as subject-matter for a thesis, his very title suggests a vital objection to his case. He confidently speaks of "our frustrated, split and alienated characters" as a matter of course. "Restlessness, disquietude and unsettledness" are the common lot. This, as a Euro-American, seems to him beyond argument, though how he'd fit a Winston Churchill into it is hard to see when he says "personalities have shrunk to 'hollow men' and to schizoid characters." It probably means that the hell which fascism and nazism brought into the world appalled the man of good-will in him and, seeing psychic aberration in fascism as well as economic law, has turned him to Freud as well as Marx, since he thinks we are only free to "cognize necessity."

But which necessity? To take an armistice like Pétain or go on fighting like de Gaulle? Dr. Slochower quotes Harold Laski's counsel of despair: "In the last resort, liberty is always a function of power." Democracy denies this. It may also be a function of love. The slaves had no power of their own to gain liberty. Iceland had no power to secure liberty from Denmark. It is a half-truth to rule out choice and ethics. It is also an illusion that "psychology as a special study is a modern phenomenon." The apparatus is modern, not the phenomenon. And even the apparatus did not save Freud from saying "the goal of life is death."

But in any case "no voice is wholly lost that is the voice of many men." And Dr. Slochower defines the "modern" on one-sided evidence. If Joyce was an exile, Yeats wasn't; if Henry James was, William James wasn't; if Martin Andersen Nexö was, Johannes V. Jensen wasn't; if Céline was, Bernanos wasn't; if Hemingway was, Pearl Buck wasn't; if Proust was, Anatole France wasn't. These too are voices.

July 5, 1945

TWO DRAMATIC CRITICS

TASTE is incalculable. Some men choose to be coal miners, others to be dramatic critics. Like the miners, the critics have to forsake daylight, to drudge in the dark, to light the scene from their own heads and to take the run of the mine. Once, in the crusading days of Bernard Shaw, it was like gold mining. In these sober days, with the theatre encroached upon, it seems decidedly coal. But if you look at the year books of Burns Mantle and George Jean Nathan you are with men who have given their lives to it, and the yield is stupendous.

Burns Mantle is no crusader. When I first met this benign man, forty years ago, he was trimming his lamp, not for battle as I had hoped, but for busy wayfarers who were going this way and that. Burns wasn't worrying so much about the City of God as about municipal lighting, and he was digging for public utility. He never seemed to be agitated by imperfection. Admitting its inescapability, expecting no miracles, he still enjoyed and celebrated the theatre's triumphs, and brought to them the balm of his temperament. By the side of Percy Hammond, whose headlight bored into the Shuberts until they squealed, Burns was as serene as an altar light. And he has persisted in this relation to the theatre, indefatigable, kind and inclusive as a bus.

In *The Best Plays of 1943-44* he publishes the twenty-seventh of his theatrical round-ups. Here, with his short professional introductions and all kinds of summaries, are the ten plays that he deems the best. He is permitted to give them in compressed form, a piece like *Jacobowsky and the Colonel* taking forty tight pages and *Outrageous Fortune* about the same. The other eight plays selected and represented and lightly reviewed are Moss Hart's *Winged Victory*, Lillian Hellman's *The Searching Wind*, John van Druten's *The Voice of the Turtle*, Edward Chodorov's *Decision*, Ruth Gordon's *Over 21*, Maxwell Ander-

The Best Plays of 1943-44 edited by Burns Mantle. Dodd, Mead.
The Theatre Book of the Year 1943-44 by George Jean Nathan. Knopf.

son's *Storm Operation,* Elsa Shelley's *Pick-Up Girl* and Paul Osborn's *Innocent Voyage.*

Where Burns Mantle conforms to the industry by sampling the goods and telling us how the customers like them, with mild words of deprecation about overemphasis on sordidness and misery, George Jean Nathan in *The Theatre Book of the Year 1943-44* retains far more of the crusading spirit. He is with the consumer rather than the producer. He is grim, vituperative, personal, gross, sarcastic, alive. He doesn't select plays or give us a précis of them. He reviews the lot, from *The Student Prince,* June 8, 1943, to *Hickory Stick,* May 8, 1944, when he went home and took a breather.

George Jean is both Nathan the Wise and Nathan the Wise Guy. He has seen so much of the theatrical world, from basement to skylight, that the cheapness and cynicism of its tricks have driven him, not to despair but to defiance. It is hard to tell whether he has a mind like a card index or a card index like a mind, but whenever any playboy puts a novelty on the market, Nathan can reel off its unsuspected antecedents like a prosecutor. Sometimes he bludgeons the innocent. He is so anxious to hurt an offender's feelings that he occasionally behaves aggressively. He defends taste with a complete lack of it. He carries knives, knuckle-dusters, tommy guns, pruning forks, hand grenades. He is a one-man commando raid, and he dances on the corpse.

But if you do not weary of blue noses being called muckmoochers and snoopers and pure boys and so on, or having a play's appearance burlesqued as its "epiphany," or if you can accept one play as "a little on the travesty side" and another "on the routine theatrical side" and a third on the "light entertainment side," then the substantial judgment that resides in George Jean Nathan can be recognized for the real thing. The smudge of the mine makes his smile like a demon's rictus, a grin from the black gang, but he has been digging almost as long as Burns Mantle, and with a much sharper sense of unrequited love.

Where Burns Mantle writes himself out from under *Outrageous Fortune,* for example—"a household of unhappy and slightly abnormal humans"—Nathan calls Miss Franken's people merely "befuddled and distraught." He sees an "inner wisdom" in it, which Mantle could debate, but he shows that its dignity and seriousness command his respect. This responsive gravity in George Jean Nathan attends any and every play that calls for critical acumen. And he can be extremely perceptive about the implications of *The Voice of the Turtle*, at the expense of people with asphalted minds. Burns Mantle treads lightly, even when he treads on their asphalt. Nathan comes along with crowbar and hot pitch, sometimes to pave a new way, and sometimes to touch up the trade. How much a trade it is, and how little an art, is an obvious inference, but each of these critics is an incorrigible, an admirable, devotee.

December 30, 1944

EARLY AMERICAN

MONEY is sometimes well spent on apparently useless things. When Henry Clews was amassing his fortune as a broker he could not have imagined what it would mean for the work of his daughter Elsie. Elsie Clews inherited from her highly gifted sire the ability to hold firm to anything that interested her, but where he respected money for its use she was acquisitive and possessive of facts that were mere rags and bones to most Americans. Had she been forced to earn a living it would have been impossible for her to study the Zunis and the Hopis. That wasn't then and isn't now a commercial proposition. But being her father's daughter she was able to follow her bent as a laborious investigator, to live with the Indians in the Southwest, to gather their myths, to piece together the patterns of their culture, to elucidate their religion, their sex life, their behavior as citizens and as lawgivers. From the Southwest she carried on into Mexico, then down to Ecuador. Her work as an anthropologist was teamwork, part of a world-wide disin-

Mesa Verde by Christopher La Farge. New Directions.

terested exploration that has made race prejudice about Indians
or anyone else a nonsense only proper to a Hitler.

One of the friends who shared Elsie Clews Parsons' interest
in American Indians was Grant La Farge, but it was the artist
in him that the Indians set afire, and this fire has been passed
to his sons, Oliver and Christopher. At a time when travel in
Europe was drawing most Americans who could afford it, the
Southwest called a small number to pursue a deeper knowledge
of the Indian past and present. Mesa Verde in Colorado had
Indians dwelling there for ages before Columbus sailed into
the Caribbean, and at the close of the thirteenth century, for
unknown reasons, a community of Indians "suddenly left their
high caves, their beautiful utensils, their cloths, their food and
their dead, in the cliffs of Mesa Verde." The empty shell remains intact, the tomb of a departed civilization.

Christopher La Farge evokes this civilization in a play called
Mesa Verde, written to embody the tribal fugue from its
center of life and well-being. He has studied the researches of
Dr. Washington Mathews, author of *Navaho Legends*; of Dr.
Ruth L. Bunzel, who put *Zuni Indian Myths* into poetry, and
of John Louw Nelson, who wrote *Rhythm for Rain*. But this
scholarship he has turned to the enrichment of his poetic
drama. It drapes his Indians idiomatically, as blankets used to
drape the Irish in the time of Elizabeth and still fall in stately
folds from the shoulders of Ecuadorians. The object is not to
parade a special information but to invest in their own peculiar
dignity of style the dark and intense figures that Mr. La Farge
imagines, happily respected in the decoration and typography
of the volume.

Verse drama on the radio teaches us to dread mouthy
speeches about the heroic past, peopled by roaring bores forever in the act of defying flood, fire and famine. They vocifer-
ate and vaticinate with a lugubrious eloquence. Mr. La Farge
cannot avoid the monotony of natural disasters. A drought is
a drought, and the resultant hunger is a wolf in the tissues. But
Mesa Verde has nothing in common with the hackneyed or-
atory that makes the radio so resounding. It has the quality of
speech that is elevated and yet private. The blatant image is

omitted, and while dramatic gesture would certainly heighten Indian references to "the house of the Sun Bearer," "the house of the dark and the sharp knives," which is the heavens ripped by lightning, very little cooperation would be needed to give its third dimension to the drama.

Mr. La Farge helps a good deal by many explicit directions —some readers will never overcome the apparent bleakness of a printed play and in this one the Indian names are so utterly unfamiliar as to be additionally difficult. Nayenezgani and Tobadzischini are jawbreakers. But *Mesa Verde* does successfully suggest a whole world of strange and somber tradition. Under a pitiless sun the cave-dwellers are just as terrified of drought as any Italians who must harvest their corn. No priest is patient with a young leader who goes to build a dam rather than the church, first loitering with a forbidden girl when the enemy is threatening. *Mesa Verde* does not attempt to overcome austerity by being natural and colloquial. It creates in a very few words the shy intimacies between the young, the hardness of the Old Governor, the conflicts in counsel, the sudden threat from the enemy, the fire, and then a flight to the south, seeking for water. "In the blue of the south," a breathless envoy reports, "I found a village risen, house upon fair house, the stones cut to true measure, growing as the seeds grew, as the corn flourished in the wet fields, as their beans drooped heavy from the vines, as squash grew round and full in the sun." Words like these draw all away except two who sacrifice themselves. These "lovers are joined forever in loving in the dark world of death."

America's thirteenth century may seem far from the Europe of Chartres and Mont St. Michel, and yet these Indians sought to propitiate their gods with much the same division between the arbitrary priest and the good old shaman. Mr. La Farge has found such beauty in the legends that his first desire has been to devise a mode of expression that would retain it. This he has done exquisitely. His figures of speech and his dramatic figures have something stylized and ceremonious and gentle about them, but the result, a little archaic, is never sterile. Colorado nursed these children once, and only a sensitive poet could have so drawn them back from the dark world. Their eyes are still dim with it, but their voices have a sad echo of their own later follies and misfortunes.

July 31, 1945

H. ALLEN SMITH'S LATITUDES

To COME late to the party is never very wise. The newborn are always doing it; they are always arriving late into a world warmed up by their elders, and not always finding the old jokes as good as their elders did. They have to pick up at a point where they are cold and where the old show is in hilarious progress. H. Allen Smith, for example, is as established as burlesque. He began with his public a good while ago. *Low Man on a Totem Pole* started the show. It went on with *Life in a Putty Knife Factory*. Now it continues with *Lost in the Horse Latitudes*. For a person who comes in late, assured that Mr. Smith is no less devastatingly funny in the new book than he was in the old, the proper mood should be one of suspended judgment and humility. The new arrival knows that if you laughed yourself sick over the first books, here is another chance to be sick. But is he compelled to be sick with you? In the thick of the horse latitudes and the horse laughs, how much must he yield to Mr. Smith's latitudes?

The mirth that overwhelms H. Allen Smith is old-fashioned —it is right from the Inhibition era. Mr. Smith was born in the Bible Belt, and he has just learned to unbutton it. He goes into kicks at the mention of a privy. He is contorted at the thought of a toilet. To call attention to the female anatomy by slightly or grossly obscene names seems to him just as uproarious as to refer to blackheads, pimples, acne or any other humiliating little complaint. As for the business of mating, the Sex Life of the Date Palm is almost more than he can stand. If he should ever go into the sex aspect of the hardware business, and discover

Lost in the Horse Latitudes by H. Allen Smith. Doubleday, Doran.

that threads are male and female, he'll probably die in the dithers or end as a funny man at a hardware convention.

Since most of his humor deals with Hollywood, he cannot help telling us about Hollywood horseplay, and much of it convulses him as it might convulse the pimpled boys behind the barn. He tells with savage glee of a swanky affair at the Medbury home where, as the guests entered, they saw in a little room facing the door an elderly bum, unshaven and poorly dressed, sitting publicly in a state that is usually kept private. This is only one of innumerable attempts to count on the reader's inability to withstand a shock to his decency. And with it there are puns on personal names; jokes about supposedly comic food ("the Algonquin Indians invented succotash, for which the hell with them"); comic cuts about the recently dead (Sir Arthur Thomas Quiller-Couch, compiler of the *Oxford Book of English Verse*, lived to be 80 years old, was hit by a jeep and died); and anatomical caricatures about beautiful girls who have pimples.

This kind of humor is lazy, self-indulgent and dissolute. Occasionally Mr. Smith has a spark, and occasionally he has a quip, but in general he thinks it is enough to stick out his tongue or thumb his nose. When he wishes to be genuinely appreciative, as with Jim Cagney and Ed McNamara, he omits the humor of such stories as McNamara's about Caruso and Scotti, or the revelatory Norwegian side of Jim Cagney's character, and the whole fascinating and essential tale of his childhood in Yorkville. Mr. Smith's mere mention of celebrities is not enough.

Grant that to be a comic in print is difficult, and that to be vulgar is often amusingly human, the use of this vulgarity easily becomes tedious. It ignores Anatole France's great dictum, "I am polite to you, in order that you may be polite to me." Vulgarity has always rightly served to relieve the boredom of correctness, and to reduce priggishness and cant. For that the kings had court jesters and the Christians had carnival and Mardi Gras. But when vulgarity goes out of its way to violate human dignity—as, for example, at Tod Sloan's funeral —the reader is revolted. "Human" respect is fair game, but not self-respect; and Mr. Smith is not artist enough to see the need of sparing his victims.

Ah, then, you are a highbrow? That is the obvious retort. No, a clown is too great a gift from nature for anybody to be a highbrow. But no comedian can put over his inspiration unless he adroitly and socially controls it. Once I heard a comedian with a line like Mr. Smith's try to outdo the rest of the company, which included John McCutcheon, George Ade and Dick Little. His stories were as broad as they were long, and simply no one could laugh at them. In the end the embarrassed clown said to the waiter, "A glass of water, please." Dick Little added, "And a toothbrush." That gave us a laugh, and these were not censors; they were professionals.

October 5, 1945

SOLDIER AS WRITER

To CRITICIZE books after they appear is one duty of the newspaper reviewer. He can take literature as a kind of gladiatorial show of which he is a spectator, turning his thumb up or his thumb down, as it pleases him. But a more remote duty of the reviewer is to think of books before they are written. The friends and relatives of soldiers don't want to wait till their boys come into the literary arena. They want a word of advice beforehand. What about the war book that hasn't yet been written?

So here with deference to all creative talent is a word of suggestion to soldiers. After your tension as a soldier you'll possibly want to put words around it. You've been separated from civil nights and days by a barrier that is as real as a burning river. You've come near death. You've seen your best friend killed. How to get that into a book?

The shock of war is a tough fact. You are like a golf ball that a strong driver has hit for 250 yards. You are flattened out of recognition at first, become a queer misshapen spheroid through whom the shock is passing. But you've been trained. You don't stay looking or feeling like a consternated egg. You carry on, with the shock absorbed.

As a soldier, that is, you recover from the shock. Discipline gives you back your rigidity. But the writer in you cannot be identical with the soldier. If he was, you could not want to write. The shock you absorb as a soldier must be converted by the writer into words. And you cannot accept any of the standard poses that exist for the absorbing of the shock.

The pose of being hardboiled and callous, the pose of being a bundle of nerves that writhe like severed wires, the pose of being humorous, tragic, base, heroic—these are the regular ones. But you've had a private experience, the shock of which is unique. The indignity within its dignity, the dignity within its indignity, will be the result of your personality. These sensations, part of them absorbed in discipline, part gripped in independence, must be caught by the lens of your own self.

If the lens of your eye is a good one, you'll capture the outer scene in your own way. The sea of mud in Barbusse's *Le Feu* can never be forgotten, nor the entombing trenches in *All Quiet*, nor the splintered woods imagined by Stephen Crane in *The Red Badge of Courage*. For the sake of the soldier's emotion they were dramatized, brought under his control in order to heighten the dismay or joy of the fight, the dullness of it, the engulfing boredom.

But it is the man himself who makes the war his own. Socrates, a conditioned soldier, walked barefoot on the winter march. A word or two made that discipline forever memorable. Montaigne, who loved the shock of war and said he loved it, was not devastated like Tolstoy, for whom war was a tragic shock, as it must be for an evangelist. But each of them transmuted the experience.

The young American went into warfare unprepared. He had been living for the most part in a post-war world that had the callosity of England after Cromwell, the hardness and wit of the Restoration period. The Puritan conscience may have had to cope with hip flasks, petting parties, a panic and a depression, but it had no concrete war philosophy, as the Germans had. That itself makes a theme for writing soldiers. The Germans had been "bunked" so that they would exclude those humane notions of which young Americans were debunked without knowing it. Hence part of the writer's job, if he is an American, is to make a moral adjustment under the shock of war. Tolstoy, with Russia as his heroine, made his greatest book out of it. If the war that a young American has lived is to live for others he must face the inwardness of his adjustment.

It need not be a turmoil. Good soldierly Americans, like the late Justice Oliver Wendell Holmes, could not, as veterans of the Civil War, enter into the turmoils of Barbusse. They were entire in their feelings as democrats. There was no division in them, nothing unseating and deranging in their moral adventure. The crust of it was so firm that Walt Whitman could, without a doubt of its moral majesty, write "when lilacs last in the dooryard bloomed." The Civil War merged with a Northern evangelism, a Southern patriotism.

But this war has not been spiritually legible for most young Americans. They have gone out of a framework of society that was already being questioned. They had gone under the surface of peacetime. To kill other men, to see men killed, puts to them the ultimate meaning of their lives, whether ironic, laconic, sardonic. If a young writer can go under the crust that soldierly custom hardens and tightens, if he can use the lens of his mind and of his soul, as well as the lens of his eye, then he'll have something to say. How it happened and what happened can come first, to secure the vivid news of it. But the meaning of the news to him is the essence of it. The writer has to catch the unique personal revelation that springs from his having been employed in the oldest of trades. His own revelation has the root of art in it; the war is but its meat and its nourishment.

August 4, 1945

English Esthetic

THE POET ERNEST DOWSON

SAILORS in Singapore as well as high school girls in Iceland found themselves looking at the title, *Gone With the Wind*, and wondering about it. What did they make of it? Where did those strange words come from? Who first thought of them? The only place I have seen them is in a poem by Ernest Dowson. He wrote in "Cynara":

> *I have forgot much, Cynara! gone with the wind,*
> *Flung roses, roses riotously with the throng....*

Yes, he flung roses, roses. And four of his words, little known as he was, were carried to the far corners of the earth.

It is about fifty years since the young poet wrote that evocative line. He was already something of a modern Villon, and "Cynara" was famous in literary circles. Being a proper little gentleman by birth, Ernest Dowson did not directly shoo away his fame. At Pont-Aven, in Brittany, Gertrude Atherton asked him to tea. Though he was nearing the end, he pulled himself together to please the lady, attached white collar and cuffs to his black sweater, wore a pair of white shoes and was freshly shaven. "He drank three cups of tea before he left, and finally consented to read his 'Cynara' poem, which he recited 'in a low monotone that never varied for an instant.'" Later Mrs. Atherton thought of renting a big stone house for the winter and asked him if he'd come every day. "He stared about him as if the bare little room were a vision of paradise. 'Will I! Last winter I had no one to talk to.'" As he laughed, it was seen that his front teeth were gone; he was about 30. He procured new ones, but when Mrs. Atherton changed her plans and de-

Ernest Dowson by Mark Longaker. University of Pennsylvania Press.

parted for London, Dowson, in torture from the "clip and grip" of those cheap teeth, threw them away.

Nothing would be easier, in view of human avidity for romance, than to prepare a spicy dish of it from a life like Dowson's. He did what squalid bohemians do—he drank, he neglected his teeth, he didn't wash, he went with the wind. To be disreputable like this, sentimentalists suppose, is halfway to being a genius. But to give an important subject its due, to show what the man was like, and what a dangerous trade the writing of poetry really is, Mark Longaker has written *Ernest Dowson*. Dr. Longaker is as honest as they come. He has not set out to compose a Dowson "blues." To a complex theme he has brought a full fund of imagination, but a cool and level head. He has labored with love. The absence of coloring matter takes away from the big show of emotion to which the subject lends itself, yet for anyone who wishes to go to the root of the matter, *Ernest Dowson* is a fine piece of work, and it should endure.

The method employed by Dr. Longaker is a help in this direction. Dowson died in 1900, but a number of people still living had known him, and Dr. Longaker went to London and Paris in quest of them. He so gained their confidence that they entrusted him with their memories of Dowson, their clues to his movements, unpublished materials, gossip that had to be sifted—in fact, all the straight stuff out of which a life can be conjured. Dowson, for example, had tried to pull Oscar Wilde out of his old ways after the prison term. Dr. Longaker publishes for the first time twelve letters written by Wilde to Dowson in 1897, and only the biographer's evident probity and tact could have won these vivid scraps of histrionism from Capt. Vyvyan Holland, Oscar Wilde's son. It is enlightening material.

Enlightening to what end? To the enduring end that we should have the truth about Dowson. And what a terrible Dostoievskian story it is, for all its English quietness and lack of blah-blah! Dowson was dead at the age of 33. His father had inherited a drydock on the Thames, at Limehouse, from which he derived two things, a dwindling income and an increasing tuberculosis. The elder Dowson was no ship-caulker. His uncle was that brilliant "Waring" of Browning's witty poem. He was himself a refined, sickly gentleman who wintered in the South of France, a moth around the literary flames of his time, acquainted with Swinburne, Meredith, Rossetti, R. L. Stevenson. He should have been in a drydock rather than owning one. He and his wife were both touched with disease. They took Ernest with them to Mentone and the Italian Riviera, which during peacetime winters is a prolonged English sniffle and cough.

For the puny boy with enormous eyes this exile was formative. He picked up French and he learned Latin from an Italian priest as a living tongue—that is to say, he prepared himself for the lyric as most of the great ones had done before him, by purifying his taste at the source, and by merging the discipline of the classic with his own nervous, original line. Ingenuous and ignorant in many ways, he was already bitten by Schopenhauer, Stendhal, Baudelaire when he went up to Oxford. Several of his lyrics had been published, and he was writing elegant stories, too soft and yet inexorable, like a dagger on a velvet cushion. This asymmetry was not corrected. Dr. Longaker gives a forlorn photograph in which Dowson visibly shrinks from a balanced education like a lovesick maid from a balanced diet. He left after five terms.

London was pullulating with poets. At the Cock on Shaftesbury Avenue, at Henekey's bar, at the Crown, at the Cheshire Cheese, at the Café Royal, Ernest Dowson was to find a score of them, the ambitious and indefatigable Yeats, Lionel Johnson, Arthur Symons, Ernest Rhys, T. W. Rolleston, John Davidson, Richard Le Gallienne. They appreciated him, and very often he left his bookkeeper's desk at Limehouse to look with burning eyes on this whirling life, to binge and swinge with his kind, but without physique or other reserve force. The management of young poets is always food for thought, and no wise woman took him in hand. He fell in love with a Polish girl whose father ran a Soho restaurant that stank of garlic. She was a child. He became a Catholic, probably on her account, but Missie was above him, in a high niche, and he drank

and slept with the dulcies. To earn a living he did hack translations, getting £50 for doing Zola's *La Terre*. The pasty-
faced publisher Smithers took him on, and was patient, but
life hit him. His father, nearly on the rocks, swallowed chloral.
His mother hanged herself. His Polish girl married the waiter.
Dowson fled to the Paris of Verlaine and Toulouse-Lautrec.
No good at self-help, he disdained pity, but the kind Sherards
at last gave him shelter at Catford, E. C., where he died.

Dowson's lyrics still afford delight. Narrow in range, of
course, they are pure in feeling and integrity. He left English
verse richer than he found it. Dr. Longaker sheds light, not
simply on his weak mortal nature, but on the travail of a strong
spirit. It takes strength to have a literary ideal and stick to it.

September 16, 1944

AGAINST VICTORIANISM

A GOLD mine of material has been asking to be exploited. From
the first purrings of Pater and whirrings of Swinburne, the battle against Victorianism became a famous one, and now-it-can-
be-told. Though Oscar Wilde died in 1900, a few months ahead
of Queen Victoria, time had to elapse before what Shaw calls
his "giantism" could be seen in perspective. But "art for art's
sake" was a battle-cry initiated or caught up by others than
Wilde—by Whistler, the whole "fleshly school" and a host of
minor figures. It was a counterpart of another struggle, science
for the sake of science, and followed on a religious upheaval.
Some who took part in the new orientation were led to measure their strength against Victorian conventions and ideals,
prejudices and prudery. The fight is not finished, and whether
it be taken romantically or critically, its realities are still a living part of our history.

William Gaunt, an English writer, christens this upheaval
The Aesthetic Adventure. He builds a lively and rapid ac-

The Aesthetic Adventure by William Gaunt, Harcourt, Brace.

count of it in terms of war—muster of forces, battle, débâcle, aftermath. The biggest engagements, taking the affair on these bright terms, were two sensational lawsuits. The first, in 1878, was about the merits of a picture, an action brought by Whistler against John Ruskin. The second was about the merits of a writer when Oscar Wilde risked a libel suit against Lord Queensberry in 1895. As mere piquant quarrels, apart from their significance, these lawsuits lend themselves to the chronicler, and Mr. Gaunt makes good copy of them.

Whistler had come jauntily on the field to the sound of trumpets, soon after the days of *Trilby*. John Ruskin, qualified to swear by the beard of the prophet, called Whistler an impudent coxcomb "to ask two hundred guineas for flinging a pot of paint in the public's face." A good story in 1878, it is still as fresh as paint. Mr. Gaunt keeps its freshness but though he organizes the material ably, he lacks real convictions about the points at issue, and he hasn't even the courage of his lack of convictions.

Whistler preferred to name St. Petersburg as his birthplace rather than Lowell, Mass. This was a bit of his coxcombry. But he and Wilde irrupted into an era of peace and prosperity. In a sense, they had to be bootleggers. English talent had never kept pace with French talent in painting. As for the drama, if Sheridan had left it for politics long years before, it was for excellent reasons. There was even less English genius in the theatre than in painting. The original Beecham was making pills, not music. The Victorian Frys were not making pictures, they were making chocolate. Bohemia was not so much the invention of Bohemians as a condition forced on dashing creators whose powers were hampered by existing timid academies and pundits. If the theatre was to be revolutionized, it depended on galloglasses like Wilde and Shaw. Art invited the dissolute as well as the devoted, since it was a lawless province for outsiders and upstarts and parvenus. Their first requirement in an epoch so fat and upholstered as Victorian England was to tear the stuffing out of it.

Wilde joined issue on another score. He thought that he as well as the aristocracy should have personal license. Here he collided with convention. A society that is built on Church, Army and Aristocracy may be extremely corrupt, and Victorian England had its putrid spot, but in a court duel with Lord Queensberry, Wilde was no match for a man who could hire a gladiator like Edward Carson. The effrontery with which Wilde tried to carry it off was perverse, but what caused his effrontery? That is the crux of *The Aesthetic Adventure*.

Mr. Gaunt carries water on both shoulders and argues at will on either side. The artists were "unsocial" at the same time that the bourgeois "scented revolution." Whistler was an imp, while Ruskin was "disordered." On the issue itself, however, he relieves England of responsibility. He blames Whistler on "a continental state of mind." The "infection" began with Gautier and Baudelaire. "The inroad of foreign ideas and uncongenial aims" came when "books, pictures and thoughts crossed the narrow sea." France, that home of decadence, was at the root of it. Art for art's sake was a "foreign doctrine." And in the end Whistler, who hated academicians, was to run his head against unalterable law. "He found, as other brilliant foreigners have found, an attitude at once indulgent but at bottom unyielding."

Mr. Gaunt is a polite fraud. It was not the narrow sea that caused this revolt. It was the narrow mind. Mr. Gaunt may say "decadence became a watchword. Opposition was aroused." This might be turned around. He may trace "decadence" to brilliant foreigners from France and Ireland and America. But the unyieldingness of any country to its artists, and the "cult of sensual and senseless ease" that Wilde came to deplore, go deeper than that. Byron was no foreigner. He was a home product. Mr. Gaunt is superficial on the main issue, but he tells a story for the story's sake and the respectability is trimming.

May 17, 1945

IN THE COOL OF THE TIMES

SINCE 1942 *The Times* (of London) Literary Supplement has been giving a page to Charles Morgan. He had been drama critic up to 1939 and then went to the Admiralty. "Having granted me a free hand in the choice of subject," he says, "the paper afterward intervened only to give encouragement. No greater kindness can be done a writer." Indeed, no. And for a new book Mr. Morgan had many kinds of essays to select from. Holding his mirror up to nature and to literature, he made five or six groups which in sum he calls *Reflections in a Mirror*.

The author of *Sparkenbroke* and *The Fountain* is not what one would term a frantic mixer. His novels have had great success, but that success was as much due to his powers of withdrawal as to his expansiveness. What outer offices, guarded by doorman and secretary, are to a modern chief executive, or what moat and drawbridge and boiling oil were to the executive of 1500, Mr. Morgan's apparatus of exclusiveness seems to be in his literary thinking. He was captured at Antwerp in 1914, for example, as a young navy man and was a prisoner in Holland for four years. His essay, "On Being a Prisoner," refers to this. Captivity was hard, but he delved deep into himself and out of his forced withdrawal, being a man given to reflections and searchingness, an extremely sensitive man, he burrowed and excavated and assayed his own inwardness until he had *The Fountain*. His object is not to be inaccessible, in short, but to become accessible on his own terms.

To mix easily and frequently has its advantages, but there is something about Mr. Morgan's vivification of literary experience that says a lot for aloofness. As he turns over his ideas of Emily Brontë, of Thomas Hardy, of Turgenev, of Tolstoy, especially in the nostalgic atmosphere of the war, his sense of those greatnesses seems wonderfully alive. What he says, of course, is part of that prolonged conversation on masterpieces

Reflections in a Mirror by Charles Morgan. Macmillan.

for which another name is culture. When the company is conversing, we are aware that if there is a latch on the door, there is also a spy-hole, and not everyone breaks in. Virginia Wolff is sure of welcome. Lord David Cecil has the floor. Lytton Strachey and Max Beerbohm are much complimented. Clutton-Brock is remembered from the old days of *The Times*. But it is all to the right effect, the effect of releasing the spirit, a spirit not spared by the pestle of war.

One feels underneath these essays how Germany has injured Europe, and how Charles Morgan fears that Russia will do the same. Hence he turns to France with that nostalgia for the very rivers and towns which now asserts itself as the perfection of experience. France achieved a cleanness of line, a levelness of vision, a gift for truth, that remain untarnished and imperishable. Mr. Morgan picks up a serene and charming book, *Why Birds Sing*, and vivifies it so that Jacques Delamain is almost of "our race," whatever that is. Pascal's *Apology for Religion*, chosen from the *Pensées* by Dr. H. F. Stewart, is another book that enables Mr. Morgan to enlarge on France. Still another is C. M. Bowra's *The Heritage of Symbolism*, with its elucidation of Rilke, George, Blok, Yeats and Valéry. Baudelaire in this context has his proper, his monumental significance.

To catch the bird on the wing, the emotion of that civilization so injured, Mr. Morgan ventures on an essay, "*La Douceur de Vivre*." It is Max Beerbohm's "subject within all his subjects," and into it, though Mr. Morgan can at times be irritated and infuriated, he puts more than the pelicans in St. James' Park. A day at Lord's is at the back of his mind. Why not? "And when it is over and you are calling a hansom, what will the newsboy slip from under his arm—a green Westminster or a pink Globe? And at what time will the curtain rise on Lehar at Daly's?" And who was she?

Max Beerbohm's table-talk has the ring of it, the "sense of it that gives to his prose an unsurpassed mingling of grace with tenderness, so that an essay of his produces the illusion of sunlit conversation when it is near evening and the great heat is gone from the day."

To capture that loveliness and yet to be capacious enough

to take in *War and Peace* is quite a facility. Mr. Morgan is not a burly writer who writes like a man of action, and sentiment would be his danger if he did not go deep. But from the leaves he distills come the extract and essence of life itself, its quality, its meaning, its value. When he attempts, under provocation of a familiar kind, to bow-wow with the publicists, he sounds too sharp and impatient. But he is vigorous in asserting that "an artist is, in his nature, the antithesis of the mighty strong beast —a corrective of the evils to which a democratic society is exposed." There he is with Socrates, and of all the conversationalists to whom he gives his fine ear, Socrates still beats anyone in Bloomsbury.

May 19, 1945

INSIDE QUILLER-COUCH

IF ANY writing man has a tear to shed let him shed it over Quiller-Couch. For five or more years his friends were urging him to write the "life" that had begun in 1863. He shied away from it. "There ain't going to be no Reminiscences, never— never." But by July, 1939, he was getting down to it. "I write almost daily a paragraph or so." And this he kept up until he had four chapters. By that time, as anyone who reads *Memories and Opinions* can tell, a priceless story was being unfolded. A fifth chapter, not quite revised, was being written, still with the penholder that he had bought in Mr. Thornton's shop "across the High" fifty-odd years before. Then came a fatal accident. He was hit by a jeep. Only these five chapters survive him.

Q was not the type of literary man from whom reminiscences would spout like a geyser. They are drawn from a deep well and come up in a slow bucket. As he brings them to the light of day something groans in him. The little Q that was buttoned up by his nurse and his class in the days of Victoria fumbles hard to undo the buttons. At the age of 7 his grand-

Memories and Opinions by Q. Macmillan.

father took him swimming at Dawlish, and when he cried after two heavy waves had smitten him to the shingle his grandfather said, "I hoped better of your pluck." That night he cried again, praying God to make him braver. The forces that thus mold a boy do not make for the man's unbosoming himself hilariously.

But if he recalls his bruises as a child, and one brute of a schoolmate who bullied and tortured him, "mincing before authority, cruel to the weak," he is at pains to admit that frequently the authorities "prevailed, and rightly." He instances the choleric injustice of one teacher, Miss Sylvia Townsend Warner's grandfather, quoting someone who dryly said, "a boy naturally demands justice, which is the last thing in this life he will ever get." Yet he says "a queer affection still tinges my memory of" Warner. His is no sob story of youth, but neither is it callous. And he recollects from far days two surges of wonder that poured on him a "drenching sense of beauty," one of them in a place later identified as the woods that had held Tristan and Iseult. It is characteristic of Q that he can reveal these inmost secrets which are his, while the first we hear of his own Iseult is the curt line, "That same evening I asked the lady of my affection to be my wife," and then it hurts him to be so voluble.

English self-consciousness is obvious in Q. It is often called shyness, a double tie between the Englishman and a stranger; it ties the tongues of both, since behind English modesty and delicacy and reticence there may be a severity of private judgment that goes with unbending strength of will, and in the stupid much inflexible prejudice. And yet this same "shyness" does preserve the integrity of heart that nothing, not all the Luftwaffe, could weaken or break. Q's people lived by the heart. He tells how his grandfather, Elias Ford, spent his substance on others until almost ruined. He tells how his extravagant mother gave up her drawing room for months to neighbors who were Wesleyans and had typhoid, doubly afflicted. And he recalls how his father, a doctor, brought Catholic Sisters of Mercy into a community rancorous about Papists. In a nation like England, "nation of shopkeepers," this fiber of disinterestedness is not the least tenacious of its roots. Q's grandfather, a provincial, wrote a classic *History of the Fishes of the British Islands,* illustrated by his watercolors. His father's last efforts were to complete *The Ancient and Holy Wells of Cornwall,* both of them labors of love.

With such urgency of talent and slight gifts for vending it, Q was just the man to edit his renowned *Oxford Book of English Verse.* He was not the typical bookworm. He was keen about rugby and cricket and rowing, and he won the House Cup in a ten-mile steeplechase, "to my own and everybody's surprise." But this sort of thing he took, it may be said correctly, in his stride. To the classics he took as some men do to drink, not in his stride but in his thirst, a glorious thirst for Greek and Latin and "an insatiable thirst for poetry." In the temple of great literature he learned proportion, the liberal art. Once in a while a lovely phrase slips from him that obeys instinct, as when he says, "we talked of many things . . . as the Channel at our feet melted, league upon league, into an embracing gray." But the surveillance of taste and considerateness are so innate that even with inspiration he behaves shyly. He isn't of the pioneer breed.

Many of the men he eulogizes will be unknown to us, and some of his book is about such odd fish as his grandfather might have painted. But from the well of his memory he was hauling in his clear, cool style a refreshment dipped from a deep native source, not merely of the kin that left him a heritage but of amenity in Abbotskerswell and Plymouth and Bristol and Fowey, of beauty dawning for him, and of an Oxford that enchanted and fulfilled him. "At 14 I beheld the City of my young desire, which it surpassed." He did not give his heart lightly, but when he did it was for keeps.

June 28, 1945

JOHN MASEFIELD, APPRENTICE

A BOY of 13 is seldom held to be ready for the rough-and-tumble world. He is supposed to be schooled for it. But school on H. M. S. Conway fifty years ago was in itself a rough world. A lad was flung into it like a dog into a millrace. He had to fight for himself, one against the universe, the prey of his seniors, the legitimate victim of all the pirates and terrors on board, the "new chum" who had to be licked into shape. Either he learned to take care of himself or he was warped into a sneak or a bully. His education was not meant to break him but to toughen him and make a man of him. The process had little leniency in it, in fact it bordered on the heroic.

But a wonderful book John Masefield has made of it. He was 13 years, 3 months and 3 weeks old when he became a "new chum," or apprentice, on the old Conway. No one ever had more natural courtesy than John Masefield. He went aboard that ship with starry eyes, or, as he says himself, "He had the phantasie very strong." He was new, "puzzled, excited, confused," just the sort to be scared and have pins stuck in him at service, to be damned and hazed and half-drowned, to have men of terrible countenance say, "Here, you," "Come on out, you," to be sent on idiotic errands.

But while his memory of it is still blazingly vivid in the exact sequence and startling impact of event, he does not recall it with any self-pity whatever. The captain of the hold saw the hammock he had tried to make neat. "What the hell d'you call that thing? That isn't lashed up. Take it back on deck and lash it up properly." "Please, I've done it as well as I could." "Take it to hell out of here, and do it a — — — lot better. That thing isn't going into one of my racks, my cock; so scatter." This was discipline. He records it as he winces from its pain, but with no resentment, no frustration, no indignation. The wood didn't splinter.

Why? Because he loved the ship. He marveled at kindness

New Chum by John Masefield. Macmillan.

and help. He was ravenous to learn, to go aloft, to master his chores, to get the better of it, and if his hammock was loosened at night or his face daubed with filthy blacking, if "terrible old hands" gave him what-for, there were others for whom he was the eager apprentice, and for them his heart was not less eager, overflowing with its wild worship. He got the hang of things through H. B. "I know not what became of him; but I have thought of him every day for more than half a century."

This generosity of soul in John Masefield has never been contaminated. "Surely all the generosities of the soul," he says, "come from the arts; and they alone bring life," but *New Chum* has something else in it. He writes of persons as they indelibly impressed him, whether good or bad, and he writes of ships with a lover's scrutiny and avidity, distinguishing them, living into them, proud of them, "the firm, exquisite, sweeping, curving sheer," and all else that fair ships inspire, "in all their beauty, in all their tragedy."

But beyond this, and beyond the rhythmic ardor of game and song and dance, intoxicating for the young, he puts into *New Chum* his special elation. Masefield has always been simple, buoyant and unforced. It is his power to feel uncomplicatedly. Take a line from a description of giant gray dray horses, "All day," for example, "the hoofs stamped the blocks of the road, with a clash, a clink, and a spurt of sparks." But this art embraces much more than immediate impressions. It brings mankind into an order that has its social generosity. He sees, for example, a big ship's crowd on its way to be paid off. Among them would be the tough and the terrible. But the ship's crowd are men of his kidney. "They had the indescribable look of high endurance, which used to mark the sailing-ship seaman. . . . During and just after the last war one saw the same look on the faces of some of the infantry. I have seen it on no other faces."

And back in Liverpool "these men were like children"; they were going to be robbed, "scum and sneak-thieves" lying in wait for them. "The crew passed by, with those maggots of corruption clinging to them. (They had the faces and minds of maggots.) Several times in my childhood I had been appalled by the callousness of life: I was appalled, then; it was a scene most frightful to me. Well, later, I was to see other instances of men who did the work at the risk, or cost, of their lives, for the benefit of harpies. The game goes on still," and from Thomas Wyatt through William Blake to John Masefield it has seared the English poet.

It seared him on the day his leave began when he went aboard a small and very filthy steamer. "This is where the men live," said the watchman. Masefield was appalled. "I wanted to be clear of the type of man who gave iron walls and a shelf, and a little daily offal, in exchange for a life's work."

So that, beside "this place, where joy doth sit on every bough—and every cross-tree, and every sail," John Masefield has woven into *New Chum* the valor and tenderness of his nature. Every moonsail and fiferail is real to him. The zest of his youth is still gleaming.

August 2, 1945

NOEL COWARD TRIPS

TROUPING for the troops is a fashion in this war. Hundreds of entertainers are doing it, and little books of reminiscence may become as common as war babies.

But writing is also an art, and one that Noel Coward practices with a fine hand. An actor all his life, a singer and comedian, he happens to have a literary gift of a special order. His war baby, *Middle East Diary*, may seem a casual amorino, but it has an older brother in *Present Indicative*, and while it covers a war effort for its own sake, it arrests a slender and nimble figure for us in a way that is worth any reader's discrimination.

Noel Coward thinks of himself as "a successful playwright." This is not untrue. To have used *In Which We Serve* to show that the common Englishman wasn't the comic relief of *Cavalcade* marked an advance and a success with himself. But

Middle East Diary by Noel Coward. Doubleday, Doran.

Coward's successes with himself are not to be measured by political perceptions. Coward is first of all a virtuoso, a man of his métier, like a kind of Cellini.

When he went from Plymouth to Basra on this brave and prodigious tour of his, he caught the experience as theatre. Its backdrop was theatre. The triumph was theatre. The Middle East was a theatre of unconquerable English spirit. It is all stylish and conditioned, Coward not being a Renaissance Italian, but it carries on a writer's self-story.

The scene is always dramatized. "I looked out of the scuttle and there was the convoy; gray ships, gray sky and gray sea, not a scrap of color anywhere." He comes to Oran. "There it was again, the good old French North African atmosphere, laid on thick," and all like a set from the Boulevard Raspail. In Cairo the oriental courtyard "with a tinkling fountain in the middle of it reminded me forcibly of the second act of *Kismet*." At the Yacht Club at Alexandria "there were a number of elderly, mauve-looking ladies sitting on the terrace when we arrived. They were thickly coated with rice powder and were hissing." They hissed him because he was in shorts. He offered to remove them, but the management removed him. By the Nile, good theatre since Plutarch, he lay on Alexander Kirk's roof in a chaise-longue. "Once more the moon silvered the Pyramids and the stars glittered and graceful peace descended on me." On Malta he tenderly observed an old theatre, perhaps the oldest in Europe, the Manoel, "curly and rococo."

And there, as it "reeked with atmosphere and the sense of the past," he "tore off *Trafalgar Day*" for "unbejeweled British sailors fanning themselves in the boxes."

In often magical words Noel Coward recaptures the performances he gave. Some missed fire. Some were as good as could be. He had acquired an accompanist en route, as well as a fever and many mishaps. He knew "black inward rage." But he is terse, self-critical and all alive to the contagion of it. These are thrilling pages, his strong but evanescent emotion impaled lightly and inescapably.

The British at the top passed him along from Gibraltar to the Gulf, obviously delighting in him and soothing him. Lord Amherst, a Jeff today as formerly, was Jeff to Noel. Lord

Mountbatten was Dickie to him. They, like Coward, are cast for a public part. The actor helps the aristocrat to feel he can create illusion, and Coward in turn goes aristocratic. So graphic, autographic and autobiographic are his roles to him that, as he laughingly says, he almost shoved the captain off his bridge to re-enact *In Which We Serve*, and he tours hospitals almost like a queen. He is as much at home in a wardroom as a palace, but when really at home he is light-hearted, impish and inimitable. Kings and princes are attracted to Prince Noel of Greasepaint. Genial artists are like this, dipping color from the palette in front of them, though if he were as violent as Cellini was, they'd bounce him out, as they bounced Cellini. And he'd understand it as little as he understood André Gide.

In the rude air outside, as might be expected, our successful playwright can be both rasped and rasping. At times he is infected by The Tatler. "Went with Lilia before lunch to have a cocktail with Prince and Princess Paul of Greece in their beach hut." Fancy that! He can think of grouse-shooting on his way to Sicily. "The 'Glorious Twelfth' and here I am about to go and watch some of the shooting!" He identifies himself with the Navy, the Old School Tie and the Rock of Gibraltar. "I have always had an affection for it." He is petulant about incompetence and a dirty roller towel and a dreadful fellow who called him "Nole." He evidently does not vibrate to doughnuts. In a world where the Lion still roars, the Eagle may feel like screaming at this, since there is so little else to scream about.

But he has the good English qualities. He is as loyal as a lamb when he meets any other English actor. Dear Bobby Flemyng, who "popped over from Nazareth," warmed his heart. His heart responds with English sweetness, than which nothing is sweeter. He has a way of reestablishing a world for which one has a longing. "Gammon waited on us and it felt quite like old times." You almost forget that Noel's Old School Tie was donned at the Old Vic, such is the warmth and cheer of his imagination. *Middle East Diary* should dangle and twinkle on many a Christmas tree, with a star on it.

November 9, 1944

War-Torn World

TOM TREANOR'S MONUMENT

D ON'T be misled by the inconsequential title. This is not an inconsequential book. It has imperishable stuff in it. No sensitive reader should miss it.

Tom Treanor was society editor of *The Los Angeles Times*, but he wanted to see the wars. He looked on *The Times* as "unquestionably" one of the half-dozen most important papers in America, and *The Times*, with the prudence that comes of long years of overseeing eager youth, arranged with him to mail his stories. "It was not because *The Times* lacks money." It was because it positively did not want cable-type stories. So off he went, long on eagerness, short on status. "The Only Correspondent Representing a Newspaper West of the Mississippi Ever to Visit the Middle East."

Tom Treanor was as eager as a spring freshet, and in Cairo he must have been nearly the nuisance he said he was. That he was ready for action he soon conveyed to Public Relations, and also the "stupefying fact" that he was the Only Correspondent, etc. This left the authorities quite cold. But by hooking and crooking he attached himself to something still farther west of the Mississippi, a New Zealander. So he made his unaccredited way into the Desert. He made his way to El Alamein.

Those who have seen the famous moving picture may wonder what it was like to a young American to walk forward with the advancing British that night at El Alamein. Here it is, warmly felt, singularly honest. Tom Treanor saw things for himself. He had seen the Amazon from the plane as "a mighty flowing acreage, a long lake on the move." He could see as a

One Damn Thing after Another by Tom Treanor. Doubleday, Doran.

casualty "a truck which seemed to be kneeling on the desert with its front wheels blown off." But it was the British Tommy that made him live it at El Alamein. "Probably he's the solidest, sincerest, happy-go-bloody lucky little man who's ever existed." He saw him with his crooked grin, his "appealing briskness just short of gaiety." He was with him under fire, flirting with the death to which the Tommy was engaged, and taking his course without being on the books.

By playing "Tom-the-fun-loving-Rover-Boy," he left "that cool feel and musty smell of an old dignified bar made of heavy, polished dark woods" at Shepheard's Hotel, and went on unauthorized flights to Malta and Gibraltar. Yes, he was cocky. But he "went to the well once too often." He was expelled to India.

So far, "unaccredited to anybody, broke, grounded, writing my news by mail, threatened with expulsion and finally expelled," this boy needed a break: he got it. Another *Los Angeles Times* man put him right in India. To him it was all new and confusing, *One Damn Thing after Another;* and India was like the "gully, gully man" of Cairo, confusion worse confounded. Yet, unconscious as he was of the process, just by tussling with his tough human assignment he made an amazing success of India. What a marvelous Indian ingression it is! No one asked more incisive questions. No one etched it more firmly or lightly. He used sympathy, showed detachment, moral courage and brains. At any time he could see a lovely picture—"the wind was driving the dust through the moonlight"—but he began to see the patterns. He was organizing his thought.

After nosing through the mud of Burma, in the jungle fighting, and having a stare at the bleakness of Chungking, he returned to the serial of Sicily and Italy. He was there for the worst of it. He was out with an isolated company in Sicily, where men risked death for a drink of water. He was the only newsman to be right there for the hard slugging on the Rapido. It was beginning to be grim for him. He was pretty well expended. He made nothing of it. Before that his mind had played with such engaging items as the superb American Negroes eyeing the African Negroes and exploiting them. He had seen things for himself. Now he took it in step with the individual soldier, watching him "start forward for an attack with that strange hurried expression on his sweating face."

There is a lot of the real America in this book. It isn't tough; it is laconic; and it is sensitively individual. Tom Treanor made little of his generous spirit and he spent all he had, he lost his life in this tough and costly companionship of war. He paid the price that all war correspondents risk paying, to give us straight truths that make us, or should make us, responsible. The pity of early death was stark for him. "Nobody can help the dead with tears or praise or monuments," he said. But that is not true. He helped with this rough chiseled and finely profiled work. This book is his monument.

October 7, 1944

STRONG NATION

THE Basques are an anomaly in the modern world. They form a real nation, intensely aware of themselves, but so small that their desire to exist as a nation comes into modern politics like a figure out of *Green Mansions*. The Basques are extraordinarily fine-looking people, and they live in that lovely country that flows down from either side of the western Pyrenees. They have a language behind which they are as secret as a garden behind thorn bushes. It is an impenetrable barrier, if they wish to exclude you. But they are a singularly upright and democratic people, intensely Catholic, rather austere and self-contained and disciplined. They have, in brief, a way of life, a very old civilization. Were there twenty or even 10,000,000 Basques, they'd be quite eminent as a western European nation. All they lack to be a free nation is an island.

Their most terrible moment in recent history is summoned in the single word Gernika (Spanish spelling is Guernica). That is the name of their afflicted capital in the north of Spain.

Escape Via Berlin by José Antonio de Aguirre. Macmillan.

It may be assumed that the Basques offered no visible threat to the German Reich in the years before the World War; but they offered what the gentlemen of the Reich were looking for, a target from the air. While England and France and America stood by, the Germans demonstrated a first chapter in the lesson that the RAF and the American Air Force were to continue —namely, what unopposed air force can mean. Picasso's terrible picture exposes the disaster that the German heroes willed. As a work of art it is as modern as dive-bombing, and quite as effective.

It would seem that after Gernika the Basques could not survive. Soon afterward their army had to surrender to the treacheries of the Italians and of Franco. But in this age of dangerous living the odd thing is the resurgence of feeble, or apparently feeble, elements of civilization against the incredibly destructive forces that grind this agonized world. Anyone who wishes to learn how such things can be must look into *Escape via Berlin.*

The man who wrote it, Mr. de Aguirre, was the young President of the Basques. It does one good to read a book by so explicit a man. You say to yourself, what except death can happen to a cumbersome group of over forty Basques caught in the whorl of the thundering German war machine outside Dunkerque? Mr. de Aguirre had taken his mother and his wife and two small children to La Panne, which had been so safe in the last war. When the Germans broke through in 1940 he and his tribe, provided with the few hundred dollars left to them after Franco had beggared them, were swept to their knees by the floods of war. They were joined by other Basques. They were just a bunch of powerless refugees. But if one of them, Mr. de Aguirre, were captured, he had nothing to expect but Franco's firing squad, after a rapid transfer by the Gestapo.

No better description of this wallowing in the flood of refugees is easily to be found. Mr. de Aguirre has one of those extremely clear minds in which facts stand out without fuzz. Only two of his group were killed. His wounded sister died of gangrene. Their amiable treasurer was killed outright, and the funds on the dead treasurer's body had to be rescued from among mounds of dead. These details, narrated by a feeling and warm-blooded man, are very telling. We are enabled to be there with him. But a family council has to decide on the course of action open to the Basque President, and he elects for the audacious and dangerous decision to go in disguise to Berlin.

He became a Panamanian, cultivated a new personality and a mustache, won the collaboration of Pan-American diplomats, and, after months of weary dissimulation and narrow squeaks, made his way to Unter den Linden. No novel by Vicki Baum, who knows her Berlin, could hope to rival this true narrative. For one thing, Mr. de Aguirre sees it all with an honest lens. He doesn't distort or foreshorten or play tricks. And this dignity lends to each encounter with the Gestapo or the diplomatic corps a tension such as one feels when any valued human being has to tread his way through mine fields.

We find ourselves wanting him to come through, but at every turn there are hazards and disappointments. There is something about conservative consulates that is like a disease, as if iron filings had entered into their souls. He was up against this, as well as "the tragic mysticism of the Germans." That's a polite word for it, but out of his narrowed eyes he observes German conventionality, even under the Nazis. "Mention a name of a diplomat and they are filled with awe."

The dawn comes when, through his generous friends from Pan-America, he and his family reach Sweden. It is the Swedish Social Democrats who cut the red tape, with help from the British. The day breaks in glory when he comes to Brazil, and the United States, through Jefferson Caffery and Columbia University, extend a warm hand. He feels how good the humble can be, but there is also a bureaucracy that can be good.

This Basque is honest about the conflict between the Church in Spain and the Church Universal. He is a lucid and tireless exponent of his whole philosophy. His book is a democratic document, but he scarcely knows that it is the grim story itself, and the nobility and nerve of it which do most to plead and to manifest for the small, strong nation he belongs to. Against lurid skies he is an upright figure. The Tree of Gernika is a tree of life.

November 11, 1944

THE WINNING OF ASIA

RUSSELL Brines of The Associated Press is a young man, reckoned in years. He was born in Denver in 1911. But not much of his carefree youth has withstood his contact with Asia. He went through the fall of Manila.

Already in 1939 he was on the front in Manchuria, learning how, in spite of their wish to save face, the Japanese cannot resist sticking their neck out. "Give me a Japanese division armed with bamboo spears," said Gen. Sadao Araki, "and I'll wipe out the entire Russian Far Eastern Army." Mr. Brines foresees a Japanese war with Russia, "so deep and so encrusted with hatred and suspicion" are the issues in abeyance. But it was not Manchuria which led him to write *Until They Eat Stones*. He has built it up from all he saw and heard of the Japanese imperialists, from 1939 till he came back in 1943 on the Gripsholm.

"We will fight," he quotes the Japanese as saying, "until we eat stones." His painstaking, somber, impersonal book is his testimony that they mean it. He was interned himself, with his wife and daughter, at Santo Tomas, and had nineteen months of it, but so overwhelming is the importance he attaches to Japanese grimness that he has sunk his own story, which happens to be particularly honest and informative, so that a "national hypnotism" should be made memorable. And he surveys it, not only in Tokyo where he saw peasants dedicate their grandchildren at the Shinto shrine, and in the Philippines, where he learned it through bitterness and Japanese "polite, almost patient, condescension," but also in squalid Shanghai,

Until They Eat Stones by Russell Brines. Lippincott.

and from those who knew Thailand and Burma and Indo-China and the Malay Peninsula.

Once in a while, as in Santo Tomas, Mr. Brines pierced through hatred. "I learned to like you," said the first Japanese commandant, a stern-faced, old-line officer. "I learned to like you, against my will. I found that underneath you are very much like Japanese people, and you are not at all what the papers say about you." Except for this single human touch, an expanse of flint spread unbroken around this informant, and wherever the secret police took charge he learned of rule by torture, of hideous and venomous cruelty, kidnapping and blackmail.

Though the Japanese themselves are at the mercy of their secret police, Mr. Brines piles up evidence of their war fever. "Death before dishonor" makes little of pain and less of suicide, and though he believes "the average Japanese peasant is not bloodthirsty or aggressive," he does not doubt for a second that they must be smashed. "We must fight, in fierce union, until they eat stones." We must match their doggedness.

For all the ruthlessness he describes, he gives no great impression of true Japanese discipline or efficiency. To kill Filipino workers, in order to preserve a military secret, seems both dastardly and stupid. The Filipino collaborationists are in danger of assassination. The majority of the Filipinos cannot be stirred to hate Americans. They "are living primarily for the day the Americans return." Detailed as the Japanese blueprints for conquest may be, it is slightly idiotic to produce a Japanese "Catholic" bishop who grants divorce. The Filipinos scorn this nonsense. Night clubs and black markets and Japanese drinking Scotch and soda do not remove the feeling of blight and disease, of starvation and "sullen indifference." And Mr. Brines gives warming instances of Filipino loyalty.

The miseries of internment were much lightened by American ingenuity. Mr. Brines got out a paper. There were engagements, babies, poker, cocktails, a building boom and baseball. But he passes over this community of several thousand to expose the tentacles by which Japan takes strangling hold on its

conquests. The white men have not only to defeat Japan. They
have to win the Asiatic.

Mr. Brines is able to reveal a figure like Admiral Decoux in
Indo-China, and to gather some solid facts about Malaya. His
lust for exact detail gives practical value to his book. But it
has another value.

The unpremeditated earnestness of his manner and the almost
unrelieved, pitiless desolation of the outlook, with famine so
near and death so casual, leave a sharp and lasting impression.
What a heritage for America! Who said the "frontier" no
longer exists? There are more thankless jobs to be done than
ever Abraham Lincoln dreamed about.

December 28, 1944

WOMAN-MADE AMERICA?

WHEN an American who has been an active war correspondent
comes home to tell us we are poor deluded imbeciles, we can
hardly fail to lend him the only things we don't seem to have
lent to anyone else. Let's lend our ears to George Weller.

Mr. Weller has read Admiral Mahan, Homer Lea and Hudson Maxim. He knows Fafak and Pago Pago and Dang Dong
at first hand, is familiar with Sad Sack and Dogfaces, and has
a powerful argument that he spreads before us in *Bases Overseas*.

The American of today has Mr. Weller's deep pity. He accuses him of being "feminine," of being "mulcted," of not
understanding international politics and not wishing to practice
them. "Like a 'teenager in love, he has a sense of moral superiority mixed with an inadequate sense of his interests." "Never
one to stint himself in self-pity—another of his many feminine
attributes—he has attained a state so degraded in his international political adjustments that he glories in his own sucker-
dom."

Bases Overseas by George Weller. Harcourt.

Mr. Weller, concurring in part with Mr. Lindbergh, thinks the American is a sucker for Britain.

"If there were no British Empire to be sustained as an ally," he says, "America would have holed herself up for the winter of the world's discontent in the Western Hemisphere, leaving Europe and Asia to fight it out." The Western Hemisphere, at any rate, is an armadillo. But we forgot that "strategy is a system of logic, not of ethics." We went to help Britain. We have poured out billions "to uphold British hegemony in the Middle East." And for what kind of a Britain?

Mr. Weller shows no awareness of that pacific Britain which had no more use for spending on Singapore than we had for spending on Guam. He tells us "the war was already all but lost by the time that the United States entered it," but lost by a Britain that, without paying its debts, still has Greece in hock to its bankers, has Portugal for its washpot, and makes a tool of Abyssinia by lending it money. We might help ourselves to the Portuguese Empire, but we are mollycoddles. We are "a literate and susceptible population, politically inexperienced but highly idealistic and emotionally vulnerable." Starry-eyed mystics with a craving for goldbricks. We pay for our feed to an Australia we are "defending" and lashing out our pay under the Southern Cross. "Do we get value? Sometimes."

As for lend-lease, he thinks it an orgy of "messianic internationalism." Secretary Stimson took a different view. He held that "we are not seeking to make a loan to Great Britain. We are really seeking to purchase her aid in our defense. We are buying—not lending. We are buying our own security while we prepare."

Mr. Weller pooh-poohs this as "American incantation and self-persuasion." No, we are suckers. The "wife-mother" has bamboozled us. Look at the booty Britain got out of the first war! What booty did we get? We were offered a mandate for that "tearful pauper," Armenia. Britain and France are "fat with territorial acquisition." And lend-lease is "like a man in a cold railroad station who does not know where he is going, burning dollar bills to warm his hands while he waits for his train." But will he have any fare left, the poor spendthrift?

And remember, "Britain rejected an American-born Queen."

Many a man with an ardent temperament is loose and flamboyant. It would be news to a Jesuit that "the only civil institution in which common property really works is marriage." You can't dogmatize to Stalingrad that "cities are cowardly places." Nor to Sicily that "an island is well-nigh invulnerable." Nor to Quisling that "every man is bound by his allegiances." But while Mr. Weller gushes with whirling opinions that fall in cinders almost as soon as they rise in fire, he does rub in the practical consequences of our intending to hold the Philippines.

"Once containing bases are established, there is no problem of 'governing' Japan, 'policing' Japan, 'occupying' Japan or 'teaching Japan to be a democratic power.' Contain Japan in a permanent system of bases." He argues this for Japan, and for Europe from the Skagerrak to the Balearics. Unlike Gerald Johnson, who would give the Skagerrak to Russia, Mr. Weller would earmark it for America.

Books about the "soft underbelly" of Europe which forgot the knobs on it have served to remind credulous readers to keep faith with themselves by not yielding it freely to the glib. Mr. Weller is too glib. He says, "Who holds the bases, holds the peace," though we held Corregidor, and Britain held Singapore. More and more bases is his answer. The cure for preparedness is shrewder preparedness. Perhaps it is. But his smashing criticisms of Britain and France, his arguments that "armies are for powers that want to keep the lands they conquer," rather force one to ask, why all these bases for rival empires? Why not international bases? He does make a case for bases in themselves.

January 6, 1945

ENDURING PEACE

POLITICS is not just a science, and America has never had the formality in politics that science likes. If a mad statesman desires facile, untrammeled action on an ideal level, where all is high and clear, with little friction and less human nature, he can pull his nation into a stratosphere, but America cannot give it to him. A democracy can create a community and liberate every member of it, but not by this method. It can do it only by living in the density of the real world, by nurturing the sense of real people, being mature in that sense, and striving for a cohesion of things consented to, things loved and desired and willed.

And when a blow descends on this community, like the death of President Roosevelt this week, it is not political science that suffers most, it is the heart. A member of ourselves, loved for a supreme sense of great reality and his power to work disinterestedly, is lost to us. He had worked on an agreed pattern, by an understanding of human nature, shuttled backward and forward.

How does democracy arrive at the pattern? Dr. Gardner Murphy, president of the American Psychological Association and professor at City College, is a star in his profession, and probably nothing would better suit him, given the scholarly cast of his mind, than to fly high in the schematic. But one sentence in the new volume he has edited, *Human Nature and Enduring Peace*, tells how humanly alive he is to our present world. "In a period of war," he says, "we clutch desperately at the hope held out by our political and military leaders—and respond with surging faith to the addresses of Mr. Churchill and of the President." This faith, this surging faith, can never be again sustained by the voice we knew well. But *Human Nature and Enduring Peace* is no vague science. It is an attempt to substantiate that faith from every angle, by an intellectual community.

Human Nature and Enduring Peace edited by Gardner Murphy. Houghton Mifflin.

Dr. Murphy acts as its monitor, working out the method by which human traits can be disentangled in politics. But instead of stringing fifty essays together, he has proposed sharp questions to individual colleagues and made them cohere. This carries forward a searching inquiry. He begins with "The Impulse to War," fifty pages of keen analysis by himself. "The Obstacles to Peace" come next, with no attempt to exculpate Germany, but with five forthright essays, the one by Charlotte Buhler being a most valuable contribution on German youth and the German unconscious. R. N. Sanford is brilliant on "Relapse into Old Habits" of American thought, while James L. Graham, in a scathing examination of our "educational failure," sees a real obstacle to peace.

Dr. Murphy opens the floor to "A Positive Program," political and educational. The book ends with a further affirmation, "World Order Is Attainable."

On the eve of the San Francisco Conference, where decisions must be made, *Human Nature and Enduring Peace* does everything in its editor's power to throw light on "trouble spots" as they appear to men and women trained in "the psychological study of social issues." By the manner in which he has put his questions and shaped the discussion, he has clarified a great deal, working heart and soul to put the resources of a particular skill at the service of American policy makers.

What impairs a lengthy book of this kind is obvious to anyone interested in exposition as such. While Gardner Murphy does not give biographical notes on his contributors, it is evident they are working psychologists, most of them highly trained. Now to write well costs time, and time is money. America does not pay psychologists so that they can afford to write well. Those who happen to write well, as Dr. Murphy does, give their maximum energy to a book like this out of their bounty. This is a much better book than a recent one by anthropologists, but much of it is muggy, abstract, evasive in the interest of textbook decorum, and beneath the level set by the editor.

Top-notch magazine writers arrest the attention of busy politicians. But while America bribes high school girls by giving them free trips to state and national capitals and by sending them in herds through museums at a mile a minute, it stints its psychologists. It expects these intellectuals to give national guidance at 2 cents or no cents a word. This is preposterous. The slick writers become entertainers, the loyal ones become sleeping pills.

But if some of these fifty contributors are dull as the dishwater with which intellectuals are now familiar, three times a day, *Human Nature and Enduring Peace* has burning faith in it, and in some essays it has wisdom and extraordinary pertinence. Here is priceless aid from psychologists who explain how the sadists, the cynics and the wayward can be sorted out. If our own ego can stand the jolts, we learn how we can work for a world order, about which there is nothing vague or visionary.

Our salvation can be put into action, but, after April 12, we are on our own now more than ever. Reader: "The problem of implementing the findings, developing national policy, is yours."

April 14, 1945

BHAGAVAD-GITA

The Razor's Edge, by Somerset Maugham, did not make a great hit with many critics, and yet the American public, or more correctly one of its publics, has given it a strong and sustained response. Why? As a story-teller Mr. Maugham is as adroit as they make them, but while his story and the setting must have engaged his readers, *The Razor's Edge* was not solely compelling on that account. The elderly snob was droll, with his flair for art and his mania for titles, and the girl in Paris whose depravity dooms her to be murdered was a shockingly vivid piece of debasement and vice. But it surely wasn't

Bhagavad-Gita translated by Swami Probhavananda and Christopher Isherwood. Marcel Rodd Company, Hollywood.

for this that the book climbed to the head of the national list, in spite of a cool reception. It was, in all probability, for Larry, who traveled to India from Chicago, and went religious.

Larry was particularly unconvincing to those critics who have long since learned to dislike and distrust the elated theme, whether in *Resurrection* or *The Blue Bird*. But in Larry, it seems to me, the public did find a salt that it craves, and this urgent craving, if not satisfied by Mr. Maugham, was certainly quickened by him. In the Maugham labyrinth there must be a Larry, and by some dogged English quality in the author the elusive quest after divinity was not abandoned until Larry was on paper. Divinity may have outdistanced Mr. Maugham. It does most of us. But his pursuit of it in terms of Larry made his book a stirring event for thousands.

Among these must be many who, for poignant reasons, which become more poignant every day, wish to go farther with it. Two other Englishmen of letters, Aldous Huxley and Christopher Isherwood, have lent a hand to making it possible. Mr. Isherwood has devoted his fine literary gift to a new translation of *Bhagavad-Gita*, working with Swami Probhavananda. And to this Hindu scripture, "The Song of God" as its title would express it in English, Mr. Huxley has written a brief introduction.

The little book is a self-contained one. A complete stranger to the Hindu gospel can pick it up and in one or two evenings follow the great poem from its inspired beginning to its sublime end. Mr. Isherwood has joined with the Swami in making a version which, as Aldous Huxley says, "can be read, not merely without that dull esthetic pain inflicted by all too many English translations from the Sanskrit, but positively with enjoyment."

The poem is very old, not as old as the Pyramids but maybe as old as the Parthenon, and it applies to 1944. It begins with a soldier who might be seated in a tank, "his heart overcome with sorrow." It is his duty to fight and he cannot bear it. Why must he fight?

The driver of his tank is the Lord himself, Krishna, and he, who stands for peace on earth and good-will among men, turns to Arjuna, and talks about war to him.

"I cannot see where my duty lies," says the fighting man. "Krishna, I beg you, tell me frankly and clearly what I ought to do. I am your disciple. I put myself into your hands. Show me the way." Krishna answers him. He had begun by saying, "Is this hour of battle the time for scruples and fancies?" But it is not to the soldiers' pride the talk is confined. It opens on the meaning of war, the meaning of life and death, of killing and being killed. And never hesitates to say, "Go forward and fight."

For soldiers, and those who love soldiers, this is a living word. It is part of what Aldous Huxley strives for in his introduction under the name "Perennial Philosophy." The introduction is much compressed, but in no sense confused, and the reader who can labor with it and hydrate it with the sweat of the brow can see what Huxley means by urging that contemplation should not be a means to action. "Contemplation of truth," as Larry gropingly understood, "is the end, action the means." Emerson, and Emerson's America, had insight into this. Probably Lincoln had.

But it is the Army, the Navy, the Air Forces, the Alex Dosters, for whom "The Song of God" speaks to the heart. Somerset Maugham led us to the threshold. Huxley calls from within, and this song harks to us from beyond a horizon.

December 23, 1944

Biography and History

APOSTLE OF TEMPERANCE

A LIFE of *Father Theobald Mathew* might easily be tame and flat, and certainly Dr. Patrick Rogers uses no coloring matter in his story of the so-called "apostle of temperance." But this meek biography, so judicious and sober, happens to have a remarkable man for its topic and it does well by him.

Over a hundred years ago Theobald Mathew was a young friar in Kilkenny. He was so kind in the confessional that all the poor were flocking to him, but one Saturday as he was about to hear confessions a document was handed to him and he had to tell his penitents that his powers were suspended. Hurt to the bone by this reproof for zealousness, the young Capuchin sought his transfer to Cork, where two other Capuchins had a small chapel and a friary.

The gentle, ardent young Mathew had been born on an estate of 1,500 acres and in a grand house of fifty bedrooms, where his father was agent for his cousin. Cork was full of poor people not immune from cholera and typhus—and the poor so deprived that the dead were exposed in their coffins outside their hovels until alms had been collected to pay for burial. Labor was crushed down. Liquor was so cheap that a man could get drunk for 10 cents.

The city was still Gaelic speaking, and Father Mathew had to learn Irish in order to hear confessions, which he began at 5 in the morning. The toilers of the city came to him, men who cured fish or made sausages, chandlers, sailors, lamplighters who mingled the smell of whale oil with the odor of sanctity. "The

Father Theobald Mathew by Patrick Rogers. Longmans, Green.

way of it is this: the worse you are in the beginning, the more he'd like you and the better he'd use you, but if you didn't improve very soon, there's no usage too bad for you."

Was Irish drunkenness beyond remedy? A Quaker on the poorhouse board kept saying: "O, Theobald Mathew, if thou wouldst but take the cause in hand! Thou couldst do such good to these poor creatures." Theobald resisted the call. His brother was a distiller and his sister had married a distiller. Poverty was the basic evil. "Give, give, have no fear of giving" —that was his paternal impulse. But the "total abstinence" movement, up till then rather Methodist, invited qualities in him that others could value. He had a florid way of speaking and used poor gestures, and his voice at the beginning was "slender, weak and almost infantile," but he was so warm, so earnest, so "simple and unaffected," that the friars made him their provincial, and by the time he was nearing 50 left him free to begin a crusade. The situation had awaited him.

Seldom has such overwhelming response greeted a missionary. Human beings of all sorts and kinds fell under his spell. He went from Cork to Limerick and Waterford, saw thousands of men and women, poured out advice and help, and to Catholics, Protestants and heathens. To give the pledge to 40,000 in a day was soon no novelty. Courted by every politician and agitator, he held single-minded to his mission and carried it to Scotland and England. "No man has done me more injury than you have, Father Mathew," said the distiller George Roe, "but I forget all in the great good you have done my country."

Thackeray saw him as benign. "His features are regular and full of a noble expression of mildness and indomitable firmness. He has a fine and delicate hand and dresses well, almost elegantly." Thomas Carlyle came on him at a meeting in Scotland Road, Liverpool. "A very ragged and lost-looking squadron indeed. . . . The very face of him attracts you. . . . I almost cried to listen to him." Jane Welch Carlyle saw the hordes in London. "When one looked from them to him, the mercy of Heaven seemed to be laid bare." He gave the pledge in England to 200,000.

But who was to pay for the medals, the halls, the music, the band-players and their uniforms? The apostle was a pauper. A legacy from Lady Elizabeth Mathew went to others. A benefit in Dublin took in $10,000 and cost a swollen $5,000 for expenses. Birmingham overcharged for medals. "Give" was his motto, and he refused to ask cash for the mercy of Heaven. But the great Famine came to tax his strength. He had a stroke, not of luck but of paralysis.

Yet he carried the crusade to America. The South blamed him for once having denounced slavery, and William Lloyd Garrison blamed him for not denouncing it again. Henry Clay and Lewis Cass did him honor, however, and so did the Senate. The total who took the pledge reached 7,000,000. Homesick, insolvent, mortally ill, he lived to complete his American mission. A few years of invalidism and he closed his eyes on a country in which hard drinking was recommencing, though perhaps 80 per cent of the distilleries had gone out of business.

The man was no economist, no psychiatrist, but he had a heroic heart and was curative. It is a singular fact that his kinsman, the Right Rev. David Mathew, now Auxiliary Bishop of Westminster, writes an introduction free from the parching vice of sectarianism. He dares to hint that Theobald had a father whose "Catholicism was rather shadowy," and in the family burial ground Catholic and non-Catholic "lay side by side." Bishop Mathew, who turns a pretty phrase, reminds one that nobility of temper may transcend creed. "Grand George" and other Mathews kept open house, but Theobald opened his soul to the helpless and hopeless, enabling them to save themselves. It was romantic, and shortened his life, but it remains impressive.

February 8, 1945

GUIDE TO MOZART

WHEN he was a youth Mozart spent some time in a German
military town and he was amused by it. "At night I hear perpetual shouts of 'Who goes there?' and I invariably reply,
'Guess!'" This light-heartedness he brought into the world
with him. When a biographer says to him, "Who goes there?"
Wolfgang Amadeus Mozart answers, "Guess!" He said it in *The
Magic Flute* and in the *Requiem*. He said it when he died at
the age of 36, in 1791, nine weeks after the first performance
of that aerial opera.

Between this unhappy date, 1791, and our own time there
have been many biographies in which pathos was dominant
because of Mozart's brief existence. The Professor of Music
at Smith College, Dr. Alfred Einstein, has not added to them.
Dr. Einstein is a famous musicologist. His *Mozart* leaves no
doubt of that. His is the kind of book, someone has said, that
you should play on the piano. But his microscopic knowledge
of the 626 works in the catalogue is only an indication of something that transcends scholarship. Between himself and Mozart
there is an almost religious intimacy. He has brought to this
intimacy a massive intelligence, an impatient and even irascible
exclusiveness, a jeweler's eye, and a steady discrimination that
bars sentimentality. The result is a great handbook, written in
German and translated by Arthur Mendel and Nathan Broder.

Dr. Einstein's love of Mozart is at once severe and jealous.
This little Mozart did not go about life in a way of which Dr.
Einstein approves, and at times he almost grunts his disapproval.
His instinct of self-preservation is outraged by Mozart's lack
of it. Mozart fell into the hands of women, including a mother-
in-law, and Dr. Einstein is an unhappy uncle about this, as he
is about Mozart's defeat in the second Paris campaign, a defeat
on the terrain where Gluck was wearing medals. All this is
inverted apprehension and solicitude. It makes the story live,
though the biography is less a correct and ordered account of

Mozart by Alfred Einstein. Oxford University Press.

events than a keen interjection. You have to infer much for yourself, but you are inspired by a desire to read the other biographers with whom you feel that Dr. Einstein is not infrequently irate.

But anyone who knows the music so completely, who has botanized in that forest so searchingly, cannot help impatience with those who merely pass through it on a highway. Mozart, as anyone can tell in five minutes, was one of those supernal creatures who moved into perfection like the month of May itself. Winter could not hold him, and he flowered. That he did this without visible egoism, and yet with complete humanity, is obvious. Putting this together with the fact that he died before he was 36 and was buried in a pauper's grave, you have material for one of those Hollywood biographies that have the sweetness and tenacity of fly-paper.

Dr. Einstein's knowledge of the Mozart achievement was won by years of labor. It rules out facile tears and the concert commonplace. His examination of the scores is inevitably professional, not literary, but it provides the reader with the most concrete sense of Mozart's work, vast in its quantity, infinitely inflected. This exhaustiveness is essential to full undertanding.

Like everyone of his naturalness as a human being, Mozart set out with light-heartedness almost in his infancy. Only one of the portraits that Dr. Einstein reproduces catches any likeness whatever. That is the Josef Lange profile, with its sensuous mouth, its proud dominance of brow, its apprehension of sadness. Here one sees that the road he chose has no handrail between him and the precipice; for him it was agonizing and breathless with danger. It took heroism to pursue it, but his father knew he was gifted to compose—that is to say, to order the spirit he liberated, and create form for the adventure he elected. He did not flinch from it. Born to music as a mystic to sainthood, he made of it an art that came to correspond to his own entirety, as racing to a horse of Arab strain or the ocean to a salmon. This was the felicity to which he was born. He had joy in it, even in his duet with death before he finished.

He worked hard, "hard for himself and easy for his listener." Perhaps his purity of form came less from serenity inside tradition than from the manifold outlet he found, such as dramatic prowess inside opera. He mastered an astounding variety of forms. In this he was aided by the fact that he was musically and socially acclimated, fond of his family and thus able to expand at home. He was afflicted by inclemency in the world of German princelings, but he could bundle himself up for that variable weather. He stood it because loyalty was natural to him, however lively his spirit and mature his esthetic independence. Dr. Einstein, impatient with those who compare him to Raphael, says "Mozart could be compared only with Dürer," but, to qualify this exasperated comparison, Dr. Einstein later mentions Watteau and Boucher. Haydn's noble tribute, when Mozart was not yet 30, uses the right word. "Before God and as an honest man," he said to Leopold Mozart, "I tell you that your son is the greatest composer known to me either in person or by name. He has taste and, what is more, the most profound knowledge of composition."

In close analyses that allow Dr. Einstein to specify his appreciation, the depths of Mozart's art do not go unplumbed. Though *Mozart* is not a work of art itself, it offers a companionship and masterly guidance to anyone who wishes to know Mozart better. It has treasures of pure discernment in it, and for a genius.

March 1, 1945

HE KNEW THE TOLSTOYS

Tolstoy kept a diary. Without it we could still know him, as is proved in the period when he let the diary lapse. His own works are rich in the best kind of biographical material. He was the center of Russian interest for a long generation, all the keen writers visiting him, talking with him, observing him. There never was such a source of copy. His widow gave her version of him. His daughter Alexandra wrote a book, which

Tolstoy and His Wife by Tikhon Polner. Norton.

is second only to one of his own. But for each of the endless
series of crises that shook him to the roots, each calling for the
seismograph, the diary traces the curve. Just as he took off his
tunic every night, so he bared his soul.

Nicholas Wreden read a book in Paris in the late Twenties,
written in Russian, that made him "more aware of Tolstoy as
a human being" than any other. It was by a Russian, "a typical
public-spirited liberal in pre-Revolutionary Russia," with the
unusual name of Tikhon Polner. Polner called his book *Tolstoy
and His Wife*. Mr. Wreden asked for the right to translate
this book and has now got around to publishing it. This is certainly no literary or analytical concoction. Polner knew the
Tolstoys. Feeling Tolstoy's dignity and nobility to start with,
and the wife's lifetime of devotion, he has at the same time the
implacable diary that sets down the soul-rocking quarrels, the
titanic writhings and accusations, and yet the sad, timid little
birdsong after each terrible storm. *Tolstoy and His Wife* is an
irresistible account of tragic marriage. By his refusal to veil the
facts Polner risks harshness, but from first to last he manages,
without any attempt to gild the lily, to be wise, calm and kind.

Perhaps Sonya, as Tolstoy called her, did "capture" the great
man. Count Tolstoy though he was, already famous, he was
a hulking fellow with something of the backwoodsman about
him, and more himself with people slightly inferior in the social
rank than with less awkward, less spontaneous, more courtly
Russians. The three daughters of Dr. Behrs, who lived inside
the Kremlin, gave this original, highly self-conscious giant the
wooing warmth in which all of him became sweetly soothed
and expansive. He sang with them, basked in them, dreamed of
them. But as the oldest of the three waited for his offer, it was
the 18-year-old Sonya, at once soft and hard, who signaled to
him. He went through agonies of doubt and love. He was
"old," almost 34. His diary (which he eventually showed to his
Sonya) exposed how he had previously aspired to women of
the beau monde. Something in him feared Sonya's sway, but
he was more afraid of proud, sophisticated women. Delivering
a crushing blow to the older girl, he married Sonya.

Long afterward Gorki was to say of Tolstoy: "He has very

vague relations with God. At times they remind me of the relations between two bears sharing a den." Many malicious words were to be spoken of "the old sorcerer." But Tikhon Polner has his one purpose, to give us Tolstoy and his wife, and he manages most skillfully to include only the revelatory, the crucial, issues in Tolstoy's fantastic development as they affected the marriage.

Sonya was a matriarch. Having come into possession of a genius, she did not deny him herself in any essential. She was fiercely jealous and honestly faithful. She bore him thirteen children, and did her best to nurse them under his command. She worshiped his talent. She copied *War and Peace* from his blinding, tortured script as many as seven times. She sat up late and got up early, proud to serve his creative genius. She couldn't stand the smell of cowsheds. She forced on him a clean bed pillow instead of his creased red leather cushion. But with her bundle of keys she toured the domain, such as it was after his gambling had shrunk it.

But he was an eagle, she was a cage to him. Faithful himself for forty-eight married years (they kept the dockets), and loving Sonya through the birth and death of five of the brood, through the education of the others as young aristocrats, he passed from this paternity into a phase beyond her. From first class he went down to steerage, as it were, and she couldn't follow. He wanted to redeem the world. He wrote an *A. B. C.* that sold a million and a half copies. She couldn't bear it. From steerage he went to the black gang, the stokers. He found the derelicts, the epileptic, the vagabonds. He embraced the lepers. Sonya could not incorporate lepers into her matriarchy. At 82 he ran away from her, having deceived her by signing away his copyrights in a sort of economic nudism. He died in a station-master's house, with Sonya kept from him in a car on a siding.

They tore each other to pieces, these two. But having brought thirteen children into the world, it was a bit late for Tolstoy to go celibate. He gave up liquor, tobacco, meat. He became a Fundamentalist. He gave it up. He was as fiercely jealous of his daughters as if he were an oriental despot. And yet, with lidless eye, he gazed heroically into the eternal. Sonya, half-German, said: "Yes, I lived with Lev for forty-eight years, but I never really learned what kind of a man he was." You try it.

July 7, 1945

FOUNDER OF DUTCH LIBERTY

MIRACLES do happen. A generation ago the young English woman historian was often tethered to a dry theme until she had nibbled it bald. Today she dares much more to select a major subject. She behaves as though history has direct meaning for life no less than for the uses of professional method. Courage, as Miss C. V. Wedgwood proves in her *William the Silent*, is not the least of a historian's moral equipment, and she carries off her newest enterprise with the quiet verve of a well-disciplined but wholly responsible author at first hand.

Hers is the noblest of subjects. The Netherlands possess in William of Orange one of those unforgettable heroes who fathered a nation and moved from a Mount Vernon to a Valley Forge. The names of Haarlem and Alkmaar and Leyden are imperishable. Miss Wedgwood has not faltered before the intricacy or magnitude of this checkered struggle, and hers is a glowing, substantial, ingeniously organized book.

The reader who knows nothing of the "great founder of Dutch liberty," as Baedeker used to call him, can count on easy initiation in these pages. With a tolerant hero to dramatize, the author allows her pattern of the man to emerge from the action itself. The problem for a scholar in a crowded historic landscape, with so many lines interlacing, is to keep the huge peak forever in view, bridging ravines with a word and leaving crags to the eagles. In spite of the masses of detail that she has to dominate, Miss Wedgwood unwaveringly pursues the essential drama to which her ripe sympathy gives her the clue.

William the Silent by C. V. Wedgwood. Yale University Press.

William the Silent had an almost impossible task. Momentously alive to political reality, he saw a union of states as his goal, but to achieve it against the Spanish overlord had to be painfully induced from within his people. William was a German noble by birth, and a Lutheran. Inheriting the pocket princedom of Orange at 11, he became a Catholic and a favorite of Charles V. Not till Charles' pea-green son imposed the Inquisition on the Netherlands did William deflect his allegiance by degrees. The dike against the Inquisition was to protect a nascent individuality; he had to net the states together while seeking to leave religions free to slew around inside the net.

His mother, Juliana, among the plum blossoms at Dillenburg, is Miss Wedgwood's gracious keynote. William was never a self-denying hero. He had four wives, moved from altar to church-yard in correct rotation. And he had all three religions, though still believing in God. What Miss Wedgwood makes of him, with an art that so incorporates the document that she is almost never impeded by it, is a man with an inexhaustible power to give himself, the kind of man who cannot be licked because he doesn't know when he's licked.

The Catholics and the Calvinists were just as impatient then as the Communists and Fascists are now, but he sought untiringly to make a sovereign state, to do it by the reverse of cold ambition, by a warm, tenacious, pliant process that used force as little as possible. His courtesy was an instinct. Sitting in his wool clothes among his burghers, as Fulke Greville saw him, he was no less himself than when clinking a gold goblet with the Duke of Aerschot. He pursued, with men of every tempo, the object of broad sovereignty for a whole people, to save it from groaning under Spain or fretting in rebellion. William the Silent to us, he was actually William the Sly to contemporaries; he had the slyness of de Lannoys and Roosevelts when the terrain calls for the amphibious. But he grows steadily until the day he is assassinated, at the age of 52 (1533-1584).

Miss Wedgwood never forgets that daffodils and high skies are historical documents. She makes us see and feel the scene he lives in. She is perhaps too shy of legend, as though a Hitler

could not prance and smirk at the downfall of France unless
there was an archivist at hand instead of a photographer, but
she actually uses innumerable documents so as to capture the
living man. Where Motley was cumbersome, she is quick and
terse. Her style is a harpsichord. Some of the vast and somber
music is outside her scope, while she uses words like "extrem-
ist," "die-hard," "exhibitionist," "egocentric," "Gestapo," to
speed the streamline narrative, even to the point of ticking off
William's enemies too summarily and handing Don John of
Austria an unfavorable report at the end of his term. But she
knows the great story in loving detail. She has lucid color and
a command of all the rival forces, tooling her four-in-hand
through the narrowest streets. The dignity and majesty of the
drama are inherent in her fine sense of it. The self in William
of Orange is grandly revealed in its transmutation into a national essence. It is remarkable to have so consummate a career
respected in such detail yet lifted into a symbol and a promise.

November 30, 1944

POLITE HISTORY OF A TURK

THE operations of professional history are a little like develop-
ments in real estate. About forty years ago Prof. Roger Bigelow Merriman began to improve a section, which lay in the
first half of the sixteenth century. His friend Archibald Cary
Coolidge was working in the same field, down around Turkey,
and they shared their interest in these enterprises.

Professor Merriman's pioneer job was on the "hammer of the
monks," Thomas Cromwell, the man who did dirty work for
Henry VIII until Henry VIII did him dirt in return for it, and
callously killed him. This salient bit of development Professor
Merriman followed with four competent volumes on *The Rise
of the Spanish Empire*. Inheriting from Coolidge an unfinished

Suleiman the Magnificent by Roger Bigelow Merriman. Harvard University Press.

manuscript on Suleiman, and still believing that "few periods possess such fascination," Professor Merriman now caps his work with a most readable narrative of *Suleiman the Magnificent.*

Certainly, no vacant lot gaped and grinned more defiantly than the Turkish one. Everyone knew that Suleiman was one of the Big Four. He was born in 1494, the same year as Francis I. He was enthroned in 1520, the year of the Field of the Cloth of Gold. He outlived Henry VIII and Francis I by about twenty years, and where they went from monogamy to the harem, the Turk went from the harem to monogamy, though one can see in his sultana Roxelana many of the traits of Anne Boleyn. Suleiman, gouty and perhaps cancerous as he was, did not die until 1566. After battling with Charles V for over thirty years, he survived him by eight. What a collection of gouty despots these four, when they congregated among the millions of ghosts with which they had thickened the battle-fields!

Professor Merriman has a claim on sincere appreciation for laying out pathways and signposts through a wild, unsubordinated region. His narrative is smooth and flowing. He brings into intelligible focus the vast contributions of German history a hundred years ago, the French diplomatic surveys, Venetian annals, private diplomatic letters, translations from the Turkish and recent American research. He has arranged it like a buffet, so that you can help yourself to the first big drive to Vienna, to the relations with France, to Turkish government, to Suleiman's private life, to the Mediterranean struggles with Charles V, to the widening of the land empire and the further invasion of Hungary and the failure at Malta.

There is no set drama of personal history, but for lively details Professor Merriman is particularly grateful to a diplomat, de Busbecq, who left candid private letters. He calls the diplomat "a charming, open-minded, tolerant, humorous man of the world"; and when you have sunk into a chair in history, you tend to be riveted to the de Busbecqs and to be no less charming.

But a glance at Suleiman's grim portrait in the Metropolitan

Museum in New York, engraved in Constantinople by the Dane, Melchior Lorck, suggests the limitations of this kind of history, valuable as it is in the polite world. The iron doesn't enter into the soul of the de Busbecqs. In a diplomat's soul you may find iron ore, but it is usually oil—and in a whale of a diplomat you'll find the whole equipment—the blubber of charity, the whalebone of flexibility, the oil of commodity.

But history from Foreign Offices, from state documents, is too oily a substance, and Suleiman was a sinister statesman worthy of the man who wrote *Thomas Cromwell*. Where are the Balkans today? In the tertiary stage of that imperialism of which Suleiman was the spirochete. His was an imperialism without commerce or carrying trade, an imperialism of janissaries, of slaves, of bakshish, of corruption, of torture, an imperialism of bureaucracy, of permissible murder, of laxity and negation. Suleiman extended his empire. His mother was a Tartar, and he had the grim resolution to conquer, so that for three and even four hundred years the empire held firm. But Lawrence of Arabia was a witness to its fundamental character, and Suleiman the Magnificent might well have been viewed as one of the decisive and sustaining agents of history. History without a sense of its determinant agents is spineless, vinelike and crawling.

This is Turkey, but just its smoked breast, for polite consumption. There must be somewhere in the United States a student who knows Turkish—let him be a Greek, an Armenian, a Syrian, a man from the Crimea, it scarcely matters. With the skeleton map that Professor Merriman has so competently and tolerantly drawn for him, he can go to work on Suleiman's janissaries in the flesh, Suleiman's corsairs, Suleiman's massacres. Suleiman murdered his very able eldest son to give empire to Selim the Sot. He was one of those despots we should study. This is an engaging and worthy biography in the professional manner. We should have the whole rude story.

January 4, 1945

FRENCH AID TO AMERICA

In Col. Stephen Bonsal's long life he has seen much history in the making, and fortunately this influences his latest book, *When the French Were Here*. He has not spared himself a historian's immense trouble. His research has been among unpublished reports and letters, which are often intractable material. But where others are most concerned to relate their research to the existing texts, Colonel Bonsal cares especially for the movement of life itself, and for the striking men and women who promoted it. Hence this volume on French aid to Washington is no stiff compilation of data but a well-defined episode out of early American life, a delightfully graphic and easy one.

He calls it a "narrative of the sojourn of the French forces in America, and their contribution to the Yorktown campaign." The word "sojourn" suggests its smooth and agreeable texture. The French regiments that arrived from Brest bore famous names and were commanded by men of notable family. Their soldiers paraded Newport wearing white coats and long waistcoats, faced with crimson and pink and green, sky blue and yellows.

The author likes the vista of French history. Vauban, Saint-Simon, Chastellux, Lauzun, Noailles, Berthier, Bougainville, Deux-Ponts, Damas, Dumas—these, with the Swede Fersen and the Bavarian Closen, with Rochambeau if not de Grasse, were brought into the culture of a New World on terms of alliance and intimacy. Some of them were to defy revolution a few years later, many of them to die on the scaffold, not so many to be Republican. Knowing their courtly tradition, Colonel Bonsal wisely shows the eagerness and warmth with which they entered into America. It was their first glimpse of "sweet equality." The Americans were hospitable to them, and while the ladies had no court life, did not dance or dress in the French

When the French Were Here by Col. Stephen Bonsal. Doubleday, Doran.

style, and were by no means "given to gallantry," there was something in their mode of existence that stirred esteem and tenderness. Such marvels as the hummingbird were novel, but no more novel than the gentle gravity of the Quakers.

After a tentative period, in which the choleric Rochambeau had to repress Lafayette's impulsiveness, French collaboration was put to the test. An unguarded letter written by Washington fell into British hands, and they were not slow to use it. They shrewdly asserted that nothing could be more abhorrent to "the sour and turbulent temper of the Puritans" than a royalist and Roman Catholic France. With Americans exacting cash from the French for every service, it was no secret to Rochambeau that "these people are at the very end of their resources." Washington was even more blunt about it. "We are at the end of our tether."

Of 6,200 recruits for his army, "pointedly and continually called for to be with the army by the fifteenth of last month, only 176 had arrived from Connecticut," said Washington privately, "and two companies of York levies—about eighty men." For this reason the long march from Newport, through Hartford and Farmington and Newtown and Ridgebury and Haverstraw, brought no chance for the French to break into Manhattan. There were skirmishes. Washington saw Closen stubbornly turn back, under heavy fire, to retrieve his hat, and the same Closen said his heart ached to observe an army "almost without clothes," the greater number without hose. He was "horrified at their emaciated condition and amazed at their unwavering fortitude."

Most unwavering of all was General Washington. Colonel Bonsal reveals in repeated citations how Washington imposed himself by his dignity, his simplicity, his greatness. He was a man of honor, dealing with men of honor in the French, and Rochambeau took his role as loyal lieutenant.

Washington's resolve "to go southward" was hazardous. Without the French fleet he had no frame for his bowstring. But word came that de Grasse was nearing land. Rochambeau "caught sight of General Washington waving his hat at me with demonstrative gestures of the greatest joy." Deux-Ponts beheld him at the same moment. "Of a natural coldness and a noble approach, which so well adorns the chief of a whole nation, his features, his whole bearing and deportment were now changed in an instant." At last the patient general was rewarded. He could strike at Yorktown. And Colonel Bonsal relates in exciting detail how Washington sped his French and his "ragged Continentals" to the attack, with Hamilton going into action. The French Navy made victory possible.

Louis XVI, indeed, made it possible, one of the grand ironies of history. But if French valor and loyalty were at American disposal, it was mainly because George Washington knew how to avail himself of it. He had the same habit of amenity as these Frenchmen. He enabled them to give their best, and not one of them missed his significance.

Colonel Bonsal has made enlivening history of a many-sided collaboration, from which something emanates that lifts one's spirits. It was a martial gamble for the French, magnanimous and gallant in execution. No wonder Clemenceau was fired by Colonel Bonsal when they talked of going over the ground from Newport to Yorktown. Could anything show more vividly the deep-rooted French tradition than the pride of this defiant Republican in the deeds of the monarchy? But France itself was the ally so ardent and generous in these pages. Washington knew its contribution.

February 15, 1945

HISTORY ON WHEELS

IT WOULD be hard to find a better title than *Caesar and Christ*. It is meant to be instantly provocative, and it produces the desired result. By mentioning two proper names it starts to life the first question in every sensible person's mind, the clash between power and goodness, and brings history down to two supreme representatives of an irreconcilable war. One stands

Caesar and Christ by Will Durant. Simon & Schuster.

for empire in its prowess, a dictator with a strong military state under him, and making a place in the state for the common man; the other represents the wish to be good and to be saved.

This clash of principles may not be explicit in the present war, but the United Nations are trying in some way to extricate themselves from the Caesar principle and to bring into politics a concept of pervading responsibility and solicitude. When Dr. Will Durant gave his book this dazzling title he raised expectations.

It is a huge book. The minute you look at it you feel tempted to say, Body by Fisher, with its 752 pages, its admirable fixtures of maps and illustrations, and its formidable black-bound size and weight. But it is not the size that matters. It is the engine. Is the title justified?

Taking it literally, no. On the Caesar end of it, this book begins with the very origins of Roman civilization and carries it from the Etruscan epoch, which was wiped out with modern thoroughness, through the Republic, the struggles with Carthage and Greece, down to the internal wars and Sulla.

Caesar steps on the scene after this prolonged first act. The next two acts are occupied by the development from Augustus, the Queen Victoria of his pacific age, through Murder, Inc., to the Philosopher Kings, with a full account of the empire. The last quarter sketches Rome and Judea and gives us the emerging of Jesus, with a finale in which the empire embraces Christianity. Dr. Durant elaborates, not Caesar and Christ, but "a history of Roman civilization and of Christianity from the beginnings to A. D. 325." And he furthermore plainly repudiates the drama inherent in the title. "No moralist should write history," he says.

Shakespeare's imagination and art, he thinks, "were too creatively active to let him ponder quietly the meaning and possibilities of life." And while concluding about Christianity that "all in all, no more attractive religion has ever been presented to mankind," he still thinks of Julius Caesar as "one of the ablest, bravest, fairest and most enlightened men in all the sorry annals of politics," "the most complete man that antiquity produced."

With such reserve and ambiguity, ruling out the kind of partisanship that marks history in Thucydides, Michelet, Macaulay, Acton, Dr. Durant has to sacrifice a sweeping current in the narrative, with all the logs pointed in a given direction.

He is content, in fact, to slope along in Lucian-like skepticism and moral indifference. "The people rightly preferred laughter to philosophy," he can say in one place. The moral standpoint, he says elsewhere, "is always a window dressing in international politics." And, even if concluding that the essential cause of Rome's decline "lay in her people, her morals," he would rather evoke a smile by saying Cicero "trimmed his wind to every sale" than be consumed by Carlyle's "fire in the belly."

And yet, with all his apparent sophistication and professional detachment, he dishes up those mounds of scandal and gossip on which Gibbon first glinted, with that light sweat of sedentary concupiscence on his brow. Suetonius, Tacitus and Dio Cassius were full of bias, Dr. Durant admits. "These are stories that we have no means of disproving and must record as the tradition."

But *Caesar and Christ* is just as great a success in its organization of material as it is disappointing in its "shallow sophistication." It is for the expert handling of its immense baggage that the book is impressive. The fact that Dr. Durant has systematically ordered his material, amassing it with diligence, grouping it with keen discrimination, classifying it by subject and making it extremely direct and intelligible, is a service to any reader who wishes to control the facts. The book is indispensable for its honest labors and the vast stuff of history it makes accessible. The style has no pretensions, moves easily and draws one on, but what imposes on the reader is the lesson itself, that lesson which school histories remove from contagion of sympathy and credibility.

Dr. Durant has brought contemporary culture to his aid—philology, anthropology, science, literary criticism. There seems to be no considerable person or no important trend that he has not reported, and this encyclopedic knowledge he has fused, not into a symphony, but into a completely lucid and warmly informative compendium. Except that he calls the Cimbri Celtic, when they were from Jutland, no mistakes leap to the eye. For some the book will be furniture, but for readers who lose heart in the sultry mazes of Gibbon or on the dusty highways of school histories, here is an inviting chance to correlate the story of Rome with the story of Christianity. These same Romans are always with us. It may be news to Fiorello that nearly all the men are handsome, "nearly all the women beautiful, strong and brave," but if the Romans had not understood statesmanship our Archbishop Spellman would not be shuttling the Atlantic, and the city of Rome would not be intact at this moment. The political genius in the Romans, Caesarean and Christian, is still a most powerful factor in the world, and the old story has contemporary meaning. Dr. Durant puts freight on wheels.

October 28, 1944

HENRY CABOT LODGE

ONLY the other day Walter Lippmann was deploring that few histories written since 1919 give an "adequate account" of the argument of President Wilson's opponents—"men like Theodore Roosevelt, Root, Knox, and even Lodge." Well, the word "adequate" is like a duffle bag; you can put anything into it, from a bolster to a tommy-gun. In view of Mr. Lippmann's own spiritual travails since 1919, and his present though not necessarily permanent conviction "that Clemenceau was right and that Wilson was wrong," Karl Schriftgiesser's account of Henry Cabot Lodge is scarcely likely to have the adequacy he is looking for. Mr. Schriftgiesser is a liberal. He stands today pretty much on the moral platform that Mr. Lippmann helped to erect in his radical epoch, before he resigned to "the world as it is" and saw those stars which leap from a collision with

The Gentleman from Massachusetts: Henry Cabot Lodge by Karl Schriftgiesser. Atlantic Monthly—Little Brown.

hard facts rather than a vision of the universal. Today Walter Lippmann is constrained to believe that Wilson went to Paris "to impose a Wilsonian peace on the Allies," despite the sage warnings of Cabot Lodge, whom he now cites with approval. Strongly at variance with these assumptions about Woodrow Wilson are Mr. Schriftgiesser's, and whether or not he seems adequate will depend on the moral bias of the reader—but with one important reservation.

That reservation is entirely in Mr. Schriftgiesser's favor. He knows politics from Washington and Capitol Hill. He is a hard-headed reporter, with an intimate and concrete sense of the record. He offers very little on the side in the way of refreshment. He never says it with flowers. He is, in fact, just as little esthetic as one of those modern hospitals that have pitiless lighting and ruthless telephone bells. But, ignoring the nerves that a literary man might soothe or coddle, he goes to the essential point with a surgical devotion that neglects nothing. The political record is everything to him.

With the private Cabot Lodge, who emerges mainly as a gentleman with pressed trousers and pressed flowers of speech and pressed ideas of class and country, he has little to do. We learn nothing of "Bay" Lodge, the poet of the family; and Nannie Lodge, the cousin whom Cabot married, is just one of those concave wives who follow the contours of their husband's career with the warm fidelity of a blanket. What engrosses Mr. Schriftgiesser is not the private byplay. He even bluntly summarizes the clear-sighted Henry Adams as a "cynic." His is a prosecuted inquiry into the eminent Senator, with grim attention to the party game. He never strays from that absorbing but specialized topic. He fortifies his position with a zeal for documentary evidence that never flags. Cold as Henry Cabot Lodge is, to begin with, by the time you finish the book he is hanging like dead mutton from a meathook.

Yet no doubt about it, this was a smart and versatile politician. He had a library of from 15,000 to 20,000 books, and he was no less equipped in this world's goods than he was intellectually spurred and booted, but he sprang from adventurous traders, and in politics he was no more a dilettante than

Sidney Hillman. After toying with civil service reform and the poll tax issue, which was alive and kicking sixty years ago, he very soon made terms with "the world as it is," and became a confirmed and expert machine politician. On Mark Hanna's part it was affectation to say to this dude Senator, "Who in hell are you?" Both of them were at home at the rodeo. They knew how to round up and brand the voters, and neither was ignorant of the price of cattle on the hoof. It was Lodge who prevailed on Boss Hanna to put the gold plank in the Republican party platform. As a machine politician he was forceful, adroit, dogged and regular. When Theodore Roosevelt went off the reservation, aware of new pastures to the left, Lodge parted company for the time being with his dearest friend, and, superb wrangler that he was, he stood on his record in a masterly speech and kept his accustomed seat in the Senate.

This was all defensible. If to accept "the world as it is" means to be anti-woman suffrage, to be anti-English with an eye on the Irish vote and the German vote, to be for a high tariff and a low immigration, the room for discussion is still open. But Mr. Schriftgiesser exhibits proof that Lodge himself narrowed the discussion on the League of Nations, at the start. He delivered no warnings to Woodrow Wilson when a league was first mooted. He was for it. He did not shrink from its utopianism. He defended its utopianism. He and Woodrow Wilson interchanged amenities. But the bosom companions Theodore Roosevelt and Cabot Lodge had long schooled themselves for the direction of America as a world power. They steadily grew exasperated with Woodrow Wilson's conduct of America during World War I. They grew frustrated, embittered and polemical. Had Woodrow Wilson known anything of Abraham Lincoln's open secret, his assuaging goodness, possibly these two vengeful men might not have become wreckers, but Lodge outraged the proud and stubborn Wilson by a prevarication, and into the conflict there entered Lodge's mammoth egoism, his toplofty style, his still nimble brain and his powerful venom.

Perhaps Senator Jim Watson gives us the truly adequate account when he reports Lodge's final dodges about the League.

"My dear James," said the wintry Bostonian with his smile, "you do not take into consideration the hatred that Woodrow Wilson has for me personally. Never under any set of circumstances in this world could he be induced to accept a treaty with Lodge reservations appended to it."

Thus Lodge gave to party what was meant for mankind. Only a free lance like Mr. Schriftgiesser, tenacious and devoted, could have disengaged this intricate and rather appalling story from such scattered records and testimonies.

September 21, 1944

THE WOODROW WILSON EPIC

IN HIS stimulating book, *Woodrow Wilson and the People*, Prof. H. C. F. Bell chooses the political rather than the biographical angle. This is a good choice today. Wilson's foray among world institutions was essentially a fight for moral ideas by unyielding methods. Wilson strove to give them shape in Princeton, to bend Boss Smith to them in New Jersey and to carry them from Washington to Versailles. He dipped the young William C. Bullitt into Russia to see how the Soviets assayed, and at a time like the present, when world order is so in view, Mr. Bell does extremely wisely to pour into easy narrative the confluence of many living ideas, many sprawling events and much political evidence.

His book is rich and discursive. It is also slily opinionative. But he writes equably, with his pipe in his cheek, and he disarms the irascible by not putting himself forward. He is never "virtuously indignant." Even John P. Marquand hasn't fixed the thermostat for a steadier living room temperature.

We are not shown Thomas Woodrow in swaddling clothes or boyhood complexes. We begin flush with Dr. Wilson's inauguration as president of Princeton in 1902 with the doves cooing. Mr. Bell uses this as a preamble. All that Mr. Taft expressed so well in a few words—"Mrs. Wilson was a very sweet

Woodrow Wilson and the People by H. C. F. Bell. Doubleday, Doran.

woman and offered an antidote to his [Wilson's] somewhat angular disregard of other people's feelings"—is sensitively and informatively filled in. It prepares for the crusader's entry into a political America in which Mr. Taft had been blandly rounding out himself and his career.

Thanks to Taft and the Old Guard, Woodrow Wilson snatched the role of Galahad from Theodore Roosevelt. W. E. Dodd was soon to say that Wilson was "the only man who had given the Democratic party a real standing in the country." But many Democrats, their hearts in their gumshoes, were aghast at their Galahad. Mr. Bell recalls how Tumulty became his sword-bearer and how Dudley Field Malone was his minstrel. But the skyline drive on which he took the boys made 1912-14 the years of a great divide. It was not the spoils that were divided.

When the time comes for a Woodrow Wilson Memorial, the sculptor will unfortunately not be able to represent Woodrow Wilson in a kilt or a Montgomery beret. He was nominally the very picture of a fastidious, most respectable, high-brow liberal of the nineteenth century. The old Adam in him had apparently been completely macadamized. But neither manse nor campus had eradicated the fierce Celtic redshank in him. It was preserved in him by Calvinism, and many who had no truck with Calvin, including Honey Fitz, Tom Taggart, Charlie Murphy, Roger Sullivan, found themselves trotting on the moral skyline after a Covenanter. This made history.

Eventually it came the turn of a French Tiger to be chastened like the Tammany one. Clemenceau, Lloyd George and Orlando had their chance to fall in line as the Democrats did. Mr. Bell groans at the "exaltation" and angularity that Mr. Taft noted. Forgetting how Mr. Taft had exclaimed, "I feel like bursting," Mr. Bell wonders why Wilson had not incorporated Taft in the peace negotiations. But all war was an ebullition of the devil in Wilson's eyes. Not until he could forget the bloodshed that some Republicans had itched for in Mexico, and not until he saw in the World War a means of redemption for the peoples of the world, a way to a League of Nations, could he sanction association with Britain and

France. With a new Covenant in prospect, this pacifist cried aloud, "Force, Force to the utmost, Force without stint or limit, the righteous and triumphant Force which shall make Right the law of the world."

It was of this potent zealot that Theodore Roosevelt had privately said: "I do not regard him as a man of great intensity of principle or conviction, or of much reality of sympathy with our cause. He is an adroit man, a good speaker and writer, with a certain amount of ability," etc. It took a tarantula in his boot to tell T. R. what was biting him in Brazil, but Woodrow Wilson needed no tarantula and no Brazil; he had Lodge at home. Washington was his jungle, his Africa and Brazil combined, the theatre of his moral drama. And the institution of war quite as much as the institution of poverty seemed to him the ultimate enemy of the people.

Mr. Bell is no apologist for a crusader. As an ample professional historian he takes no sides. Even Senator Lodge is not condemned, "impossible as it is to know the motives of any man." But he does add, "There is almost conclusive evidence that Senator Lodge was moved throughout by partisanship and personal animosity." Mr. Bell is not inflammatory. He does not venture to talk of motives. "Who ever really knows the motives of a statesman?" "Apparently even House did not fully understand the President. But who did, or, for that matter, ever has, or ever will?" Here is no irritating omniscience, but he is less above the battle when the Irish are in question, or Mr. Bullitt, or the Soviets. Even General Ironside is clear that in 1919 "the Allies had espoused the cause of the White Russians." Mr. Bell wraps it in wadding.

But he silhouettes Woodrow Wilson as a great, a towering, figure against the horizon of world order. Eventually the Soviets may see virtue in that, as they did in nationalism. In history diverse roads that lead to great goals draw pilgrims from all camps, and Mr. Bell substantially and movingly indicates that in Woodrow Wilson he sees not "an ignominious and dismal defeat," as Karl Menninger did, but one of those angular pioneers who gave all he had for a vision and a deliverance.

June 7, 1945

Russian Affairs

DALLIN'S RUSSIA

PARTY regularity is a grand ideal. Theodore Roosevelt hated a Mugwump until he became a Mugwump himself. After that break with Taft, party irregularity became the grand thing for about six years. And then he sank his differences with the GOP, and party regularity became an ideal again. It was all highly confusing.

To avoid this sort of confusion about Russia, which is now the big "if" in the world, we simply cannot think in terms of regularity and irregularity. Stalin's Russia is no more finally Russia than Trotsky's Russia was Russia, or than Napoleon's France was France. Friendship between the American people and the Russian people does not exact our blind acceptance of any propaganda or our hoodwinking ourselves about the Soviets as a finality. It depends on our grasping the inescapable realities of the Russian situation, without binding ourselves to a Russia which may be here today and gone tomorrow. The Russian nation is a permanency, and it is this permanency with which we must be dealing fifty and a hundred years from now, either to make war on Russia or to be friends and collaborators with it.

Dr. David J. Dallin has written a compact and apparently dry book called *The Real Soviet Russia*. He is said to be a political exile from Russia, and consequently he cannot be a buddy of Stalin's. It is obvious from his text, however, that he is a hard-headed, tough-minded, professional thinker, a man thoroughly conversant with his subject, terse and clear, extremely able and relentlessly concrete. The impression he gives

The Real Soviet Russia by David J. Dallin, translated by Joseph Shaplen. Yale University Press.

of the Soviets is argued from a close scrutiny of the measurable facts, and it is so coherent and telling that one feels it is responsible. To study this book is to take hold of Russia as a comprehensible evolution and to go forward with one's own political education.

Start with a fact. "In 1937 a census was taken in Russia, and it showed such a deficiency compared with Stalin's predictions and the assumptions of the Five-Year Plans that the directors of the Census Bureau were executed."

An American is dizzied by a fact like this, but, whether it is disputable or not, the reader of *The Real Soviet Russia* comes to feel he can understand it. The author says, "History knows no perfect analogies," but, as Edmund Wilson suggested in his book on Russia, Lenin was something of a saint. He was an Ignatius Loyola, if you like, one of those Marxist saints who think in terms of a revolution carried out by the initiated and consecrated. "Russia used to be ruled by 150,000 landlords," Lenin wrote in August, 1917. "Why could not 240,000 Bolsheviks do the same job?" That is the acorn from which modern Russia grew, though the real initiated remain a small party within the party of five millions.

The "blind obedience" of revolutionaries is diametrically opposed to democracy, as is the ruthless fidelity of any oath-bound secret society. It was Lenin's root principle. "Give us an organization of revolutionists and we will turn Russia upside down," he said. And that organization, which uses the workers but is not composed of workers, still holds its own in the Politbureau of fourteen and the Central Committee. "The Politbureau is the party's real brain," elected from the seventy-one members of the Central Committee, which, with its half a thousand administrative officers, "constitute the brain trust of the Russian Communist party and of world communism."

What used to be the Ogpu is now called NKVD. This is the fang and claw of the administration. The "party" is 43 per cent NKVD. It is nominally a police, but actually it is an army of more than a quarter of a million, a secret service, a system of spying and bullying unparalleled. If our shuttle airmen were offered prostitutes, it was because the NKVD uses prostitutes as spies. The Red Army is up against this multitudinous police. Prisoners of war, outside the Geneva Conventions, are ruthlessly mishandled, leading to the corresponding abuse of captured Russians, or else the prisoners are indoctrinated.

Americans cannot credit this sort of manipulation. They cannot credit that a human rubble exists of from seven to fifteen million slaves in Russian labor corps that carry out public works, treated worse than any other slaves who ever existed. But Dr. Dallin traces the evolution of these labor camps from the first idealism of the Bolsheviks that labor was honorable to the final exigencies of war shortage and war sacrifice. Essential to this abuse of the powerless is the doctrine of "blind obedience," so beloved of Hitler and Mussolini.

The result of this party system is incredible waste. A Soviet economic journal shows that where a South Amboy electric station employed fifty-one persons, a comparable Russian station employed 480. "In Russia, eleven men are required to produce 1,000 kilowatts of electricity; in the United States, 1.3." "Political considerations" govern industry.

The Red Army is used with hideous waste of human life, counting on Russian bravery and docility. (They fought with broomsticks in 1916.) "The whole world will be grateful to Russia," says Dr. Dallin, but "the Russia of the future will have no reason to be thankful." And, in conflict with a government that has never captured its intelligentsia, though it shackles it, will be "many Russian workers discontented with the low standard of living, the unbridled power and control exercised by plant officials, and the unlimited power of the police in private life."

Dr. Dallin's version of Russia is not nostalgic. "The ending of the revolution would not involve a return to the past. Hardly anyone dreams of the restoration of the old Russia. But the revolution must be ended. All that is beautiful in it, and all that is ugly, must be relegated to history. In realizing this, the Soviet intelligentsia expresses the urge of virtually every class of the population."

Is this book a fingerpost to a new, even though "tortured, desperately tired" Russian people? Is Russia to free Russia?

Dr. Dallin's book should make us walk around the Kremlin
and look at this great, grim nation.

November 25, 1944

W. L. WHITE'S RUSSIA

ONE ugly episode stands out in W. L. White's *Report on the
Russians*. That is what happened after the Eighth Air Force's
arrival in Russia. He was on the spot when they flew in, and
he was in his pajamas when the German bombers came after
them. For reasons that Mr. White explains elsewhere in the
book, the Russians could not put up night fighters. The
destruction of the Fortresses was a complete job, as Mr. White
guessed from his trench. The Germans got in when the American guard was down and before the Russians could put up
one.

Mr. White was traveling with Eric Johnston as a guest of
the Soviets. On the basis of his proved ability as a reporter and
narrator, W. L. White had been allowed to accompany the
president of the Chamber of Commerce. He had six weeks in
Russia, filled with banquets. Had he written a book called
Vodka Vodka, on the systematized hospitality he endured, it
would have been funny. Even a guest who hooked a ride and
"three lush gorges a day" might reasonably take a crack at
cynical public relations. But the mouth he opens, in spite of
the caviar in it, is a loud one. Mr. White gives the impression
that he has it in for Russia.

That he has a keen eye for the loss of human freedom is a
good thing. He thinks of Russian workers as slaves to their
jobs. "Absenteeism seems to be as rare here as it would be in
the Atlanta Penitentiary, and for many of the same reasons."
He notes disparities in pay, hard working conditions, the use
of compulsion, "sloppy engineering." He cites much of the
same evidence that David Dallin piles up in his excellent book,

Report on the Russians by W. L. White. Harcourt, Brace.

The Real Soviet Russia. But he also has a good word to say for Russian race ideology. He reports that the transplanted factories do well, exceptionally well at Tashkent. And he has high praise for Russian theatre.

It is the strictures on the Russians as people that surprise one in this book, as distinct from a liberal's strictures on dictatorship. Nothing makes bad blood or sets up stolid, ugly opposition more than to malign an ally. Hitler's worst offense in *Mein Kampf* was to poison international relations by irremediable hostility. It is in nose-thumbings across the fence that hostility displays itself, thus making for fascism. Mr. White fires no guns for fascism, but he rolls ammunition for it. This is the offensiveness that fascism utilizes, where liberal criticism tries to keep the monkey out of it, in order to keep the ape-minded out of it.

In his short introduction Mr. White takes out insurance. "A word about the Russian people," he says. "I like them very much." This is how much he liked them: his protocol companion Kirilov "always stared at us with the solemnity of a frog lost in reveries, unruffled as a pail of cold lard." Kirilov took him to a concert. There he saw Russians in "ill-fitting clothes, poorly cut, often flashy and always of tawdry material." A comparison discreditable to the Russians leaps into Mr. White's mind. "Before our WPA home relief cases would have appeared in public as shabbily dressed as this Socialist Soviet aristocracy, they would have gone down to the court house and torn case-workers limb from limb."

Considering war hardships in Russia, this is a smear, of course. The Russian officers were undersized, he says; "their unsmiling Slav faces and clipped bulletheads" reminded him of Prussians. He noted their "shabby, undernourished women." If he liked the famous Moscow subway, he took pains to note that "in the Western world no one expects effortful beauty in a subway, which is as functional as a can-opener." Is this a plea for effortless ugliness? He met Russian movie stars and had a laugh—"a bevy of bouncing girls in their early forties, who show the effects of their extra ration cards. Because in the Soviet Union a double chin or an extra roll of abdominal fat is a mark of caste." He met a Russian girl at a party. The stars had "billowing Russian busts encased in pastel sweaters," but the girl had "the usual sallow, pimply Moscow skin and shabby clothing." How about legendary Russian beauty? "Does not exist in the absence of adequate amounts of fresh fruit and tomatoes. The women are drab, sallow and tired, and on the street dismally unattractive."

As for primitiveness in hotels and elsewhere, Mr. White never seems to have heard of Chic Sale. He is bitter about toilet facilities, and just as frank about sex surgery. He is joky about garbage disposal—the Russians "eat it." They "are tremendously formal people—not because they are Communists but because they are Russians. They may be innocent of the use of toilet paper, but when they throw an official shebang, everything must be just so, from oyster forks to medals."

When one thinks of the grueling and murderous war waged on Russia, it seems odd to malign the Russians for being ill-clad, slovenly in their factories, shabby, thin, tired, sallow. But the Russian girl who warned Mr. White that a book like *Martin Chuzzlewit* would be injurious evidently made no impression on him. To him the Communists at home are "misfits," the people in *Grapes of Wrath* are cited as "curious, insubordinate malcontents." How much better his father, William Allen White, carried America abroad when he and Henry Allen visited Russia at the time of the revolution. There was no food for fascism in *The Martial Adventures of Henry and Me.*

March 15, 1945

LAUTERBACH'S RUSSIA

AT THE Taft convention in 1912 a little old man kept crying "Louder, louder," until Cannon Ball Smith took the floor; then the old man screamed, "Not so loud, not so loud!" This same petulance would move the same kind of man to exclaim at

There Are the Russians by Richard E. Lauterbach. Harper & Bros.

Richard L. Lauterbach's book, *These Are the Russians.* When W. L. White had the floor he underdid it. Now his companion Dick Lauterbach overdoes it. Mr. White served the Russians with sauce tartare, and Mr. Lauterbach serves them with jam. The golden mean is hard to arrive at.

But this jam is for public consumption. While Bill White's discords were unnecessarily rasping, his report of a dance that he attended with Dick Lauterbach is from off the record and behind the scenes, but it gives us an inkling of their mutual American candor:

" 'Oh, hell,' said Lauterbach, 'there it begins.'

" 'He's just a friendly Red Army guy.'

" 'Red Army, hell. NKVD. You tell them by that blue hat band.' "

Thus, according to W. L. White, he and Mr. Lauterbach looked with democratic eyes on the Russian secret service man. "Every minute we expected the NKVD man would lead us back to the concert but he didn't. Then he said something to Dick in Russian. 'I can't believe it!' said Dick. 'Know what he said? Asks us wouldn't we like to go up there and dance with some of them.' 'Tell him, sure.' And then Dick said, 'It just can't be true. It would be impossible in Moscow.' "

The frank words, "It would be impossible in Moscow," and "A thing like this could never happen in Moscow," seem to give a fair idea of how these two reporters privately felt about espionage and surveillance. But when it comes to Mr. Lauterbach's own report of the small episode, he is one of the most demure and prudent of public witnesses. " 'This is certainly different from Moscow,' I said to Bill, indicating the NKVD captain. 'And how!' said Bill. 'Tell him it's been awfully nice and thank him for everything.' " According to White, the captain was told in good Kansan that he was "the most regular guy we have met in the Soviet Union."

These Are the Russians draws on much greater knowledge and insight than W. L. White's story. Mr. Lauterbach knew enough Russian to talk to ordinary people. In 1943-44 he saw close up such amazing sights as shattered Stalingrad and staggered Leningrad. He strikingly reports the unique plans for restoring the beauty of Leningrad. He discerned the appalling role of children in the Red Army, the hazards of the catacombs of Odessa, the horrors of Maidanek, the grimness of war criminals on trial. He observed the outpouring of Russian energy for reconstruction, the absolute passion of good men and women living into the future as if total sacrifice was not too much to pay for it. Nothing can stop these Russians. Mr. Lauterbach caught their grandeur and really felt the flame in them. Their superlative faith, their magnificence, seem for him to justify their vast overriding plans for civilization.

But while he saw infinitely more than did W. L. White, felt it more deeply, went into it more susceptibly and more sincerely, Mr. Lauterbach at the same time gives us a map from which he has omitted the scale in democratic miles. Glad as we are to have statistics, to hear that 600,000 head of cattle were shifted from 1,000 to 2,000 miles, or that in a broken town 900,000 yards of finished fabrics are turned out daily, we'd be better satisfied if the ultimate bearing of this report helped us to see Russia as an honest partner in the international situation.

In a narrow sense he means it this way. We must bear and forbear with the Russians. "It's something that has to be worked on hard by both parties all the time, like a successful marriage." Why? Because as Moscow correspondent of Henry Luce's papers, *Time* and *Life*, he foresees trade to the tune of "many billions of dollars." "We are interested in long-term credits," said Stalin. "We can get along without them, but it will be slower." But Stalin must have them. "I have traveled 20,000 miles in the Soviet Union," says the author. "I have seen what they have done, and I think the country and the people are a good investment regardless of politics." And he adds, "We must and can get along with the Soviet Union."

In order to get this trade, do we propose to give Russia carte blanche in eastern Europe? Where W. L. White took pains to emphasize plenty of small things that stuck out like a sore thumb, Mr. Lauterbach refuses to admit it when a thumb is stuck in a democrat's eye. He is selling us, not telling us. But much as America wants "a good investment regardless of politics," he repeatedly demonstrates that absolutely nothing in

Russia can be "regardless of politics." If we cheerfully take trade as an end in itself, we need only acquiesce in Russia's politics, hook, line and sinker—its hook in the Baltic States, its line in Poland and its sinker in Bornholm. The Russians who now "strongly resent" our doubting Moscow will then get along swimmingly with us. Mr. Lauterbach's book certainly throws brilliant light on Russia's simple demands in these matters. Our role in the marriage is evidently to be the Mother Heroine. Russia is content to be Poppa.

May 31, 1945

S. N. HARPER'S RUSSIA

A CHICAGOAN who gets shingles because of Russian foreign policy is a man to look into. Samuel N. Harper did not live to finish his memoirs, but his brother Paul has given them shape in *The Russia I Believe In*. Had an artist written the book, it would have been a panorama of two civilizations. But very early Russian civics got into Samuel Harper's blood, and at this moment his testimony on Russia, covering forty years of acquaintanceship and study on the spot, has value for the problem of faith it embodies. His father, the "dynamo in trousers" who presided over the University of Chicago with the backing of John D. Rockefeller, certainly did not rear Samuel to be a Bolshevik. Hence his love of Russia, his belief in it as exhibited in this story of his life, is all the more worth examining.

Harper's passion for Russia owed much to the *Chicago Tribune*. Half a century ago Chicago opened his eyes on Russia because Mr. McCormick was Ambassador to it, and a whole flock of his townsmen, the Ryersons, the Hutchinsons, the Cranes, found their way to St. Petersburg. It was Charles R. Crane who took President Harper along. President Harper re-

The Russia I Believe In by Samuel N. Harper. University of Chicago Press.

turned "with a tremendous enthusiasm for all things Russians."
And this, transmitted to the boy, was fanned by Charles Crane,
who urged him to learn Russian, gave him introductions, put
up money for his studies and decided his life for him.

So on "Bloody Sunday," 1905, young Samuel was on the
scene at the American Embassy, in company with Joseph Grew
and Robert Bliss, when the Little Father betrayed the little
people. He was far from revolutionary, but he refused to write
"simple drivel" about Russia's complexities. "I have concluded,"
he wrote his mother, "that it's better, after all, to stick to scholarship." Content with small pickings, he and Bernard Pares
made a team, to travel, to interview all and sundry, to write
everything down. Pares, "of course, always thinking of the
interests of the British Empire," and Samuel "in search of
truth," never sparing himself, bitten by countless fleas and
bedbugs, talking Russian to everyone.

What really bit him, however, was Russia itself. In a boyish
blurt of candor he had written, "these blamed Russians lack
backbone and stamina." Gradually, with the growth of his
knowledge, the wealth of his connections, native assiduity, and
drive and freshness of nature, he became, if not "the first authority in the United States on things Russian," as his friend
Pares declares, at least the kind of pertinacious specialist to
whom the State Department could turn, as well as David R.
Francis, Elihu Root, John D. Rockefeller, Sidney Hillman. And
in the same way that he himself had passed from being a weedy
boy with weak eyes under the thumb of his father, the under-
lying Communist Russia grew in self-assertion and power.
Samuel Harper damns Chamberlain in 1938 because he "did not
offer the Soviets anything that a responsible Government of a
strong power could accept."

His advocacy of this "strong power" developed gradually.
He began cautiously about the Soviets. He did not think recognition would be "constructive." But as the new Russia made
good after heroic struggle, this pragmatic observer ceased to
be detached. He considered Stalin "hard and ruthless." He
calls him a Tammany man, "an able and resourceful revolutionary strategist and machine boss." But in Trotsky he saw a

dangerous prima donna, a pathological egoist. "Trotsky, Zinoviev and Kamenev were the three leaders for whom I had not been able to eliminate a personal feeling of resentment and even hatred."

The "search for truth" eventually passes into missionary fervor. Minimizing the policy of world revolution and overt anti-religion, Samuel Harper shows himself intolerant of critics. He accuses William Henry Chamberlin of being "sour" and Eugene Lyons of being "cynical."

Scrappy as the material of this book is, it is lively, personal and varied. We can see the whole human being, with the mind in abeyance as Harper lost the democratic norms and "steeled himself" to ruthless political processes. He admits the "purge" went too far, "overreached," but he is cold-blooded about it. "While the purge started constructively, it unquestionably became destructive later on." But he adds indulgently, "methods such as those used in the purges are, of course, not easily controllable."

He argues that Britain and France let Russia down in 1938, and then poor little Russia had to look out for its own security. That his Chicago friends could "spit at the Bolsheviks" made him so angry he shouted, "Can't you be gentlemen?" But couldn't the Russians also be gentlemen? Probably knowing that his line of argument about Russia's alliance with Germany would excuse any hard and ruthless expediency at any time, he was torn by conflict. He had "a serious nervous breakdown, confining me to bed for some months, which took the form of what doctors diagnosed as dermatitis—a type of shingles, but which I translated as 'the doghouse mange.'" In the local doghouse he got shingles. What would he have got in a Siberian doghouse?

What made him sick, and makes this reader sick, is his trying to absolve Stalin for things he deemed inexcusable in others. Chiding Poland for not seeing that Russian power was self-justifying, he could still as an American citizen be so sharp about Bullitt and Roosevelt that he would undoubtedly have been purged in Russia for similar lack of loyalty. He never reconciles these contradictions. Russia was his romance. After

two days in the "bourgeois luxury" of Warsaw in 1939 he was
bored. "Fact is I'm homesick for the more real life of sovietism."
So spoke his heart. "A great boy," as his friend Pares says. "The
Russians loved him."

June 21, 1945

KEEP OUT OF TROUBLE

FOR the journalist who keeps step with events the bound volume has one drawback—three or four months may pass before
his text can appear, and in these days this is more than awkward. When William Henry Chamberlin finished his new book,
America: Partner in World Rule, "unconditional surrender"
was still a "mouth-filling phrase" to him, T. V. Soong had not
come to the fore in China, and he still felt he had to chide
Franklin Roosevelt for his way of handling press conferences.
The Yalta talks were being reported, but San Francisco was
not foreshadowed.

Obvious as this is, it is a surface defect. More serious is his
blunting the compulsion of time on his politics. Mr. Chamberlin
knows what events are pointing toward. He accepts "the risks
and sacrifices of a philosophy of global interventionism." But
while he has written this book for the express purpose of
shouldering these responsibilities, he still quivers under them
with aversion. If the American conscience had its origins in
withdrawal from Europe when the Puritans took a walk,
William Henry Chamberlin is sorely tried by having this same
impulse. His mind tells him that America must become a "partner in world rule." But while he advocates it, he hates it. And
for this reason his book is profoundly confused in its thinking.

Or, rather, its thinking tends one way and its feelings another. At the root of Mr. Chamberlin's feelings is an American
fraternity with the weak, a wish to help them and a resentment

America: Partner in World Rule by William Henry Chamberlin. Vanguard Press.

of power politics. Power, in fact, is abhorrent to him and he
does not hesitate to head one chapter, "Power Is Hell." There
are times when, like the late Randolph Bourne, he deems we
were mistaken to fight in the first war. He wishes we had
promoted a compromise peace with Germany, rejected con-
scription, stayed isolated, yet backed the Weimar Republic.
Thus, as he supposes, German democracy might have been
strengthened and "the evil power of Hitlerism" might "very
probably never have been born." Along with this feeling goes
his urgent desire to find "an effective barrier to the spread of
Soviet influence and Communist or semi-Communist ideology."

Those are his innate feelings, shared by millions. At the same
time his mind acknowledges that the present war was "a gi-
gantic duel between Hitler and Stalin for the mastery of
Eurasia." So strong are his feelings about Russia that he twists
and squirms to avoid siding with Stalin. Hence, though admitting the evil of Hitlerism, he thinks of Americans as unpaid
Hessians fighting in other nations' wars. He thinks of America
as "meekly acquiescing in the demands of other nations," stab-
bing Poland in the back at Teheran, bluffed and bullied into
bailing out "foreign countries" and twice coming "to Great
Britain's rescue in foreign wars." The dangers to America are
now "infinitesimal." They were always "speculative and hypo-
thetical." But America is the partner who is always "brushed
aside."

And so, though believing "power is hell," he finds himself
blaming America for not using power as a moral arbiter. He
blames Woodrow Wilson for not coolly and firmly using "the
immense potential bargaining power of America's untapped
military and industrial strength" to get a just peace in 1919,
with Henry Cabot Lodge cheering in the bleachers. Though
he is sure that Russia "cannot be restrained by treaties," he
blames Harry Hopkins and the late President Roosevelt for not
holding back lend-lease until Stalin endorsed a Polish frontier
and "signed on the dotted line." And today, though power is
hell, he demands that "America should oppose by every means
in its power the carving out of Russian and British spheres of
influence from the tortured body of Europe."

What to conclude from this? Of all our publicists, and he is among the best, none has more conscience. One must conclude that no matter how peace-loving a man may be, no matter how honest his mind, he cannot have Russia both as partner and enemy. If he could believe in a compromise peace with Germany in 1919, mustn't he compromise with Russia in 1945?

It is all to his honor, however, that he cannot "quit complaining" about Russia until "the system of government that happens to suit her" is adjusted, as it regards others, to the world of which Russia is a component. Mr. Chamberlin might himself "quit complaining," as T. W. Lamont requests, but Poland won't, nor the Baltic States, nor the Atlantic Charter, nor the Four Freedoms. The most vital part of this broad and cogent survey is William Henry Chamberlin's affirmation of tenets that make him the liberal he is. Being anxious, he is captious now and then. But America's power is great, even its power to run a partnership. It took a Hitler to suppose that F. D. R. put teeth into American liberalism simply in order to smile with them.

July 12, 1945

GIVING HISTORY A PUSH

A SHORT course in revolutionary technique can be derived from *Red Prelude*, by the English writer David Footman. It is a study of a Russian who was hanged in 1881. He and four others, one of them the daughter of a former Governor General of St. Petersburg, were executed in Semenovski Square in that city by a bungling and drunken hangman, with 12,000 troops to hold back a roaring crowd of 80,000.

Zhelyabov, the hero of this history, was "considered by Lenin to be the ideal revolutionary leader." He had made several ambitious attempts to kill Tsar Alexander II before 1881. Two days after the police had nabbed him, however, four young disciples stood ready with their bombs. When the Tsar

Red Prelude by David Footman. Yale University Press.

went back to see the place where the first had exploded, another was thrown at him from a distance of two paces. The Tsar survived his assassin by a few hours.

Zhelyabov was one of hundreds of young Russians who became socialists in the seventies. Not until he had served a term in prison was he converted to terrorism. "History," he said to a friend, "moves too slowly. It needs a push. Otherwise the whole nation will be rotten and gone to seed before the liberals get anything done."

But it was not only the liberals who made him impatient. "Osinski, the aristocrat, the acknowledged revolutionary leader, doubtless put out his conscious charm and was kindly and condescending. But Zhelyabov, the ex-house serf, with his old hatred of landowners, his egotism, his ambition, his consciousness of personal failure, must have seen the condescension, resented it, and come to hate Osinski; and his dislike opened his eyes to all the amateurishness, the lack of method, the pointlessness that lay behind the courage and idealism of Osinski's crusade."

The Secret Police in Zhelyabov's Russia met terrorism by "official arbitrariness and brutality." But where the young intellectuals wore "long hair, Scotch plaid, high boots and dark spectacles," Zhelyabov detested theatre. He, an ex-serf, measured himself against the Tsar of all the Russias and against the existing social structure. "We can do anything if we are not afraid of death." Mr. Footman greatly admires this Spartan resoluteness and he despises the Tsarist feebleness. "The Tsarist Government was too humane, or not sufficiently realist. The White Terror of the middle seventies terrorised only the timid, who in any case were barely worth terrorising."

On trial Zhelyabov said, to his later regret, "I would willingly abandon violence if there were the possibility of serving my ideals by peaceful means." But "for the common good" he had ruthlessly resolved "to organize revolutionary forces on the widest possible scale," and for an armed revolution it was necessary, as he saw it, to enlist soldiers and workers, and "to establish a strong, centralized machine."

Mr. Footman dwells on the underground technique as inevitably opposed to the liberal notions of choice, consent, individual liberty and persuasion. There were those who drew up a plan for a Constituent Assembly, but Mr. Footman believes they had "little first-hand knowledge of social experiments. Its authors still clung to the belief that social justice and individual liberty were not only compatible but mutually conducive." Zhelyabov wanted power. He loved Gogol's *Tarass Bulba*. "The saga of blood and battle and implacable struggle against enormous odds had touched his innermost being." He believed in matching might with dynamite.

A hard taskmaster himself, inordinately proud of his long black beard, friendly and easy but a driver and an egoist ("which may well have been the flamboyance of youth"), he counseled terrorist action that, "even more than war, requires meticulous training and an iron discipline to enable human nature to support the strain." He realized "that violent action of some kind would be needed to bring about the revolution, and that he must prepare himself to play his part. He had no humanitarian scruples. He never spared himself or felt the temptation to spare others."

And as a result terrorism won adherents. The young were stirred even by his failures. The movement "gave him all that any man of his temperament could ask for—a complete break with the failures and humiliations of the past, a leading role in a movement that had been his dream since childhood, the confidence that his part was well within his powers, and a vast empire waiting to be conquered."

Mr. Footman's book is not a personal drama, owing to the scantiness of the material. But it is a triumph of close and scrupulous inquiry into an obscure and extremely important development from Byronic protest to hard-boiled revolutionary dynamics. Zhelyabov hardened his heart in the name of "the common good," which covers a ruthlessness that in turn breeds fascism. Neither social justice nor individual liberty stands much chance when "hard and highly skilled" killers begin to "push" history. The workers' soundest weapon in the end is not dynamite but a constitution.

July 28, 1945

THE SORE SPOTS

NOTHING gives an author a worse pang than to be praised for the wrong thing. It was no more David J. Dallin's purpose to write *The Big Three* for the sake of showing that "Britain was the great adversary of Russia" through a long stretch of history, than it was the purpose of the Romans to leave mere roadwork for posterity. But Mr. Dallin's roadwork is so good, and the lack of concrete evidence on diplomatic history so general, that for this feature alone *The Big Three* is a job of work that should serve a big public.

Mr. Dallin is a mature Russian living over here with whom few can compete for dry and trenchant political analysis. It might have been expected in *The Big Three* that he would have pursued his analysis of the Russian Soviet Republic as a sociological danger. He still feels this danger. He thinks that progress toward peace "can be achieved only through abolition, down to the last vestige, of internal political suppression and subjection, of all forms of autocracy." But in *The Big Three* he sees Russia as a great power following the lines of expansion laid down by Tsarist Russia. He sees these lines pressed against Britain not only in Eastern Europe and in the Balkans and Greece but in the Mediterranean, in Turkey, in Iran, in the Far East, in Moslemism and in Zionism. What this means for the Big Three, but particularly for America, is the burden of his book. It makes a reader wake up.

Striking major omissions from Mr. Dallin's book are the mention of air power and the mention of Leftism in Britain. With Britain's naval inferiority at his finger tips, he assumes that from now on London must coordinate with Washington or be subordinate to it. In bold strokes that have the force of a woodcut, he depicts Britain's cool and astute selfishness in the past, and he thinks that "nothing is stronger in international relations than selfish interest." To say that "Britain openly supported the Confederacy" during the Civil War cuts the wood so that the

The Big Three by David J. Dallin. Yale.

chips fly pretty recklessly, but after so many soapy accounts of the Big Three it is well to have it recalled that "flaws in the relations between the big powers are the roads to strength and might for the weak ones," and in consequence "the predominance of the Big Three cannot be durable."

What, then, is America's role to be? It has taken a long time for America to grow from being a big nation to a big power. During that period its world politics was left to a small and initiated class, mostly diplomats and publicists, with some traders. Now dire necessity has plunged the whole American people into power politics. Congress has faced it. Elections will turn on it. The conversion is drastic and complete. And books like this by Mr. Dallin concern everyone.

Assuming as he does that France and even Germany and Japan will come back, Mr. Dallin foresees a Russia dangerously expanding. The "three sore spots" that this uncontrolled expansion must inflame will be in the Far East, in the Middle East and in Europe. In the Far East, as he sees it, "British military force can never again attain the importance it possessed in the East only a short time ago. American policy will play the dominant role." In the Middle East the hot spot is oil, and America will have to share with Britain this "hot spot of Anglo-Russian controversy, antagonism and intrigue." India is another sharp world problem. And in Europe our policy "is necessarily bound to travel more or less along the same road as the British." We must, that is to say, conflict with an expansionist Russia.

What gives force to Mr. Dallin's interpretation is his formidable array of evidence. The Soviet movement in China, for example, is summarized from Russian sources. Russian attacks on the United States are not represented as uniform. "Close collaboration and mutual understanding" have recently been achieved, but open verbal attacks in 1944 are quoted. He thinks that "there can be no automatic adjustment and readjustment of their interests. There is no cure-all for possible conflict." In fact, while Mr. Dallin admits that "the existence of political freedom and civil liberties acts as a brake on tendencies toward conquest and subjugation of alien nations," he regards power politics as basically militaristic. "Persistent effort and even wars are the price that nations pay to secure their status as great powers, and once they achieve such a status, wars become a must, and the road back to safe old isolationism is barred."

The America of William Jennings Bryan would revolt at these words, and many a thoughtful reader will resist them. But power politics, as they have existed and as they now exist, are substantially or credibly as this man describes them. Given the failure of human beings to mold a workable policy, State Departments and Foreign Offices almost invariably push selfish interests as indicated. To read *The Big Three* is to see how sore spots thus become cancerous. Mr. Dallin is exceptionally candid and lucid about it.

August 11, 1945

SNOW WHITE AND THE DWARFS

It is generally understood that the Soviet Union struggled up the hard way, and the two industrious authors of this book have written it to prove it. Up to 1914 the highest of white collar activities was diplomacy. Its chief operators had to combine a civil manner with uncivil underhand method, and this book probes beneath the tradition of suavity in power politics to expose "the secret war against Soviet Russia." By peeling off the skin and showing the raw musculature of power politics, they make a case that may shock anyone who takes Rubinstein, Pond, and Arden as true guides to the beauties of international conduct as directed by men in power. It has plenty of surprise, violence, and murder in it.

Messrs. Sayers and Kahn carry weighty endorsements on the back of *The Great Conspiracy*. Joseph E. Davies says their case is "exhaustive, authentic and fully documented." He also, by the way, says that Vishinsky is "calm, dispassionate, intel-

The Great Conspiracy by Michael Sayers and Albert E. Kahn. Little, Brown & Co.

lectual and able and wise." Mr. Davies uses words less for their
legal validity than for the contours they sketch on impres-
sionable minds.

"Around midnight on the freezing night of January 18,
1918," one of these brisk chapters begins, "a handsome young
Scot wrapped in furs groped his way by the light of a lantern
across a partly shattered bridge between Finland and Russia."
It sounds like authentic Oppenheim. This young Scot, described
as "handsome" three times on the page, was a child of privilege
going "to exploit for British ends the opposition movement
which had already arisen within the Soviet Government."
Does not Bruce Lockhart, the handsome Scot, say so himself?
Was he not a British agent? This is the sort of thing that Professor F. L. Schuman calls "sober fact, documented and indisputable."

To build up the international machinations against the infant
Soviet, Sayers and Kahn have utilized a whole library of "documents" such as these: *Britain's Master Spy, Sidney Reilly's
Narrative Written by Himself, Edited and Compiled by His
Wife;* Savinkov's *Memoirs of a Terrorist;* Sadoul's *The Socialist
Republic of Russia.* They touch on Winfried Ludecke's *Secrets
of Espionage,* Richard Wilmer Rowan's *Terror in Our Time,*
George Hill's *Go Spy the Land* and *Dreaded Hour.* They
make excellent copy of Winston Churchill's taking Savinkov
to see Lloyd George at Chequers, though it seems picayune to
say *"sic"* after "St. Just" when they misspell Lassalle themselves,
but more important to the reader is how these confessions can
be taken as "sober fact, documented and indisputable" without
deep investigation and control. Certainly the authors have not
the slightest reluctance to impugn unsupported testimony by
a Jan Valtin when it suits their argument. *"Out of the Night*
bore a startling resemblance to an anti-Soviet propaganda book
which was being currently circulated in Nazi Germany. In
preparing the book for publication in the United States, Krebs
was assisted by the American journalist Isaac Don Levine, a
veteran anti-Soviet propagandist and a regular contributor to
the Hearst Press." If this is the proper sauce for Jan Valtin,

how is it that the authors swallow as "sober fact" so much else that is without corroboration?

This book never fails to slight the character of a hostile witness. Thus Alexander Barmine is branded as "a Soviet renegade." William Henry Chamberlin is "a Hearst feature writer whose views about the trials appeared under the title 'The Russian Purge of Blood' in the Tokyo propaganda organ *Contemporary Japan*." As for Trotsky, he becomes the Axis Fifth Column. The authors of *Sabotage!* write as if the mere thought of sabotage and a fifth column never even crossed the mind of a Leninist.

Lenin, not being in the least suave, made no bones about tricks and compromises in the interests of the workers. In his letter to the American workers, 1918, he stuck to his theme that the British-French imperialist vultures were engaged in a struggle to determine which of the "great robbers," British or German, would plunder colonies, slaughter nations, and rule the world. Lenin did not pose as an injured innocent against whom there was a "great conspiracy." He never tried to nail his opponents to bourgeois morals while he himself disavowed their goodwill and chucked their morals overboard. What he avowed, and what Winston Churchill and the secret agents set out to counter, was a bitter project of international revolution. The handsome young Scot on the shattered bridge was a symbol of all that had been broken between Finland and Russia. Lenin repudiated the "despicable and bloody lie about the defence of the fatherland," the sentiment on which Messrs Sayers and Kahn based the patriotic appeal of their book *Sabotage!* Lenin classed Woodrow Wilson with Kaiser Wilhelm. He took the First World War as a greedy struggle "between two gangs of imperialist pirates," wholly useless from the point of view of the interests of the toilers, of the oppressed and exploited masses. For them, he frankly proclaimed to the leaders of bourgeois states, the only way out was revolution, civil war, a war of the oppressed against the oppressors, "the only struggle which always, in history, accompanies not only war but every revolution of any importance, the only war that is legitimate, just, and holy."

Lenin's break with the goodwill that then obtained in power politics was a deliberate one. He preached holy war. "Without such a war there can be no liberation from imperialist slavery." "There is no way out of it except international revolution." It was in view of this explicit ideology, this challenging faith, that the vultures, the pirates, the robbers, did their level best to scrap the Soviet revolution. They were later to scrap Hitler and Mussolini for another kind of defiance, and this time Lenin's Russia lined up alongside Winston Churchill in something that had been an "imperialist war" some months previous.

The Sayers-Kahn book is written by the romantic light of a red star that died some years ago. It should be clear at the present juncture that Russia has emerged from "the great conspiracy" into the great society and the great competition. While Messrs. Sayers and Kahn dwell on antagonism, open and covert, which once greeted Russia's overthrow of an organized government on class lines, the problem today has shifted. Russia is now itself an imperialism, using "tens of thousands of advanced and steeled proletarians, tempered enough ruthlessly to cast out of their midst and shoot all those who allow themselves to be 'tempted,' " but working with due regard to power politics. Raymond Robins sees no problem in this. "Stalin's policies have wiped out racial, religious, national and class antagonisms within the Soviet territories," he is quoted at the end. The operations on these antagonisms have been successful, no doubt, but the Kulaks and the Poles have died. Thus the "great conspiracy" enters a new phase. Its victims are still the weak, but Russia is no longer the exploited. Messrs. Sayers and Kahn are joining Walter Lippmann, the *Atlantic Monthly*, a Warburg, and several Lamonts on a bandwagon. It is now the Poles and other "reactionaries" who are oppressed and conspired against. That takes considerable edge off any appeal to bourgeois conscience on behalf of anti-bourgeois revolution.

March 2, 1946

Affairs in General

LIN YUTANG AT HOME

CHINA is big, baffling and bewildering. It is about the same size as the United States, has three times as many people, is boiling with conflicts like a great stew-pot, and has a history so long that a still useful irrigation system from 250 B. C. is nothing out of the ordinary. To cover this huge topic in a readable book, and give a firm handle to the stew-pot, takes a literary knack.

Lin Yutank is probably the only living writer who could do it. *The Vigil of a Nation* is a fine performance. Without having read a line of him before, or knowing much about China, the lay reader can get a grip on this momentous subject in no better way.

Lin Yutang gives his report as a personal book of travel—he returned from China ten months ago. By talking personally, he provides a human scale to measure by. His intuitions, his graphic strokes, his limber wit and neat analysis of his compatriots convey a concrete, intelligible China. His feelings on the Communists and on so-called fascism at Chungking may be attacked as biased, but his middle position is candidly revealed; and at a time when professional diplomats are so committed to national egoisms we owe a debt to any reporter whose felicity and skill are remarkable and whose tone is honest and sane.

This Chinese sanity is shown in Lin Yutang's account of the famous Taoist Temple to which he climbed. He risked his neck to do it, but once up above the "sharp, grayish-black, jagged cliffs," he balked at a final venture across the Bridge of Faith. "I scrutinized the bridge. The ropes were old and the planks not too well laid. My faith in God was not great enough, and I

The Vigil of a Nation by Lin Yutang. John Day.

decided sensibly there was no point in risking my life for sheer
bravado. Yet I was told women pilgrims had passed over
successfully. Religious fanaticism is something difficult to understand."

If he is no fanatic, no hair-shirt idealist, is Lin Yutang a materialist? His book gives no sign of it. On the contrary, while
he seems impregnably sane, he is aware that a new China,
literate and industrial and regulated, must supersede the China
that let things go, and must combine with the China that values
family bonds and human relationships. He does not hide his
warm feeling for the old China. It makes him feel gay and
adventurous to be in touch with it. He delighted in the actual
structure and color of that upheaved, outstretched, grooved,
ledged and lifted landscape whose beauty gives beauty to his
pages. He makes the provinces individual and personal, with
their teeming life and teeming rivers. He has a sense of their
shape and mass, of the way that nature slaps China in the face
or bends to caress it. But his playful and spirited narrative,
touching on Japanese prisoners, on factory management, on
food and drink, leads to the political and military means by
which the new China, the great China of the future, is to be
favored. And the book as a whole, however ingratiating its
method, is a strong plea for American understanding, and one
that ought to be heard.

In the United States, he sums up, "where democracy is well
rooted, one can hardly appreciate the Communist menace in
China, which as a nation is in the process of transformation."
He says this admitting freely that the Central Government of
Chiang Kai-shek has shortcomings, but urging reform rather
than complete overthrow. Two decades of Russian influence,
he says, have captured many Chinese youths, who pooh-pooh
Confucian humanism as feudalism and are dissatisfied with the
failures of the Central Government. In establishing a separate
regime the Communists, in his judgment, did so out of sincere
conviction, and aim to improve the lot of the "primary producer," but by doing this they have disrupted China with a
private army; and if in America the state of the Union "were
still in flux and uncertainty, Americans would be howling less

impatiently for China to grant constitutional liberties to the Communist party backed by a Communist army."

Lin Yutang believes that "the National Government and President Chiang Kai-shek constitute the pivot of this essential national unity." He thinks there has been "enough reckless talk and exaggerated claims" in America on behalf of the Communist regime. He quotes Dr. Sun Fo, who said: "Today the Communist party is in opposition. If we do not go forward, they will." But he deplores the disintegration of China, he denounces Communist methods, urges a bill of rights, and declares that, as Japan is the real enemy, "the first task of a nation at war is to fight." He thinks that the Allied plan to defeat Japan without a Chinese army was a costly mistake, and while he admits that the conscript system is bad and the army improperly cared for, he is sanguine that with big guns and tanks the situation will immediately improve.

How are pre-industrial nations, still bogged in the sixteenth century, to accommodate themselves to industrial habit—its change of pace, its impersonality, its stern subordinations and emotional dearth, its nostalgia? Lin Yutang devotes much of his book to this. He reminds one of certain Chinese pictorial artists. In Washington there is a gem of an art gallery created by a man who used to make freight cars, and one of the loveliest things in this Freer Gallery is a scroll, following the course of a river, in which the artist sought to capture motion and continuity by making his picture seemingly endless, with crags above the stream, boats laboring against its flow, hills kneeling and flattening. Lin Yutang's delight in the anatomy of China, as well as its features, makes him writhe at the profane radicalism of those who do not know it and love it as he does. Perhaps his book is most eloquent simply because he loves China and treasures its thick continuity. That makes it a book to read.

January 25, 1945

ANTHROPOLOGY IN SHORTS

THE younger anthropologists are coming to a boiling point. At one time they were content with Red Indians. They pottered around among the Zuñis and the Navajos, worked on kinship terms and restored "sibling" to our speech and measured skulls. But with other scientists vitally relating their work to events of the day and deriving what seems to be labeled as "ego satisfaction," the anthropological investigators, whose topic is mankind, show bubblings of aggressiveness. The time is ripe, Prof. Ralph Linton declares, for "a new synthesis of science," and "the science of anthropology makes a bid for the position."

Nothing venture, nothing have. But if the anthropologists mean to bag a good seat at the table, we who are on the table should keep an eye open. Professor Linton gives us a fair chance. He has collected papers from a score of his colleagues, added two good ones of his own, and issued *The Science of Man in the World Crisis*—a title that covers as lively a ferment of ideas as ever came off a university press.

Lively, but restive. In order to depict global problems before making predictions, the editor hooks in political science, psychiatry, sociology, economics and the art of propaganda. If a "symposium" were originally a drinking party, this one mixes our liquor.

The cause may reside in the difficulty of relating so broad an inquiry to so defined and accepted a base. Anthropology is happiest when it makes a "theoretic construct," but to reach the stratosphere for any cosmic view of man means flying into rarefied air. In this thin air the concept of race, for example, "may even be genetically evanescent." Race, as Wilton Marion Krogman sees it, is socially overemphasized. "Certain it is that we must no longer regard any classification as fixed, arbitrary, immutable."

The Science of Man in the World Crisis edited by Ralph Linton. Columbia University Press.

But when Raymond Kennedy later discusses race in the dense atmosphere natural to imperial colonies, he brusquely resorts to popular classification of half-castes, etc., and he is obliged to do so pragmatically. Yet when he, in turn, makes a constructive theory on the basis of the Philippines, to the disadvantage of the British with "their ineffable snobbishness and exclusiveness," he has to forget Jim Crow, the poll-tax Senators, race riots and that strange exhibit Puerto Rico. And even Otto Klineberg oscillates toward race classification when indicating a Negro girl of 9 who had an I. Q. of 200. Though unmixed races are theoretically excluded, this child was "of apparently unmixed Negro origin."

To use anthropology for life as well as pure science provokes sprightly but often contradictory ideas. A Poor Richard may say, "Habits are maintained so long as they bring rewards," but a sterner colleague observes that "unrewarded habits continue for a long time." "Verbalizing," we are assured, helps the frustrated. "That patient is more nearly well who has sentences to cover all of his wishes, fears and hopes." Yet the author of *Mein Kampf* is one to "verbalize," and the accounts of him are not good. And where a contributor casts out the word "instinct" as no longer respectable, even disdaining "instinct of workmanship," he himself falls back on its use in a few pages.

Great serenity and mastery are shown in papers by Herskovits and Hallowell, Felix M. Keesing, Carl C. Taylor. Here the "theoretic construct" is pursued frankly and sensitively, as also in the papers on Indians and nativism. A contrasting exuberance, rashness and lack of circumspection, however, spring from a bold and eager attempt to meet the demand of a world in crisis. Why? The strength of Russian racial ideology may be one of the elements of ferment. Louis Wirth's admiration for the Russian handling of minorities is highly significant and extremely cerebral. It promotes that "imbalance" which a change in American culture had already started.

One is struck by the vocabulary of machine age and machine ideology—blueprint, set-up, tie-in, technique, breakdown in the sense of analysis, gear, mesh, drive, pattern, over-all, end product. The urban influences are scarcely less marked in the interlocking directorate by which Linton, Shapiro, Krogman, Klineberg, Kluckhohn, Kardiner and Murdock lean on and cross-refer to one another, and have Freud for a point of reference, in spite of acute discriminations by Kardiner.

Yet under docile acceptance of current intellectual vogue, under a pat jargon and a disregard of subtlety in language and political ideas, *The Science of Man* still marks one of those vigorous flights in which "science as method" is transcended out of sheer adventurousness. It shows receptivity to the world at large. Disintegration of prejudice, even if the new universals may be unfeeling and cruelly insistent on "adjustment," reveals a sporting change. A science moves from the dun to the verdant. Anthropology has a new suit.

January 27, 1945

RACE IDEOLOGY, U.S.A.

A SHORT book on an inescapable theme is often the best, and Walter White has served his cause by being terse in *A Rising Wind*. The second half of it, partly a high and glowing account of Eboué, the Negro Frenchman who saved Chad for the United Nations, branches away from the main theme, but the first half of it probes directly and tellingly into dark places. It makes the book important, not simply because Mr. White speaks as secretary of the National Association for the Advancement of Colored People, but because he is possessed by one of those mastering passions to which no wise American can refuse heed and no good citizen refuse sympathy.

That Negroes have tails, useful and decorative as tails admittedly are, belongs to a type of folklore one hardly expects in 1945. Mr. White went overseas to look into the war and to see how the Negro soldier was getting on, but he could not have supposed that an English family would be providing cushions for Negro visitors, having heard from white soldiers

A Rising Wind by Walter White. Doubleday, Doran.

that Negro tails were awkward. Mr. White tells of this. He also tells of a town in England that was led to believe that Negroes could bark but not talk. At first the Negro soldiers resented the legend, but their good humor got the better of them. They began by barking softly. The English caught on. They were soon barking back, and the joke was on the white men who started it.

These are gargoyles of race hatred. Mr. White found it had also been given official sanction, not at the top but through the Army. There were "off limits" rules on the basis of race. Red Cross segregation in clubs, not in hospitals, aroused Mr. White's scorn. He quotes a fantastic document telling the British about Negro infantility, issued by a Southern commanding officer. Then there were false charges of rape and specific injustices. And in Italy there were malignant circulars and posters.

It is impossible to read *A Rising Wind* without being moved to indignation. Mr. White does it by exhibiting these blind ignorances, these humiliating examples of prejudice off the limits. Much worse is it to hear of Negro combat troops willfully deprived of combat service. Knowing how white fliers felt about their Negro fellows who won proud laurels in combat, it seems atrocious that American citizens should, because of color, have "to fight for the right to fight." This waste of generous and noble emotions in a race of native kindness and responsiveness is a smarting wound, and Mr. White does not hide it. He went right up to the front with correspondents of American Negro papers, however, and found morale high among Negro combatants before Cassino. One of them chaffed him. "I gotta be here because the draft board said so, but you don't have to!" Gay banter from hearts welling with pride, but grimness behind it.

This grimness is not disguised; Mr. White does not hesitate to close his book with a menace, and the menace is Russia. Unless the western powers revolutionize their racial concepts and practices, he says, a World War III must be prepared for, and the colored peoples everywhere may "move into the Russian orbit as the lesser of two dangers."

How any man can talk of World War III who at the same time prays that young Walter White's generation may be "wiser," I don't know. But if America can afford itself such luxuries as pugnacious and rancorous Congressmen, "unintelligent and reactionary," then Russian race ideology may win the Negroes. *A Rising Wind* is a manifesto of this, and much that Mr. White saw of the Negro's status in World War II supports him. "World War II," he says, "has immeasurably magnified the Negro's awareness of the disparity between the American profession and practice of democracy."

This disparity has to be examined coolly. The Irish fought in vain for military segregation in World War I, hence it does not seem self-evident that segregation is an outrage. Mr. White was accredited as a war correspondent with Government sympathy—he names John J. McCloy, Robert P. Patterson, General Surles. He had full access to General Eisenhower. "In having John G. Winant as war Ambassador to England," he says, "the United States is as fortunate as she is in having top-ranking officers like Eisenhower and [Lieut. Gen. John C. H.] Lee in the Army." And one telling though small instance of American idealism came in Devon when Mrs. Leonard Elmhirst (Dorothy Whitney) refused to comply with white officers who demanded that guests' cards be rescinded from Negro trainees invited to a dance. In specific instances, too, General Eisenhower impartially reviewed and corrected injustices. And English women go with Negroes, some for pay, some for love, without the stars falling out of the sky or the end of the world coming.

A Rising Wind is based on substantial reality. In this war there are six times as many Negro officers as in the last, but there are only six thousand. The barriers to military service have only been slightly lifted. Granted that woman suffrage had to fight deep prejudice quite recently, as Mr. White knows, he still has a powerful case, and he presents it honestly and unflinchingly. Without a World War III, the pride of the Negro can be respected on American lines, but Mr. White does well to tell America that Russian race ideology is in the world to stay. Russia guarantees race status. That is a new factor. It is just as big and broad and inescapable as the Mississippi.

February 24, 1945

PEOPLE'S SCHOOLS IN CHINA

PEARL BUCK is really a wonder. Though she was born with a virus, and remains an incorrigible missionary at heart, she has conquered the failing to which most missionaries succumb, the surrender to monomania. Powerful as her emotions are, almost violent as is her desire to mother mankind—the whole of it— she has not yielded to this glorious but devouring ambition. She still has the use of her head, and it is a good one. The fire in her nature might have made her a demagogue, but it is governed by a critical faculty that serves her well, and also by her exceptional capacity as a story teller. These three endowments—moral, intellectual, imaginative—make her a towering personality and yet a humble one.

She has put all three to use in a little book called *Tell the People*. It is very like that caldron of herbs described in the book, boiled and boiled until a little pill was made from it, and "if you ate it you would achieve immortality." The herbs, in this particular caldron, are Chinese. They were drawn from a Chinese, James Yen. And no priceless China tea ever had more of a kick in it.

China is an agricultural land, a land of villages. James Yen began with a village. He tells how the Village Elder was won, and how the bright ones led the less bright. He hit on the basic truth that culture, the tool of community, must come before agriculture, the tool of livelihood. But it was literacy for the sake of reconstruction. In the county of Tinghsien, where there are 400,000 people and 472 villages, there came to be

Tell the People by Pearl S. Buck. John Day.

472 People's Schools. But these were not narrowed to a single purpose, literacy; literacy was a means to history, to common feeling, to common culture. Then the people knew one another on a level where they had self-interests in common. It reduced friction when they tackled poverty.

With a few strokes of her novelist's brush Pearl Buck enables us to see James Yen, exactly as he talked this little book to her during a week-end at her farm in Pennsylvania. He was born into a ruling caste of scholars. As a young man in the last war he was in France with the Chinese labor corps. The word coolie means "bitter strength." Through learning to respect this quality in his coolies, who could neither read nor write, young James Yen foresaw what literacy could do for his people. The crowbar he gave them in France, by which to break into literacy, was a Chinese tool written with 1,000 instead of 5,000 characters. And he returned with this tool to a nation crippled by illiteracy.

"Poverty," says the wise James Yen, "is a cause of disease, disease and ill-health are economically wasteful and so a cause of poverty. Poverty and disease are in turn both largely a result of ignorance." How, then, to double the income of the villages? Grundtvig had discovered it in Denmark a hundred years ago. James Yen was doing for China what the Danish leader had done. He was asking the people to get up and walk, not by the aid of Government, not by the aid of revolution, but by the aid of their own bitter strength. They had this new crowbar, group education. A better pig, a better hen, better wheat, better cotton, and their productivity was doubled. The 200 local bankers in the county, exacting 40 per cent interest, were wiped out. "You must first stimulate the minds of the people so that they demand the thing you have to give them." With reading and writing came awareness of community.

The educationally overprivileged were not the ones to teach the farmers. Mr. Yen saw "an internationally famous European intellectual" go "back to the people." "He visited the rural parts of China. After a good chicken dinner and fine champagne, and with a pipe in his mouth, he was carried in a sedan chair by four coolies to see the country people." He came back and wrote, as our scholars did, about "the tranquillity of the farmer." This tranquillity was a myth, and James Yen found that his highbrows had to be serviced by himself. "One-fourth of my own time," he said, "was spent in lucubration."

The Mass Education Movement has become a force in politics. The Generalissimo Chiang Kai-shek took from it his total reform of county government in all Free China. And where the people have been thus evoked and equipped, their resistance to the Japanese has been much stronger. The handicaps are unbelievable. China has one doctor to 70,000, where America has one to 800. But James Yen and his friends trained "health workers." This, too, was a necessary step in a world where three-quarters of the people are ignorant, ill-fed, ill-clad, ill-housed, disease ridden.

Denmark did it. China is doing it. And the principle is the same, "first stimulate the minds."

This little book calls us to help the people everywhere to use the power latent in them. Then you have the foundation to build on. This is God's truth and no pipe dream.

March 29, 1945

AFRICA BY DAYLIGHT

WHEN people say "one world," they defer to two facts. One is that transportation makes every land accessible. The other is that, every land being accessible, no class and no race can any longer live for itself exclusively. A generation ago it was possible for an ex-President of the United States, Theodore Roosevelt, to come back from Africa or Brazil with grand trophies of the chase and relatively few words about the Negro. Africa was segregated.

Now Africa has moved from being a silent continent to a talkie. Its 150,000,000 Negroes have a fellowship with 13,000,000 American citizens, with 10,000,000 West Indians and with

African Journey by Eslanda Goode Robeson. John Day.

many millions in Brazil. The Africa that was pushed around in the early years of the League of Nations is no longer a Dark Continent. It may not yet have peeled off its European masters, but it has come into daylight and into speech. To be ignorant of it is to borrow trouble or else to leave Africa to the Soviet Union.

An easy way of testing Africa's nearness is to accompany Eslanda Goode Robeson on her *African Journey*. Mrs. Paul Robeson happens to have had African ancestry, but she is a typical dynamic American in her culture. She comes of a well-to-do family. Her grandfather, she says, the late Francis Lewis Cardozo, "was well known for his early awareness of the Negro problem." She has herself been a technician at Presbyterian Hospital and a student at Teachers College, later studying anthropology with Malinowski and others in London.

The Africa she sees is a land in which the inhabitants are as much her own brothers and sisters as are her fellow-citizens in America. "The white people in Africa do not want educated Negroes traveling around seeing how their brothers live, nor do they want those brothers seeing Negroes from other parts of the world." But Mrs. Robeson doesn't feel that way. She is a one-worlder, though she extends her ego more easily to other Negroes than she does to the culpable whites.

If a white reader can scarcely help regretting Mrs. Robeson's aversion to white Portuguese, white Boers, white Belgians and poor white trash in general, the total effect of *African Journey* is anything but unsympathetic. For one thing, she can't help making us feel we know her and like herself and her son. Hers is an extremely attractive and natural book. Another kind of woman might annoy us by traveling like a princess. It was in a "double first-class stateroom with private bath" that she and her 9-year-old Pauli went from London to Capetown. She kept in constant touch with her celebrated husband by long distance all the time she was away; the red carpet was out for her everywhere and it was from the Government House at Entebbe that she and her boy boarded the plane to Alexandria. But instead of repelling us by her evident overprivilege, we forget it in the much more pressing evidence of her aliveness to the

African people, an aliveness that in its essence is, let us say, Jeffersonian.

If the British dangle a carrot in front of an African's nose, whether it is done by a District Commissioner or a Governor, and whether the name on the carrot is "King" or "President," makes no difference. Mrs. Robeson sees it as colonial device. She sees the Negro workers in their "locations," which are economic concentration camps. She gives many photographs of mournful and patient faces. The evidence of manipulation and exploitation is exposed by her as any Jeffersonian might have exposed it. But curiously enough, it is to Russia that she looks for comprehension—comprehension, that is to say, of the Negro as educable, as endowed with his own precious native instruments of language, custom, music, ritual, technique, architecture, not to stress his own warrior caste or his own rigid class system.

Being a warm-hearted woman, Mrs. Robeson observes the needs of the African Negroes, and it strikes her to the heart to have their white conquerors so ignore them as persons. Hence her full-hearted tribute to the Russians. She and her mother and Paul Robeson know Russia from living in it; and while she salutes Julian Huxley for his wise words about African education, it is Russia that has won her allegiance. "We look at those who have enslaved us, and find them decadent. Injustice and greed and conscious inhumanity are terribly destructive. Yes, I am glad and proud I am Negro. . . . In Russia I was excited and profoundly moved to see for myself how the so-called 'backward,' 'primitive' peoples from the formerly remote wastes of Siberia and Asia have been stepped up to active and constructive participation in a highly industrialized state. The Institute of Minorities in Leningrad is a place to visit, study and revisit."

Mrs. Robeson makes us see the Mountains of the Moon, and she told the natives of Toro, in sight of those mountains, the help that "great scholars and teachers" in Russia had given to their own "more primitive tribes." Thus the headwaters of a political Nile are nourished. When one thinks of a sore like Bilbo on the face of American democracy it is no wonder that an American like Mrs. Robeson goes to Russia for her ideology. Her book may not be the most tactful and diplomatic ever written, but through its lively travelogue it transmits a clear and ringing denunciation of capitalism's tendency to rob the blind of their pennies. Her own eyes, at any rate, have not been blinded, nor was her excellent camera sealed in Africa.

August 9, 1945

SUPERMAN

WHEN God the Father disappeared for the intellectuals, taking with Him "meekness, crucifixion and love," they were left groping for a substitute. That substitute, as Eric Russell Bentley sees it, becomes a Superman if hierarchy and respect for superiors are basic for them. This is perhaps the main argument in his alert and scholarly book, *A Century of Hero-Worship.*

To have a piquant book from an American college is no longer rare. Even anthropology, as William Howells recently proved in *Mankind So Far,* can be served like a soufflé. But when the piquant writer is under 30, and his subject nothing less than good and evil, it is a bit of an event. That it should come from Black Mountain College, which is neither heavily endowed nor ponderously staffed, is in itself encouraging. Whenever teachers grasp awkward problems instead of smothering them, keen students find college not so much an herbarium as an intellectual runway.

Mr. Bentley's subject is "heroic vitalism." Not exactly an epithet to stir the sluggard, most of us have a rough notion what he has in mind. He is isolating the doctrine of power and the will-to-power, and along with its worship of the Great Man, the Hero, he is showing its contempt for, and manipulation of, the masses; its acceptance of masters and slaves; its ruthlessness. This doctrine steels its disciples to be beasts of

A Century of Hero-Worship by Eric Russell Bentley. Lippincott.

prey. It puts hardness and courage before everything, never shrinks from treachery but shrinks from surrender. It is the black drop of a will-to-evil that makes true understanding between totality and democracy seem impossible.

Mr. Bentley has not written a tract. He has not narrowed his thesis to the infected region of German nationalism. As a preamble to Nietzsche he selects Thomas Carlyle, who died in 1881, the year in which Nietzsche was outlining *Thus Spake Zarathustra.* These two dissenters, one who had swallowed Calvinism with his porridge and the other born in a caul of Lutheranism, are shrewdly juxtaposed as hero-worshipers. Not quite so aptly, Mr. Bentley passes on to Richard Wagner and Bernard Shaw, winding up the exposition with Spengler, Stefan George and D. H. Lawrence. Germany, it is clear, is touched at every point, and while the book would have been better in its form if Spengler, "the exponent of historic Nietzscheism," had been developed on a scale comparable to Carlyle and Nietzsche, yet the linking of Shaw with the tyrants, like the linking of Carlyle with Herder and Bismarck, certainly builds up the argument, though it involves some legerdemain about St. Joan.

In his sketches of the dyspeptic Carlyle and the dyspathic Nietzsche, Mr. Bentley sometimes dehydrates too much, since these men were not lengths for the sawmill but living poets in whom the sap is running. But when the subject is a master-idea like hero-worship—and the pedigree of any master-idea is a great subject—what one asks from a fresh mind is, above all, mental attack and energy. This Mr. Bentley possesses. He shows that it was imperative for these dereligionized men to worship, and that they said Yea to life in terms that have given carte blanche to scoundrels. He does this with lively sympathy for their predicament, since Victorianism for himself seems to be permeated with the smell of boiled cabbage, but he holds enough aloof to mark the social catastrophe which these men of genius incited and invited. Mr. Bentley's own gloss on them is not moralistic. His partialities can be guessed from casual remarks about liberalism. (Liberal ideology is "applesauce for the bourgeois pork.")

With similar finality he calls Shaw a go-getter, says that Carlyle was a tiger-cub for the rich, slights the humble Otto-line Morrell as Lawrence's "patroness," chides Lou Salome for her "youthful addiction to virginity" and betrays the antifem-inine bias of the thirties in seeing the pure and compassionate side of Nietzsche as "feminine." What does he mean, "fem-inine?" Lady Macbeth, Cleopatra, Rebecca West, Mae West, Clare Boothe Luce—these are no Gretchens. Only German youth are the official patentees of this cult of masculinity.

But if Mr. Bentley pulls up short at times, if he does not enlarge his inquiry to take in the worship of Marx (and Marx, like Carlyle, was himself a worshiper of history and an admirer of German military power) he still has done remarkably well in bringing scholarship to bear on the appalling German suc-cess in emancipating a whole generation from meekness and charity. Perhaps the discussion of unbridled power must there-after go back to religion. Religion has been grappling with it for thousands of years.

October 12, 1944

A POLE ON FREEDOM

SOMETIMES in a hardware store your heart leaps up when you behold a gadget. To the anthropologist this would not be a gadget, it would be an artifact, an "artificial product." But wondrous as it might be were it a washing machine, still more wonderful is to spy out a machine for one's political ideas. One of the best anthropologists of recent years came, before he died, to pass from artifacts and the rest to the significant belief that "education implants values" and that "the whole course of life is determined by values." This was Bronislaw Malinowski.

It is mournful that he was to die prematurely. He had put his great mind on the supreme topic, the topic of freedom, in

Freedom and Civilization by Bronislaw Malinowski. Roy Publishers.

the year 1942. By April of that year he had pulled his ideas down to paper, and he meant to finish his analysis during the summer, but in May he suddenly died at the age of 58. Valetta Malinowska, his widow, was completely familiar with his intentions as he wrote, and now, without adding fresh stuff or rewriting, she has put his material into shape for the printer. *Freedom and Civilization* is the result.

The first argument of signal importance in Malinowski's book is that the quest for freedom can never be made an escape from responsibility. Freedom from authority is a day-dream, he considers, and he stresses that freedom is an act, not a floating thought. "Freedom," he drums into us, "consists in the lead and guidance which the rules and laws of culture give man." It is the outcome of wise obediences. "Each member of an institution enjoys his own differential freedom in the measure to which he has a part in the planning, a full access to the means of execution, and a share in the rewards."

Malinowski takes this straight back to the discovery and utilization of fire, but he is not concerned with free-floating freedom. "Freedom is a gift of culture," and without culture, of which religion is a part, there cannot be freedom. So he says, and he draws charts to demonstrate it.

Having made this place for discipline, he then vigorously turns around to argue along the line of rewards. The abuse of authority comes when "implemented action" is restricted. "Freedom," he says, "is born there and freedom is killed there. For it is through implemented action, that gross quantum which means success, efficiency, mobility, wealth and moral control, that power is developed." And "the real abuse of authority begins when discipline has to be made chronic, permanent and pervasive."

This "abuse" of authority seems to depend on "values." Keenly distinguishing between the laws of our being, which are inexorable, and the laws of our behaving, which we can inflect, Malinowski does not seem to trace to a single root the authority through which we may inflect and the authority which inflects us. Which rules are chains, and which are harness? Granted that "the main ethical principle of all primitive tribes is that conformity to tradition is good and deviation bad," it seems well that this ethic yielded to wider knowledge. That man freed his thought and quested knowledge seems to return one to the desirability of "free-floating" freedom.

Malinowski arrives at democracy by the route of action. He asserts that monopoly is the enemy. Monopoly plays havoc with democracy, he declares, adding: "When astronomy, mathematics and physics, rudimentary yet powerful instruments of spiritual influence, become a monopoly of a priestly caste and a monopoly of its highest ranks, we see again that knowledge, scientific and mystical, becomes an exclusive and centralized power which can be used for oppression. We could quote the Spanish Inquisition, certain sects and phases of Islam, as well as of Christianity, Protestant and Catholic, as examples of monopoly in spiritual truth. Today this is represented in the religions of totalitarian systems which make the leader practically omnipotent, omniscient and ubiquitous." In other words, God-Hitler and God-Stalin.

As against the deliberate creation of political crises, which demand war, and the centralization of the tribe-state, Malinowski argues for nationhood, self-determination, plural authority, "autonomy of church, school, research, religious organizations, free courts and free discussion." He urges the elimination of too much policing, the elasticity of competing institutions, the division of authority. Propaganda "starts with monopoly in the dissemination of truth, a monopoly based on force." He condemns this, just as he condemns slave labor, which would apply to conquered Germany for anyone interested in it. And he condemns war outright, for its filthy criminalities as well as its waste, urging that primitive man never fought wars and that democracy cannot persist unless the superstate is organized to get rid of aggression.

Malinowski was an anthropologist, as his famous book, *The Sexual Life of Savages*, established for a wide public. As a modern science, anthropology is just a hundred years old, the proposition of 1843 being that "man is but an animal." The studies of primitive cultures seem to drag men to alkali wastes, out of which they drag their borax like mules. But hard as is the substratum of anthropology in this book, the inquiry is passionate and concerned. It is tough going, but a most stimulating and scrupulous inquiry, based on faith in man's powers so long as he pays the price of autonomy. This noble study of freedom is in itself liberating.

October 19, 1944

THE WHOLE MAN

ILL health changes our universe. It often poisons the will. Many victims of it cannot take the initial step toward selecting the right doctor. They fear medical etiquette if they have started off on the wrong foot. They worry about the cost of medical care. They dread the stiffness or censoriousness of the unknown physician. They shrink from action like a cat from water, and this can go on until the minnow of disease is a whale, by which time the visit may be as useless as it is unavoidable.

People in this plight should be immensely grateful for *The Doctor's Job,* by a distinguished practitioner, Dr. Carl Binger. It is in no sense a book of exhortation, although first of all a book for the patient. Mellow and spirited, like many volumes of medical reminiscence, it turns a full experience toward orienting the patient. The doctor's job is to bring "trained human understanding" to the sick person, whether he is willfully or accidentally afflicted, and the criterion of health, as quoted from Ernest Jones, is fearless and even joyous acceptance of life which marks "the free personality of one who is master of himself."

What lies behind disease? If Hippocrates were to pick up this volume he would find in it the full chart of modern ailment, from allergy to urology. He'd have a lucid though terse account of ground that has been gained for health, and the ground still to be consolidated. While disease has been much

The Doctor's Job by Carl Binger, M. D. Norton.

departmentalized, since the time of an "old-fashioned general practitioner" like Hippocrates, and while the modern internist dispatches patients right and left from his information booth to the specialists, both Hippocrates and Paracelsus would find in *The Doctor's Job* a key idea that was their own, that "he who wants to know man must look upon him as a whole."

Disease, that is to say, is not of the body alone. It is in the mind-body, for which the new word is psychosomatic, "soma" being the body. The index to Dr. Binger's book leaves out Tom, a human guinea pig. The text tells us that Tom (who was Irish) had a gastric fistula, and when anything made Tom furious, Dr. Harold Wolff could spy through the fistula and see the emotional conflagration that anger caused in Tom's stomach. Stomach ulcers, bodily a fact, often start with a hot-box in the psyche. Dr. Binger indicates how human strains and stresses can evidence themselves in eczema and even tuberculosis. A paper rose excited asthma in a man sensitive to roses. Hence the doctor's job is to be both body-reader and mind-reader.

By illustrating this reciprocation of mind and body Dr. Binger is able to give new intelligibility to psychiatry and psychoanalysis. What he calls "a splinter in your soul," which may lead to alcoholism or high blood pressure, can "produce disease." Bodily disease, however, has its own imperium, and the doctor's province is the whole man, body and soul. He gives a marvelous description of an operation on a stomach that was forced up and constricted by a gape in the diaphragm. This was a source of insomnia, and its removal was no less a victory because a bloody one. While this book admits that "worry is an elusive troglodyte," it can see a brute immediate cause for worry in a sick body, and in the end only the surgeon can deal with much that comes to the doctor's office.

The push of scientific inquiry has been so hard in recent years that the pull of the human object has been diminished for many doctors. Instead of a bedside manner some have a ringside manner, looking with a calloused eye on the patient. "Taking a beating, aren't you?" Dr. Binger embodies another tradition. Respect for human personality runs through his serene and luminous book, as well as respect for the nerves that life harasses. There are hospitals that include the sounds of dishwashing with the semi-private rooms they offer. Dr. Binger is one of those born healers, observant, astute, benign, who remind one that dignity and taste are in themselves curative.

He has no magic to offer. He does not soften the hard terms of modern life. *The Doctor's Job* does not try to take the edge off mortality or wave away suffering or even promise synthetic rubber for worn old arteries. But on every page its author recalls the final object, health. Whether we hear a neurotic excuse himself for breaking an appointment, or watch a Sicilian girl caged in submission and dying of it, or see a war hero almost faint when his finger is pricked, the value of "trained human understanding" is underlined. Hence the book is bathed in an indirect light that favors the nerves. It induces perception of many ills that are public in quantity—cardiac cases in the million, war convalescents, underpaid herds in the clinic, underpaid medicos, patients glum over unpalatable food in hospitals.

To his great book Osler brought a great quality, which was courtesy. He had solace in his touch. He showed mastery without seeking it. The same sagacity and compassion are alive in *The Doctor's Job*. Like Osler, Carl Binger can come aboard as pilot, but he leaves his patient as captain. It is a cooperation for health.

March 24, 1945

ST. BERNARD AT 88

THE brilliant leaves are going and, in bare and clean outline, we can now see the granite Bernard Shaw. The whole world has a relationship with this incomparable man, some of us since his memorable, marvelous springtime, when he burst on us over forty years ago. Even then he was no chicken, having

Everybody's Political What's What by Bernard Shaw. Dodd, Mead.

been born in 1856, and long ago he was willing to call it a day. Once he and a young actor went for a swim off the English coast and had a stiff fight to get back through heavy surf. "It would have been all right for me to go under," he said on the beach, "I've had my chance, but you're a young man, it's all before you." That was quarter of a century ago, and here he is publishing a long book, at 88. What a healthy intellect! And what a colon!

With the gallantry that distinguishes the intellectual, one searches in this book, this *Everybody's Political What's What* for signs of senility. It's no good. The Old Man does repeat himself, but the constant self cannot be supposed to change, that Marxist Quixote known to us in the prefaces. His sense of other people's sins has not become dulled by repetition. He has never had any use for a barrel except to thump it, and here, as a result of lifelong addiction to the barrel, he goes on thumping. But while it is obligatory to report the current message, it is permissible to let our minds wander for a second to the radiant Shavian edifice behind the preacher's head.

This is an Anglo-Irishman who might easily have been a crank all his life. He gives us tantalizing glimpses of his family —the uncle who removed his boots to be ready to step into Elijah's chariot, his father shouting "This will be the ruin of me" when he had to shell out a halfpenny to cross that ugly metal bridge in Dublin, or that squire of a great-grandfather who owned a pawnshop on the side. The Shaws thrust themselves against stone walls that protected and imprisoned, warped and thwarted the Occupiers in Ireland. Instead of continuing with Dublin, pulling the Irish devil by the tail, Shaw exiled himself to England, like Congreve and Goldsmith and Sheridan and Oscar Wilde before him. There he was enlivened by contrasts and had that impetus to comedy that quickens with dispossession rather than prepossession, and all was entertainment for him. Instead of seeking to titillate or orient the emotions, as if he were at home, he dramatized the intellect and sharpened his wits and his claws on English resistance. He chuckles at this in retrospect. "It is always necessary to overstate a case startlingly to make people sit up and listen to it, and to frighten them into acting on it. I do this myself habitually and deliberately." Which is the sinister truth. Every advertising man knows it.

The genius in him, full of lightning perception, never wholly conquered the Anglo-Irish crank in him; the man who says of modern war, "A duller entertainment I cannot conceive," thinks more of letting off a firecracker than he should. He indulges this side of his nature. It is idiotic to say that Dartmoor and Mountjoy are more cruel than the concentration camps, cruel as they are. It is eccentric to smear Lister and Jenner. It is perverse to link Caesar Borgia and Abraham Lincoln as men who comparably set out to unify their nations. It is downright frivolous to be angry about Pavlov's dogs when one is flippant about the liquidation of the kulaks. And it is inadequate to echo Hitler's description of England as an Anglo-Semitic plutocracy.

But while the crank in him makes him defend Typhoid Mary against zealous doctors at the same time that he consigns defectives to wholesale death, this is simply the family cut-up, Bernard with the High Hand. His book of forty-four chapters, self-indulgent in such small details, is so peerless in the large aspect that to be deterred by his faults and double-faults would be to ignore a champion game. What makes him a champion is the lively and audacious detachment he began with, the shrewd political inquest that came from it, the sense of honor and devotion he brought to it, and the natural toughness and bounce of his mind. He calls this book a *A Child's Guide to Politics*, and if the Socialist state is for him on its Marxist side "an organization of the consumers in self-defense against the organized producers," this shows his pervasive love of quality, his rabid concern for talent and genius which society flings away "through lack of the means for its fullest cultivation."

Shaw has strong and concrete ideas about these means. He prefers municipal organization to the two-party system. He prefers "sedition, blasphemy, heresy, eccentricity, innovation, variety and change" to sticking in the mud. His book insists on specialism in government, on the evils of landlordism, on the mischief of conscience without knowledge, and of knowledge without conscience. He uses the Old School Tie as a hangman might use it, and his examination of our present capitalism, in its bearing on economics, politics and religion, proceeds with a vigilance that time has mellowed but in no way dimmed.

The man is unique. He rules the crank and the zealot in himself. As aphoristic as a Pascal, he forces himself to be systematic. So tolerant that he can prefer Hail, Mary to Heil, Hitler, in spite of dyed-in-the-wool Protestantism, he still remains unyielding on the prime duty of citizenship as such. Believing "a Socialist state can be just as wicked as any other sort of state," he is still too much of an aesthete to wed the palace of his art to a social slum. This accounts for his devoting his final energy to real politics, for his striving to put Russia in an intelligible and acceptable perspective, and for his pressing against the landlord's head and the insurance man's head, not a gun but a Beveridge Plan. How superb it is to have had such vivid humane convictions, to have searched into them, to have lived by them, and to carry them like a sword!

October 26, 1944

ANDRÉ GIDE AS PATRIOT

ABOUT ten months after the fall of France, Jacques Chardonne produced a book, *Private Chronicle 1940*, which bowed to the subjection of France and made a plea for the subjection of Europe to Hitler.

Chardonne, if one may say so, was washed up at the feet of André Gide by the wave of the future. Good God, said Gide, what's this! Here, but for the grace of God, am I. "Like him the fruit of mixed heredities, with different voices arguing within me, as they do in him, I recognize in him a spirit akin to my own." But he shrank from Chardonne's obscene prostration. "Seeing him reel and stagger, at once I stand erect."

Imaginary Interviews by André Gide. Translated by Malcolm Cowley. Knopf.

From this revulsion, and reviving from French defeat, Gide commenced in the literary part of the *Figaro* to write a series of self-interviews. Later he voyaged to North Africa, and in the end was compelled to go into hiding. In the little volume translated by Malcolm Cowley, there are sixteen of these interviews between Ego and Alter Ego, and added to them the review of Chardonne's collaborationist book, an introduction to Goethe's plays, and a rather short and thin report of the liberation of Tunis.

An immense interest necessarily attaches to this volume. André Gide was 70 when the war started. He is the author of as many books as he has years. While suspect by the pro-Stalinists ever since his pellucid comments on the Russia of 1936, and of course in no way a big bow-wow in world circulation, he is still one of those hundred-eyed men who see all round and into everything. A target for the pro-Vichy snipers as well as the pro-Stalinists, it is the fashion to call him "Old Narcissus" on one side, or to chop him down as querulous, petulant, superficial, on the other. Being so quick to twist and turn, being above all things so susceptible and sensitive, Gide is a vulnerable man in the sense that his sincerity compels him to bear witness and he has no attitude which is ever quite divorced from its opposite. His ability to swivel, so admirable in an artist, making for such delight in a civilization, is no good in a party member. It doesn't make for solidarity in any politics. But for those who respect French genius it evokes intense curiosity. How has André Gide ridden out the storm?

These *Imaginary Interviews* were printed under the eyes of the Germans, and they provide an answer. Ostensibly André Gide was gassing about literature. He was saying charming and illuminating things about the novel, about Proust, about French metrics and prosody, all worth reading though not vastly exciting—a little like Melba toast—dry, crisp, crumbling. But this was the intended effect. The sous-entendu is different. In these self-interviews the Old Narcissus was going on record. He must be read patiently and with some imagination if one is to penetrate his code. He dwells on the heavy beat of Hugo's patriotic affirmations, that he may commend patriotism of the old open-faced kind. He gives credentials to all the big, imprecise words, to "my country, 'tis of thee," so to speak; to heart, to mind, to soul, to God. He says, and in so many words, "to resist is a form of action." The most daring artists, he says, seek "the most resistant material and the harshest limitations." "Not once," he pronounces judgment, "was Goethe touched by the shadow of fear that the very soil from which he sprang and on which his genius rested might tremble and disappear beneath him." This fear gripped André Gide, and tore from him messages in a code which many anxious Frenchmen must have been decoding.

Littré, for example, seems to be Vichy. Anti-Littré is anti-Vichy. Who can think that André Gide, in the six months from November, 1941, to the middle of 1942, was diddling with French grammar? "Depuis" Geneva! "Depuis" the time when Barres was bold enough to write! "Depuis" the Chamber of Deputies! He gives these broad hints at a time "when so many glaring errors stand out from our almost official texts and startle us when we listen to the Government radio." If that didn't hit Vichy in the teeth, what could do it?

On Page 70, owing to an unfortunate mistranslation, the point is missed that it is from Italy, the Vatican, that unmusical "harmony, harmony" is coming. On Page 131 this Huguenot individualist makes it more definite. "Cet ennemi de Rome," he spells it out. Oh, "perfectly correct," but "when the fruit is ripe it should be plucked." None of these essays avoids the problem of collaboration. On the previous page: "The Church reeled and tottered on its foundation. The foundation had to be changed."

At this period, we must remember, the Gestapo were pushing toothdrills through the gums and the jawbones of their prisoners. They were making their prisoners walk barefoot on upturned razor blades. Gide knew that. That is why he wrote lines like these: "Young poets," to whom on Page 12 he gives the defense of culture in general—"young poets should be concerned with beginnings; let old men weep over what is passing and the dead bury the dead." This was at a time that we were collaborating with Vichy. Obviously André Gide was saying it in code. But he said it.

November 2, 1944

GERMAN COLLAPSE IN 1918

IT IS not often that a work of pure scholarship comes along to make a violent political impact, but *Armistice 1918* has this power in it. Professor Rudin is a historian by trade, and his work is outside politics. He has taken a narrow topic for his own. With a procedure as uncolored as the decimal system, he collects from all sources, but mainly German, the history of the actual seeking and concussion of the armistice proposal in 1918, and its outcome in fact. His perspective happens to be American, but his method is flawless. What gives the book so much hitting power is that it has no bias, and we can utilize it with the utmost confidence.

Everybody who thinks of 1918 has certain questions to offer—who asked for the armistice?; did we bait the Germans with the Fourteen Points and then fail to deliver them?; should we have "gone to Berlin"? Out of these answers may spring a new power of decision. We lost the last peace. What must we do not to lose this one? With Professor Rudin's scrupulous survey in our hands, we can at least be informed on what went wrong in our previous dealings with the Germans.

Who did ask for the armistice? Hitler's legend is that the army never quit, and this assertion is basic in *Mein Kampf* and nazism. Being a pathological liar, Hitler can assert with such furious zeal that "the stab in the back" seems plausible. *Armistice 1918* refutes it in full detail and in slow motion.

The fact is irrefutable that Ludendorff's nerve cracked in August. In September he besought the Government to ask for an armistice, and without the loss of a day. Men like Rathenau

Armistice 1918 by Harry R. Rudin. Yale University Press.

heard it with consternation. He was obeyed. But once the machinery was set in motion, this scoundrel doubled on his tracks, and soon he was making out that the proposals had started from the Left, a betrayal of the noble German soldier.

Professor Rudin follows the trail of militarism at bay right into the garden at Spa, where the doomed Kaiser stood blanched with dismay, Hindenburg avoiding his wild gaze and the Crown Prince's officers passing in their hands, coldly admitting there was no further fight in the army or under the Hohenzollerns. Up to that point, by the way, the "liberal" Prince Max of Baden had played for time and the Kaiser.

For twenty years these things have been known but not fortified by all the evidence. Professor Rudin brings out that it was the "people," encouraged by Woodrow Wilson, who threw out the Kaiser. Their leaders openly opposed the militarists in Germany—Ebert, Erzberger, Scheidemann, Noske, Haase, Bauer. To besmirch both them and the armistice was Ludendorff's game. The future of militarism depended on it.

It is lamentably clear from Professor Rudin's research that Ludendorff had his task made easy for him. Woodrow Wilson had not gone abroad to unite himself with Clemenceau and Lloyd George in wartime. He did not win the Allied Governments and the Allied conservatives. He appealed over their heads to Socialists. He was well served by Walter Lippmann and others in devising the Fourteen Points and winning the Social Democrats with them. But as he had overlooked Arthur Balfour, Northcliffe, Sir Henry Wilson, not to speak of Lloyd George and Clemenceau and the Republican extremists, the support for his enticements was shaky.

The steely Pan-Germanists sat around on election night in 1918, rejoicing in the fact that Woodrow Wilson was in difficulty. They knew that Cabot Lodge, Theodore Roosevelt, Borah and Poindexter were in reality working for them, and they read the final results with glee. "Wilson stood repudiated at home just when he was being accepted abroad."

In a short time, with the Bolsheviks destroying the Social Democrats inside Germany, the stability that Wilson fought for became precarious. This enabled the Ludendorff-Hitler adventurers to rally unemployed officers and howl about Versailles. Even Scheidemann, regarded as a traitor by the Left, saw to his despair that he had deposed the Kaiser without gaining a workable peace. He prayed that the German hand should wither that put a signature to the Versailles treaty.

Armistice 1918 is a most valuable and instructive book on the eve of election 1944. It punctures the illusion that we could have gone on to Berlin—no soldier wanted it except General Pershing. He was no seer, but an innocent abroad. Neither Clemenceau nor Lloyd George nor Haig nor Foch nor Pétain dared to have any such program. The ice they stood on was too thin for that load of dynamite. And Woodrow Wilson knew that to avoid another war he had to help the forces of peace inside Germany. He was not working for chaos, for future wars and revolution.

History never repeats itself, and today there are no Social Democrats inside Germany to work with. But just as Hitler rejoices in Bertie McCormick today, as Ludendorff did on that election night in 1918, so we must ask ourselves how isolation, Republican and Democratic, can be kept from wrecking the peace again and producing a future for the virulent forces we are combating. It was not the Fourteen Points that went wrong. Wilson actually took over most of them. He lost the peace to Ludendorff because he was marked down by the American voter at a time when firm and loyal support was called for.

Anyone who reads this most valuable book must see that a vote on party lines, for party reasons, misses the point in 1944. I recommend this book as an eye-opener.

November 4, 1944

DANISH NOBEL PRIZE WINNER

DENMARK will be happy that Johannes V. Jensen got the Nobel Prize. Serious writer though he is, his very name is pervasive up and down Denmark. It rings like an honest coin the minute

Fra Fristaterne by Johannes V. Jensen. Gyldendal, Copenhagen, 1939.

it is sounded. Bankers, laundry women, novelists, house painters
—they all know his work. His most famous book, *The Long
Journey*, sold over 125,000 copies in his native country, and
that means it has been read by one out of every seven or eight
persons.

The unique quality of this book is hard to account for.
When I asked Danes about him, six years ago, the answer was
often vague. A novelist? Not primarily. A philosopher? Possibly. A biologist? Not of any school. Is he a Communist, a
Fascist, hard-boiled, soft-boiled? No exact response. Even the
content of his work somehow defies definition. But above
everything he is a great critic of human history, using his language creatively, a poet and a seer.

This poet Jensen strikes a visitor as a full, wise, ripe human
being. Like many of his unsentimental kind from Jutland, he
has a way of being silent that is a power in itself. Silence seems
to fall on him like a doom. It occupies him, as being unoccupied seems to occupy an unoccupied house. It is not disdainful,
but it is final. It is as if he had never communicated, and he
stays gravely silent, like an image carved in a hard wood.

But when he speaks—this slender, reddish blond, rather
smallish man—he is expressive like a steady fire in the hearth.
He speaks from his center. The whole man is in it. A smile
lights up, like a tongue of flame, crisp and animated. And behind whatever he says, with its irony seldom absent, there is a
rounded wisdom, a force not of the will but of a long and
beautiful integration. It is for the dignity of this deep independence that he merited the Nobel Prize.

The first time I met Johannes V. Jensen I asked him about
Ibsen. He smiled. "Ibsen did not know Asia." Later I read one
of Johannes V.'s own stories, about a coolie in Singapore. Something in it would have certainly escaped the Ibsen microscope.
Primitive hunger was in it, old fears minimized, new fears in-
tensified, and long before the war it had stark struggle and
geological ages behind it. A citizen of the globe was living it
—but also a Dane, a free man, not encumbered by a political
need to embrace an empire and yet free to embrace a world.

What would he think of America? We crossed on the liner

Drottningholm with him in the winter of 1939, when he and his wife came for a fresh look at it. They went about it simply. They wanted the full flood of people as such, stayed in a hotel on Broadway, covered the country in day coaches, steeped themselves in it, she like a golden daughter of the sagas become matron and he, at 66, as faithful as a lighthouse keeper to his own luminous task. He wrote a short book about America, 130 pages, not yet in English but incomparably good.

What arrested his imagination was the great buoyant country itself. He saw it for the future adventure of man in a free continent. He saw the fresh page that the white race had turned for itself, with Jefferson writing a legend near the top of it, a line that Johannes V. Jensen knew to have preceded 1789. But this was not a new world for milk faces alone. He was agitated less than any other observer about this race business. The adventure of the immigrant was in it for him, the Red Man, the passive Black Man, outlined in singularly few words but caught in profile, felt and understood.

Anyone who has flown in a plane over America, who has seen the same duel of land and water in Florida that can be seen in the Netherlands, anyone who has passed from rugged Oklahoma to the neat autograph of man in Illinois, must be rather amazed how Johannes V. Jensen, seated in a day coach, could detect the landscape's lineaments. He had been prepared for the Mississippi by Mark Twain and met it with living recognition, but the red of Georgia and the flora of the desert were perceived as related to other landscapes, and what he saw in Central Park were the outcropped rocks with their markings from the glaciers. That is what you call a man for continuities. Over twenty years before, the handsome Rupert Brooke, recently from Cambridge, held up America by the tail and said El Cuspidorado. Funny enough. But this older man had too broad a base for the clever, immediate point—and he had only 130 pages for 130,000,000 people. He called his book *From the Free States*, which in 1939 implied a great deal. He brought proportion, weight and comprehension to *Fra Fristaterne*. It has an untroubled tone, an equanimity, that mellows Asia into it, and links Arizona with Africa. Since he wrote it the very youths he watched with reflective and sympathetic eyes have actually enveloped a world that was already "one world" for him.

He had been in America before. He had stayed in Chicago in 1903-4, brooding on a life he put in novels; and it was a strange thought for me that in 1904 I was living in the next street to his, near neighbors long ago. We talked of Frank Norris, whose epic sweep had clearly enchanted him at that period. He has the eye for epic. He has it when he sees the Red Indian girls in California who are made for motherhood. He has it when he speaks of Walt Disney. But in the Arcady of the Far West, this lover of Herodotus is made lonely for continuous historic memory. He has lived, like so many Danes, in that country of the mind where they have made their own proud and bloodless conquests, and there dwells on it the temperate light that was first shed by Sparta and Athens. It lies benignly on this poet, but his is a Greece in which there are no slaves.

November 23, 1944

AMERICAN WELLSPRINGS

To go down to bedrock, what is the American faith for which our men are dying? Prof. Ralph Barton Perry teaches philosophy at Harvard, and for as long as he has been a thinking man he has been probing and digging for the bases of American faith. He gives his answer in *Puritanism and Democracy*.

Why not learn the answer? The only obstacle is that Professor Perry has written a book of between 225,000 and 250,000 words. If you happen to have forty hours to devote to it, saying good-by to wife, child and dog, the answer is yours for the asking. And in no easier way can you get at the heart of this lifework.

And when you have finished the book, so ramified and

Puritanism and Democracy by Ralph Barton Perry. Vanguard Press.

faceted is the argument, you might just as well begin it again. If you do this, you won't die of emptiness. You may burst.

It would be idle to pretend that, in conducting this vast intellectual campaign, Professor Perry hasn't bogged down at times. At about Page 560, I found it necessary to make myself a pot of tea. The situation arose when I read the following several times.

"They who should govern are those who are not likely to serve those for whom the polity exists. The democratic answer is that that polity exists for all those who live within it."

But every brave, exhaustive campaign has Battles of the Wilderness. This book of Professor Perry's is meat and drink for a true democrat. It will be read and assimilated by everyone who hungers for responsible thinking on the issue of all issues, this issue of an American faith and meaning. It is no poetic outburst. The author does sometimes get into the pulpit but he seems to think of it as a teacher's podium rather than a poet's crow's nest. Stay with him, however, and you have brain stuff as well as edification.

Everyone knows how Puritanism went out of repute. Superficially, it did not survive certain of its excesses—Rum, Romanism and Rebellion; fundamentalism; prohibition. The "pride of power" behind it, the "hard heart" and "cutting edge," needed a Deity backed by a Bible still unquestioned in detail. But there was also a thirst for compassion on which the Puritan frowned.

The Way of All Flesh, by Samuel Butler, gave one history of revolt. Edmund Gosse gave another. *Life With Father* brought this revolt into the region of national comedy. "What shall be done," asked Cotton Mather, "for the raising of Sammy's Mind, above the debasing Meannesses of Play?" Clarence Day answered with a play and raised the roof instead. *Life With Father* blew up the pulpit.

It was bound to happen. To love God through beauty would not have impaired the love of God, but the Puritans did not merely flee Babylon, they fled Shakespeare. Narrowed and impoverished by this, in spite of Emerson's fine radiance, many writing Americans recently took violent exception to our real or supposed meagerness. The pure loveliness of Godly desire under the elms lost its savor for them. Part of Professor Perry's work, in some ways the best part, is his recovery of the Puritan mood, its dignity, its integrity, its profundity. And America is inexplicable without it.

Between Jonathan Edwards and Thomas Jefferson he indicates Locke's philosophy as the bridgework. The Virginian was as much an American as any New Englander, and yet in nothing but his individualism was he a Puritan. More than that, the Puritan's revolt against authority was individualism for the sake of submission to God's will. Jefferson, as the motto of the book declares, borrowed God for a human end. "Rebellion to tyrants is obedience to God." Jefferson's gaze was on the tyrants.

Scarcely a modern issue, whether it be the case of Jehovah's Witnesses, civil liberties, conscientious objection, Government ownership, world organization, but has deep roots in the complex of ideas here proposed and examined. One can go back to Roger Williams from the dilemmas of Justice Jackson. One can go from modern penology to that "retributive penal justice" built by the Puritan into "the basic structure of the world."

Can we do without this harshness? Can democracy reach rectitude without rectangularity? If "irreconcilable dissent" requires coercion, how then can Professor Perry say that "the reasons which justify authority are not those which justify it to itself, but to those who are asked to obey"? Professor Perry says many witty things, such as "the true individualist will hold to his own independent judgment, even when others agree with him." But liberal independence is faced by the "antithesis between the bond of community and freedom of individuality." It has to deal with the state. "The state may be the individual's best friend," says our author. What kind of state? Hobbes'? Machiavelli's? Stalin's? One state's benevolence may be another's tyranny. And that doesn't even touch on the problem for the benevolent democrat presented by the stony-hearted who are anti-benevolent.

A philosopher who strives to bring a civilization into focus should be judged, however, in the large. Professor Perry has accomplished a great task. It was worth his heroic toil. He has gone to living fountains of our hope and wisdom. There is a Niagara of national faith and will to peace that pours through his pages. No one can see it who sees only its spray, its broken water, its turmoil.

January 13, 1945

THE USES OF LOGIC

NEW YORK has its own claims to greatness, all the way from *Carmen Jones* to its philosophers. Over fifty years ago Morris R. Cohen was brought here from Minsk by his sensible parents. He went to the College of the City of New York, and later to the Harvard of William James. That great teacher was devoted to Morris Cohen, and a luminous being like William James naturally excited the pupil's mind as much as he won his pupil's affection.

But the master's flair for drama, the artist in William James, meant less to Morris Cohen than the speculative thinker. If Morris Cohen was able to envisage a Kierkegaard very early, or to see for himself the pertinence of a John Scotus Erigena, it may have been partly due to the Jamesian catholicity. But Morris Cohen's vigilant and incisive mind gave him his grasp on Einstein because of a native discipline and severity. Devoted as he is to ideas for the sake of reality, he seems to dwell in that philosophic climate where clocks do not tick so much as thoughts, and the immediate effect is not part of what he likes to call "the calculus." All this is evident in his latest book, a relatively small book, *A Preface to Logic*.

It might be supposed, at least on the 8:15 train, that a non-student could be spared *A Preface to Logic*. Being the work of a professional philosopher, it is addressed primarily to students, and indeed it is dedicated to the College of the City of New York "and its students who gave zest to my life." But philosophers are passport officials who admit, or refuse to ad-

A Preface to Logic by Morris R. Cohen. Henry Holt.

mit, the ideas that become decisive in our lives. Any man who is supremely concerned about truth and has a supreme capacity for pursuing it means as much to ourselves as the guards on the coast of the continent.

Logic "does not provide the food which sustains our intellectual life," says Morris Cohen. "It is, however, like the hydrochloric acid in our stomach that helps to digest our food. It is the antiseptic of our intellectual life which prevents our food from poisoning us."

He does not pretend that illusions, like dancing and drinking cocktails, are not more attracting. "Unless we realize the pleasant character of illusion, as similar to that of intoxicating liquors, fumes or physical gyrations, we cannot understand the course of human history." He also agrees that "close reasoning is an arduous undertaking for which few have the opportunity, the equipment and the inclination." But he asserts with force that "the exercise of thought along logical lines is the great liberation, or, at any rate, the basis of all civilization."

Does he make one feel this? Yes. In the nine chapters of his book, proceeding from a discussion of the subject-matter of logic to the nature of meaning and probability, he reaches conclusions that are at the root of conduct and ethics.

He knows the illogicality of most moralizing, for example. "Thou shalt not steal" gives little light on surtax. "Ethical certainty is not a brute datum with which the unreflective conscience starts but rather a rational ideal which we can approach only through a process of refinement and qualification." Relativism in this sense is no enemy of ethical certainty. And logic can free us "from the twin evils of the vicious absolutism that, by ignoring the variability of human tastes and objectives, would condemn all mankind to a Procrustean bed and, on the other hand, the vicious relativism that, by denying all universal principles and objective truths, would imprison each of us in an isolated subjective world."

His power to liberate the mind works in two directions. It uses logic to assail "absolute" certainties, but at the same time to maintain that things which are not verifiable can have meaning. "The assumption that there is nothing beyond the physical is in itself essentially metaphysical." He thinks that "ethics must be able to give reasons for differences of attitude," and he also urges that ideas cannot be annihilated in a world where "norms are more than preferences." "Without ideas, nature is one big blooming confusion."

On language, too, he uses logic on the broad assumption that the "function of language is the communication of ideas." The babbling of babes and the maundering of psychotics are sure of respect in 1944, but Morris Cohen makes numerous observations that touch on *Finnegans Wake*, without mentioning it. Experts on Joyce's work might well study this.

The non-student of *A Preface to Logic* may ruefully deplore the shorthand. "Logical relations may be viewed ontologically as the invariants in the transformations of all possible objects." Sentences like this are worse than instructions in a golf manual. But since we have not paid the entrance fee, and are yet allowed into the philosopher's sanctum, we can be grateful for these discourses. They have integrity and breadth. Such logic, in his own words, "widens our sympathetic understanding and breaks the backbone of fanaticism."

February 10, 1945

WHERE ETHICS BEGIN

Nobody is likely to break Brentano's window to get quick hold of *Politics and Morals*, by Benedetto Croce. But even if it happened frequently, Croce's is not the kind of new book to stir young America to frenzy. It talks of dynamics, but in words that have no electricity, unless you are wired for it. So modulated is the text, so relaxed the translation, so slipshod the proofreading, so inexpert the editing, that the book does not take its place with any *brio*. It just slides into its pew. Nothing indicates how and where and when it came into existence in Italy. Nobody says a word to introduce it. But Signor Croce is a

Politics and Morals by Benedetto Croce. Philosophical Library.

great witness to our moral drama in the present political arena. He is a witness who deserves honor, attention and respect, and his book is significant.

First of all, perhaps, for its revelation of a liberal Italian mind, one with history behind it, and a profound appreciation of history.

Every nation goes its own way about political morality, just as it does about such a humble thing as its traffic problem. The motor car did not come into a world prepared for it. It came as an amoral fact, and one that had to be taken care of. The very notion of a one-way street, or a hospital street, or a school street, is repugnant to laissez-faire. The whole question of rotary traffic, of parking, of U turns, of green and red lights, grows out of a condition that was not bargained for in the first place. But what Benedetto Croce insists upon in laying down "Elements of Politics" is the unavoidability of much that is amoral. He is not a rebel against the changing universe we live in. He rebels, yes, against "nature apart from history and reason without reality." But the conflict of morality with politics, as he sees it, cannot storm against the practical, the useful, the necessary. The conflict is never with traffic problems as such.

Hence Machiavelli and Vico seem to him unquestionably right to start with reality. "For Vico, politics, force, the creative energy of States, becomes a phase of the human spirit and of the life of society, an eternal phase, the phase of certainty, which is followed eternally, through dialectic development, by the phase of truth, of reason fully explained, of justice and of morality, or ethics." Thus he insists on "the necessity and autonomy of politics, of politics which is beyond or, rather, below moral good and evil, which has its own laws against which it is useless to rebel, politics that cannot be exorcised and driven from the world by holy water." There must even be traffic accidents, he seems to say without cynicism, there must be brutalities inherent in the nature of traffic.

With the inexorable so firm in his Italian mind, though he darts the word "Providence" into his text now and then, he has no hesitation about ripping into Rousseau. Liberty, equality and fraternity are hollow myths to him. They are "simply absurd." And democracy, "by idolizing equality conceived in an extrinsic and mechanical way, tends, whether it wishes to or not, toward authoritarianism." If this grew out of extravagant theory, "in the century of Illuminism, in the Age of Reason, that is, of intellectual and abstract reason, and in France in particular," an equally faulty concept came out of Germany, through "understanding ethics in a somewhat partial way, as State, and in separating the State from the varied and complex life, both moral and political."

So much for the general lines of the argument, with references to Campanella, Zuccolo, Spaventa, Hegel, Haller, Hobhouse. But Croce is not hard-boiled for the sake of authority. He is a confirmed liberal. Since he thinks Machiavelli performed a most important service in bringing politics down to earth, out of the moralistic warehouse, Croce adverts to the realist's "stern and sorrowful moral conscience," but when Croce has settled his account with the moralistic, he shows his own faith in ethical concept, refers with scorn to the hard and unyielding hearts of statesmen whose names were Bismarck and Disraeli, and in a long and fascinating chapter takes issue with the whole concept of "bourgeois."

The bourgeois, as he sees the gentleman, is not the little potbellied man to whom Saint-Simon, both as an old aristocrat and as a new apostle of socialism, was averse. The bourgeois is the man from whom ethics goes back into politics. The bourgeois, or middle class, "must be understood more widely and in its pure sense as the total of those who have an ardent desire for the public good, suffer its passion, sharpen and define their concepts for this necessity, and act accordingly."

Croce even goes as far as "free enterprise" with the bourgeois, until free enterprise gets too gay. "The difficulty appears as soon as we give to the system of free enterprise the value of a norm or of supreme law of social life; because in that case it is placed next to ethical and political liberalism, which is also declared the norm and supreme law of social life. Of necessity a conflict arises. Obviously, two laws on the same level to cover the same matter are too many: there is one too many."

So pliant and refined is Croce's intelligence that his reader must be alert. At times, in the company of such an Italian, the heart is like a plaintive and bewildered pointer, waiting for his master's voice. But Croce does commit himself. He runs true to form. Aristocratic and Catholic reactionaries are just as alien to him as Labriola or Sorel. He is one of those Europeans for whom equilibrium has no meaning unless the moral springs can stand a total shock. His own intellectual springs are subtly resilient and of invincible steel. "And there are no remedies which can take the place of the intellectual and moral conscience, or that can be of help to that conscience unless it can help itself."

March 3, 1945

MARSHALL FIELD EXPLAINS

THE first Marshall Field made pots of money out of dry goods and real estate. His grandson, Marshall Field 3d, is now in possession of a colossal fortune and wishes to "contribute toward making democratic freedom more than just a word." To this end he has financed two newspapers, *PM* in New York and the *Sun* in Chicago. Besides this, he is putting money into ways of ascertaining public opinion, into using radio, and into great projects for book publishing. Considering that the old Marshall Field was a real Horatio Alger character, terrified of poverty, and tying up his millions so that no harm might come to the precious stuff, these radical activities of his grandson are striking by contrast and as compensation.

Now the grandson has written a book, *Freedom Is More Than a Word*, which sets forth his ideas. He says he has had the help of his friends, and he names Alfred M. Lee, Max Lerner, Louis S. Weiss and James Warburg. It is, on the whole, a book of copious generalizations, a labor to read, but with a personal touch at times, courage and charm, and faith that "de-

Freedom Is More Than a Word by Marshall Field. University of Chicago Press.

mocracy and human beings, given a real chance, can develop
to heights yet undreamed of."

The Grand Duke of hereditary journalism in Chicago, Col.
R. R. McCormick, has the Associated Press services there,
and when he had to think of sharing them with Marshall Field,
in the name of free enterprise, he roared. "Marshall Field is not
a legitimate newspaper man," he said, "and the *Sun* is not a
legitimate newspaper. It is part of an alien and radical conspiracy against our republican form of government." So it cost
Mr. Field half a million dollars in 1942 to get comparable services. "The AP Case" is a chapter on this example of free enterprise.

On the banks of the Drainage Canal, free speech may be a
conspiracy. In Mr. Field's book it is an open muddle, openly
arrived at. In spite of desperate lunges to break into thought,
Mr. Field may have impaired his capacity for it at Eton and
Cambridge. In spite of telling himself that "a certain lack of
gentlemanliness is a requisite of democracy," and that, for
goodness' sake, we need "more and better crackpots," he finds
it hard to escape conventional radicalism and he grips slippery
truth with no great firmness. His socialism and his capitalism
talk at cross-purposes.

For example, while he claims nothing for private property—
"there is, of course, no such thing as an inherent right of private property"—he affirms that "the long continuance of any
enterprise must be based upon its ability to achieve economic
independence." In other words, *PM* and the *Chicago Sun* must
make good as private property and have the best of both
worlds.

In the same way, extolling Judge Learned Hand's great
dictum that the spirit of liberty is the spirit that weighs the
interests of others "along with its own without bias," Marshall
Feld still openly justifies bias in *PM* in the interest of the un-
derdog and the class struggle. Similarly he talks of "freedom
of access to facts" and yet lays it down that the Soviets "have
the good sense to forswear any attempt to impose their ideology aggressively on other countries." Apparently this "fact" is
self-evident to him and "courage against injustice" belongs

exclusively to his side. If Max Lerner advocates "naked force," it makes for justice and "equality of position," while if Bertie McCormick were to advocate "naked force," it would be the crime of the ages.

The dash and daring of *PM* captured many people of generous spirit, and "the groping of one man's mind," as Marshall Field calls his book, is toward humane ideals. But the weakness of his position, as *Freedom Is More Than a Word* indicates it, arises from the sort of one-sided thinking so frequent in *PM*.

Big-hearted radicalism does win the generous. Pulitzer and Scripps and Hearst, in their own fashion, espoused "the welfare of the public." But when the class tone hardens into ideology, when modifications in "our present social system" are demanded "or else," the fact of Marshall Field's money necessarily obtrudes itself on his reader. "When the strong start a drive for power," he says meekly, "the rest of us are confronted with the sheer necessity of forming a cooperative alliance to keep the strong from enslaving us." This is sheer cant. Marshall Field is not a small, weak man in danger of being enslaved. He and his advisers are engaged in a drive for power. He, too, wishes "to push other people around," the Poles and the Baltic states if no one else, and his book is blind to one big fact about a democracy—namely, that economic categories are not made of cast iron. He is himself a proof of it.

At the time Max Lerner was a child in Russia, it was a Marshall Field who was the wicked one in Chicago, and it was Joseph Medill Patterson and Bill Hard who pursued him for breaking the city's by-laws. By a long democratic process this Marshall Field fortune is now by way of being made socially responsible. This, considering its humble moral origins, is about time. But Mr. Field turns on too much heat. He is too tough with others. If a Marshall Field can be saved, so can anybody.

April 19, 1945

AMERICAN CAPITALISM

WHOEVER named John F. Wharton's book must be something of a fisherman, because the essential words have a lure in them, *Earning a Living.* Ten million soldiers and sailors, more or less, must get back into civilian jobs, and the title is one that the fish ought to leap at. There are sentences at the beginning which seem to bear it out. "Any man or woman, with initiative, intelligence, industriousness, and health, can, if he or she learns the propositions set forth in these pages, be almost certain of personal financial success." But this isn't really what the book is about. Nor does Mr. Wharton promise success to the man or woman of ability. He is a realist, as a corporation lawyer should be.

His tart realism appears later on. "It is a pleasant theory that if, as Emerson once postulated, a man builds a better mousetrap, the world will beat a path to his door, but in the modern world the cold truth is that they will beat the path to the door of the man who makes them believe he has the better mousetrap." In other words, granted all the other abilities, you cannot possibly rely on the world to do what Emerson said it would do. You may not even have "the better mousetrap," though without it your "success may be short-lived." But you simply must have "the ability to convince people that you have the goods and services that they wish to buy." In short, salesmanship. Initiative, brains, energy, health; but you must know how to market them, you must be confident, you must be convincing. Confronted by Pontius Pilate, you must have the ability to convince him that you have "the goods and services."

But this is Mr. Wharton's window-dressing. His own goods, the goods that he really wishes to sell, are substantial and genuine. His book is one of the very best accounts of American capitalism, its virtues and its dangers, that the layman can get hold of. It is a frank, keen-minded, crisp statement of the eco-

The Theory and Practice of Earning a Living by John F. Wharton. Simon & Schuster.

nomic world we live in, in contrast to the world the Russians live in, and Mr. Wharton's ingenuity is amazing. He can show how Emerson's mousetrap, invented in the woods, can be put on the market, financed in Wall Street and given to the world, with all the gains that it promises, all the vicissitudes that threaten it. He is entirely familiar with the structure of business, but he shows it inside a social philosophy. He shows it in order to disclose what "has led to the world-wide movement for communistic, socialistic, and fascist governments," believing that "the end of the conflict between totalitarianism and economic democracy is not yet in sight."

Mr. Wharton does not think that in principle the totalitarian system of communism is either an invention of the devil or a contravention of our accepted standards of right and wrong, though in practice he admits that "the Russian Communists at one time sought to stamp out religion." But he does see the many points at which the two economic theories and practices conflict, and while leaving academic discussion of interest and profit to one side he refuses to close his eyes to such weaknesses in capitalism as bring it under fire in the great conflict. "It is possible to 'make money,' as the phrase goes, without creating any usable wealth, or without creating very much usable wealth, or even by restricting the amount of producible wealth." In these and other respects he finds our own system vulnerable.

Vulnerable, that is to say, in a basic conflict of systems. *The Theory and Practice of Earning a Living*, to give his book its full title, is founded on Mr. Wharton's belief "that American representative democracy, with all its faults, is the best method that mankind has yet devised" by which ambitious, creative people can have the freest possible scope without asking "the mass of mankind to take undue risks of insecurity." But this belief does not hide all the snags in such a phrase as "free enterprise." It does not conceal the viciousness in land speculation or the fact that Russia makes land speculation impossible. It does not gloss over the hard facts about underpaid American coal miners simply because there are dangers in unregulated monopoly by labor unions. And if Russia can solve production, "the greatest attraction of communism to the proletariat," "communism doesn't solve the other half of the problem—the desire of the ambitious young man or woman to be his own boss and select his own career."

A typewriter that had a key for every stereotype would be like communism in its worst aspect, freezing all enterprise, while our keyboard system offers the maximum of freedom to the operator. But Mr. Wharton is of an inventive turn of mind, and he can conceive of stenotypy, so to speak, which has ideographs that are not infertile like Chinese symbols but actually an improvement on single letters in the alphabet, forms of combination that save time and give a higher efficiency. "Socialized medicine," as he sees it, is this sort of stenotypy. As you read him, his candor about the hard processes of financing, so clearly depicted and analyzed, seems only less valuable than his many-sided view of its advantages. This is a good book. It hides nothing. If "basic conflicts inevitably end in war," America can at least "resolve conflict" at home by this sort of patient scrutiny. Thus democracy will earn its own living.

July 14, 1945

Poetry

EMILY DICKINSON

THOSE already aware of Emily Dickinson will wish to pursue her strange story, perhaps the strangest in New England literature. She was, as Samuel Ward put it, "the articulate inarticulate," and two volumes now added by Millicent Todd Bingham to the existing text will give much to patient readers, whether they knew of her before or not. *Ancestors' Brocades* is a story of Emily's so-called "literary debut" which came with publication after her death in 1886, and here also is a big volume of poems never before published, *Bolts of Melody*.

A "phebe" (pewee), she once said ironically, "makes a little print upon the floors of fame." She was no "phebe." Instead of going mad, as many New England spinsters do, Emily swung herself out of the dark and off the ground, gentle master of a blazing imagination. In some ways uncouth, she was to become a bold pathfinder in the infinite. Hers was a solo flight over a wilder ocean than Lindbergh's, and pursued to a heroic end. *Bolts of Melody* adds new regions to it.

Emily Dickinson worked secretively. She made only one attempt to write for the public. About 1864 she sent a poem to her cousins, "The Sweetsers." They liked it and gave it space in their periodical, *The Round Table*. Irritated New Englanders, however, began to throw brickbats because this young woman said she would rather listen to a bobolink than a sermon. It was a charming but pert poem, as so often happens with the shy young poet. Public severity drove her under cover. She cut herself off and went silent.

Ancestors' Brocades by Millicent Todd Bingham. Harper & Bros.
Bolts of Melody, new poems of Emily Dickinson. Harper & Bros.

Her brother William was treasurer of Amherst, married to a slow, rich-natured, brooding wife. Emily had a sharp-tongued sister whose two passions "were cats and her sister Emily." The mother was a meek little thing. The father was a devastating person, a storm that always seemed to impend and benumb the spectator. "Squire Dickinson," said a photographer to him, "could you—smile a little?" To which the Squire thundered back, "I *yam* smiling." "As for Amherst, Emily met an unbroken front of blinking bewilderment."

With her home a proud New England prison, amid "the welter of Dickinson animosities," and with feelings whipped to keenness by being starved, Emily Dickinson withdrew from the exterior world, writing reams on scraps of paper much corrected. "For several years," she once said, "my lexicon was my only companion." But though she remained permanently indoors, turned in on herself, the life she entered upon was spacious and peopled. She was, in truth, alert at the center of a universe, with royal sunsets in her room and memories so alive that they palpitated. She was all eyes and all ears for her adventure of the spirit. She had a grasp of inner drama that Herbert or Marvell or John Donne or Thomas Wyatt would have understood, but tenderness in it like a fleeting kiss in a dark street, and tragedy like a stab. Her emotional range had no vertical limit.

These new poems do not differ in kind from the earlier ones. They were miracles of perception and surprise in this little room of hers, where the form so seldom varied and the refusal to end with a rhyme showed her constant aliveness to life's asymmetry.

The sharpest savor of her career came with this New England salt—she did nothing to win fame except deserve it. "Shortly after Emily's death," said Mrs. Bingham's mother, "her sister Lavinia came to me actually trembling with excitement. She had discovered a veritable treasure—a box full of Emily's poems which she had no instructions to destroy." Emily, prodigal in imagination, had thus left her poems to chance, thousands of them.

Such independence of the practical world was at once set

right by Lavinia, Mabel Loomis Todd, Col. Thomas Wentworth Higginson, William Dean Howells. If love had failed to smooth her life or touch her with firm help, it certainly gushed forth to help her after her death. But of course possessiveness, the thing she most shunned, grabbed at her poems. Lavinia played a part in this that is the seamy side of the *Brocades*. "I could not bear to live aloud, the racket shamed me so." Mrs. Bingham quotes this from Emily, but the racket she herself makes is terrific. One is much in doubt, at times, whether Emily is the heroine of the story or Mrs. Bingham's mercilessly executive mother, the first foreign woman to climb Fugi, and no less eager to stand on the heights of Emily Dickinson.

Still, the Todds fought bravely for the final text as Emily wrote it. And if, out of pique, fury, animosity, Mrs. Todd kept these new poems in a cedar chest for half a century, God was good and now they see the light. It is a triumph of Emily's fantastic fate, though she was strange as a flamingo in Amherst, and her fate was really not so much to be rewarded by life as to be allowed "to die divinely." These two books will find devoted readers who will be ravished by them, for Emily's sake.

April 5, 1945

COLLECTED AUDEN

W. H. AUDEN is 38 years old. Those of his own generation have lavished praise on him, both here and in England. *The Collected Poetry of W. H. Auden* is a proof of his fame, offering a reprint of his three latest volumes in their entirety, and 225 poems besides. It gives the general public a good chance to catch up with him, without searching for separate volumes.

Mr. Auden deals in enchantment, as do all poets, and in one section of his work, "Songs and Musical Pieces," he shows that he can be a sweet troubadour in the best English tradition.

The Collected Poetry of W. H. Auden. Random House.

Sometimes he slips, as when he says in a ballad, "Only their usual maneuvers, dear." But "Song for St. Cecilia's Day" is music in itself. These forty poems dance from him—"Dance, dance, for the figure is easy."

And on another, quite difficult, level he has equal felicity. That is in the poetry that seeks the inner meaning of other creators. Somewhere he calls Tolstoy a "great animal," and he taunts Montaigne as "this donnish undersexed conservative," evidently unlike the oversexed broker he met in a Pullman. Yet a hedge-hopping poet, safe in the air but close to familiarity, quite often enjoys frightening the householders. Mr. Auden is no more above this than Byron was. But sprinkled through his collection are luminous images, images of souls. His heart moved him to speak of Voltaire, Pascal, Herman Melville, Matthew Arnold, Edward Lear, W. B. Yeats, Ernst Toller, Sigmund Freud. These are quintessences.

For his own circle, however, the Auden quality is probably best shown, not in the musical pieces or in these intellectual appreciations, but in the contorted disclosure of a spiritual drama. All through his work the word "belief" asks to be rhymed with "grief." Some might think he was a post-war poet, but he is far from that; he is a post-Darwin poet, a post-Marxian poet, a post-Leopardi poet. If he can write smooth or intricate verse as easily as some gifted youths can balance a billiard cue on the nose, the reason for his being a poet is not to sing or to cut capers, it is to discover rhyme and reason in the universe. His rejection of delight comes from "his kinship with the worm and toad," and this worm is a bookworm. W. H. Auden suffers from more than Darwin's "pituitary headaches." He suffers from the immense turmoil of his brain and the traffic congestion in his infundibulum.

His is almost the problem of a Piccadilly Circus. Mr. Auden takes too much in, from too many directions. Eros is boxed up. The tarts run wild like ragweed. The place is littered with American slang. "O pray for us, the bourgeoisie." Life is ugly; poetry is life; poetry is ugly. He cannot sing, "Tiger, tiger, burning bright!" It becomes the "locomotive beauty of choleric beasts of prey." He cannot let Keats say, "Beauty is truth."

On the contrary, ugliness is truth. "Truth is knowing that we
know we lie." It is "the drip of the bathroom tap, the creak
of the sofa spring." And when the Annunciation comes to the
Virgin Mary, she speaks like a book. "What sudden rush of
power commands me to command?" These are the penalties of
his sophistication.

Yet, unlike Siegfried Sassoon in an earlier effort, he has continued to grapple with the tortures of a poet—the injustice of
society, the curse of isolation, the enigma of guilt. "Every brilliant doctor hides a murderer." "We are lived by powers."
"We love ourselves alone." "What we love ourselves for is our
power not to love." "Gone from the map the shore where
childhood played." Yes, he doggedly chutes the chutes and
bumps the bumps and loops the loops and also hurdies the
gurdy. It is for this sour sincerity he forswears enchantment.

With such a spiritual revulsion against "vital lies," W. H.
Auden was a bleak, anxious person when the war came, as
much outside political responsibility as a cat burglar is outside
the house, though more on the inside than its inhabitants, and
compelled to mount hand over hand, though giving himself
nightmares, rather than use the bourgeois elevator. He could
not join a mob, since he was both "arrogant and self-insulated,"
to borrow his own words. He was drowning in despair, but
without reproach. "The sea misuses nothing because it values
nothing."

In truth, however, the sea misuses everything because it
values nothing. With his knowledge of "immeasurable neurotic
dread," W. H. Auden at last learns to swim in this convul-
sive sea of his. Anyone who suffered with him as he went
through the right motions in his empty tank must now rejoice
at his total immersion in a medium of belief. Only in a freedom
of surrender can these rebel English poets capture the oldest of
human release, the change from prose to poetry, from rapid
transits of the mind to an emotional transport.

April 12, 1945

POETS IN UNIFORM

POETS in wartime are tracers that throw a blazing light on their experience, against which most of them are rebellious. We may be sure that if the draft boards had rejected them for military service, as they do priests, we'd still be hearing about it. Certain French priests like to be enlisted as citizens, comrades and men. But when service is compulsory, and in a war of which W. H. Auden did not approve, the sensitive and sensuous young men are far more eager to take up arms against the compulsion than against the enemy. Then you have the kind of extraordinary anthology that Oscar Williams has edited in *The War Poets*.

It is the belief of a man like Gov. Earl Warren that "a highly courageous, steadfast heart" is standard equipment. "There is no pessimism, no defeatism, no bitterness, no jauntiness among us," he announced in a campaign speech. Mr. Williams would scorn that. He has taken care to select over a hundred poets, sixty of them in British or American uniforms, who for a considerable part see in the capitalist a darker enemy than the German and the Japanese. Mr. Williams drives this in with hammer and tongs, or perhaps one should say hammer and sickle. He favors poets who have "compassion for all who suffer everywhere, not only in combat but from the evils of poverty and social pressures intolerable to human beings," which is propaganda, not poetry.

Mr. Williams elects Auden as "the major war poet of the first half of the century." Auden's poem on Spain urged class war, "the conscious acceptance of guilt in the necessary murder." And many of the young, who gorge on the immediate issue of the class struggle, rush to disown the very notion of political democracy. War "is productive of no good," according to Sgt. Vernon Watkins. Trooper Julian Symons speaks of "the second capitalist war" and sees no national distinctions. "In the Brown House at Munich, In the White House at

The War Poets edited by Oscar Williams. John Day.

Washington, Life also continues in suffering and pity." Corp. Dick Roberts says to his buddy, "See now, dead friend, Where they have taken you, The men who persuaded you of patriotism."

A bon voyage basket is like an anthology, offering one or two items of the best. The morsels in this basket are "terrible" because this war cannot be "justified" and "my participation," as Lieut. Roy Fuller says, "and that of all the world is terrible." Hence we have items of terror, "a sailor, leg cut off," "a soldier, right arm missing," "a marine, face gone," "the hot smell of oranges and feet," while a dead ball turret gunner confides, "When I died they washed me out of the turret with a hose."

Mr. Williams thinks this is fine and realistic. He is hostile to such bourgeois as Rupert Brooke, Alan Seeger, Edna St. Vincent Millay, and carries a placard saying "Unfair to the union. Don't trade here." Which induces E. E. Cummings to say to him, "You'll never be satisfied until what Father Abraham called 'a new nation, conceived in liberty,' becomes just another subhuman superstate (like the 'great freedom-loving democracy' of Comrade Stalin) where an artist—or any other human being—either does as he's told or turns into fertilizer."

The ferment in these war poets is partly the heat of youth, the kind of thing that made the Vineyard Gazette recently observe in a nature note, "The young birds of 1945 are beginning to act tough with their parents." But there is more in this bristling book than a recoil from inept democracy and a hateful and unwanted war. We have cruel sights and grim insights —engine failure, parachute descent, mess deck casualty, officers' prison camp, troop train, Red Cross nurse, blood and whores and homesickness. But recrimination against our own society is not the exclusive note. "The greatness of the human soul," Pascal once said, "consists in knowing how to preserve the average. So far from greatness consisting in leaving it, it consists in not leaving it." And many of the poets have this allegiance to the common lot. While they show the tigerish grip that war takes on shrinking and vulnerable flesh, they do not, in the interest of new politics, blame old politicians for their violated lives.

Hence Gervase Stewart sang, "I burn for England with a living flame"; Randall Swingler sings, "Freedom is but wholeness"; Gavin Ewart chants, "the happy, tough battalions"; F. T. Prince can say, "Some great love is over all we do. And that is what has driven us to fury." These are less rebellious natures, perhaps; though smashed and pierced by the pain of war, they have wealth enough to square the conventional bill and still be poets.

No less than eleven of the contributors have died in the two wars, and Mr. Williams, though not a good proofreader, has taken pains to assemble many fascinating photographs, some personal history, and a number of contributors' comments on "war poetry." His volume is often arid, contorted and prosaic. Some writhe in the inferno. Some report with sparkle and glint. Some are contentious and sterile. But this is a manifesto of the contemporary spirit, and a few transcend its hard limits. Possessing the magic dimension of the poet, they are able to canopy a war with it.

July 19, 1945

Fiction

COLLISION WITH BOSTON

For an ambitious young writer the difficulties of a big first novel are huge. The actual form can be varied from the neatness of Jane Austen to the sprawl of Thomas Wolfe, and the communication can cover a whole hippodrome of history or settle down on a trifle, like a thimble on a pearl. The novel has no rules. It is the greatest free-for-all yet discovered in the region of self-expression, and as psychiatry and psychology open up new quarries for the digger, the hazards increase with the opportunities. But the young are fearless, and the response to their happy or unhappy experiments often depends on the fact that there are plenty of readers who are hounds for novelty and applaud it for its own sake rather than in relation to any sharp acumen.

For this reason Miss Jean Stafford can be pretty confident of excited praise for her extravagantly colored *Boston Adventure*. Her basic story is a simple one. An 11-year-old girl, the child of a German father, has to act as substitute for her Russian mother, who is chambermaid in a summer hotel that has a view of Boston in the distance. The little chambermaid attracts Miss Pride, the quintessence of wealthy old Back Bay, and eventually Sonia is taken into Miss Pride's home as a sort of companion. The "adventure" of Sonia Marburg among the Back Bay elite, and in relation to two men, one a Jew with a flagrant birthmark, the other a Bostonian with a stiff spine, both symbolic, make the story, if one omits the birth of a brother, his funeral and several epileptic fits.

To this simple tale of the immigrant in the heart of Back Bay, with the German father disappearing from his cobbler's

Boston Adventure by Jean Stafford. Harcourt, Brace.

bench and the Russian mother warehoused in a lunatic asylum, we have added the ingredient that makes *Boston Adventure* the real novelty. This is Sonia's temperament. She is an exceptional girl. Deaf to music and yet swirling in the chants and ballads that her folk have brought from Europe, condemned to chores but winged by imagination to transport herself to castles or dungeons, she is primarily and eminently a book-fed creature, and it is by the bridge of literature that she crosses the chasm from fantastic poverty to the new life in which she is at once a shrinking, quivering adventurer and a hostile and resentful refugee.

The period antedates the war, but even in peacetime this romantic Germanic girl is not quite sure whether her arm is raised in salute or in self-defense. She loves Miss Pride and holds out her hand to her, but occasionally she biffs her in the eye. Sonia is enormously centered on Sonia. She hates her mother. She detests the business college to which Miss Pride is sending her. She is afflicted with powerful solemnities and a sense of maladjustment. But the engine of this ego is eight-cylinder, so that Sonia's jarred progress throbs with the thrust and leap of her emotions, and carries her forward, parallel to the Bostonians and on a level with them, but in a different laneway.

The pleasure of this excursion in Sonia Marburg's company is handicapped. Not only is Jean Stafford determined to write literature at any cost, but she is also determined to give us tons of whipped cream on it. On the first page the storm signal is raised for any reader who has learned to fear the influence of Virginia Woolf: the dome of the State House in Boston is seen as a "golden blister." Soon the sun shines with a "rowdy blaze." Obfuscated films at the Bijou "which wavered before our eyes like dispirited ectoplasm bore no more relationship to entertainment than the lusterless exterior bore to any jewel known to man." This is the 11-year-old who observes the Bijou.

"The cold from the windows laid metallic ribbons across my back." "The heard, but unseen, white skirts of the sea fluttered sweetly against its boundaries. Just as Nathan's kisses in the fog had warmed my sorrow to its bloom, and my love, though contiguous, had only served to enhance its somber colors, so the young physician's accidental exhumation of Boston had, immediately afterward, caused me to see the loveliness of Chichester to which for several months I had been indifferent. And now, stopping to bury my face in a branch of lilac in a sudden infiltration of an unobjectified but passionate happiness, the purpose of my interview seemed to me but a tenth part of what had been accomplished, and the least important part, as if my fear that Mamma was insane had been only an excuse to know Dr. McAllister." Nathan had been her first love, before she saw Dr. McAllister. Nathan's "mouth waspishly raged over my face with kisses," and so on.

As the novel goes forward, there is less of this. But the wares of culture are packed into Miss Stafford's pages with the earnestness of a young novelist who has an argosy to unload. A nose is "raptorial." Eyes are "mammiform." A slip in speech is noted in which a character "metathetized her vowels." There is a schoolma'am in Miss Stafford not yet fully under control. And that schoolma'am might learn how to spell Agassiz and Winnetka and to refrain from a "Ruebenesque" woman. Those who mount to the seats of the scornful should always carry a reference book.

There is hope for Miss Stafford. She speaks of "the tenacity, the absorption and the humility of the artist." Tenacity she has, in excess. Her absorption is so complete that we are often richly rewarded. The Back Bay she observes, sometimes through the keyhole, is seen keenly and unflinchingly. But the sense of humiliation does not always breed humility. And she tears passion to tatters.

September 23, 1944

BEST SHORT STORIES

NOT only in Germany and Russia but everywhere in our strangely centralized and depersonalized world, the individual touch, the touch of delight that leaps from the creator to the recipient, seems to be more difficult to capture. It is simpler, because of time and space, to standardize emotions and can them. And yet, amid the bright and shiny ads that line the day coach on a suburban train, right under the scrapple and the noodles, nine travelers out of ten are touchingly personal. The human spark is still there, free, bright, unaffected. What deadens their emotion, takes away its crispness? If one says that lives as well as goods tend to be averaged, the artist makes a mistake to reproach his fellow-citizens. They, like himself, are subjected to the standard and impersonal; yet most of them spring up like green grass when the sun can reach them; they are incurably individual.

One of the signs of it is Miss Martha Foley's devoted selection of the best short stories. Here, as against the bright and shiny stories that go with the ads, Miss Foley has scoured all the weeklies and monthlies and quarterlies for a fresh and unmitigated individuality. From countless candidates she has chosen about 200, and from their stories, about 300 in all, she has actually thirty to reprint, *The Best American Short Stories 1944*, which means the best of those printed in the year previous.

They are the answer, fiercely scrupulous and exacting, to the shrewd complacencies of the standard product. Arbitrary, in the nature of things, and without the inside illumination of a St. Peter, her selection may still be taken as the cream of our individual expression, or at any rate the top of the bottle. While *The Kenyon Review, Partisan Review, Southwest Review, The New Mexico Quarterly, Harper's Bazaar, Story, Tomorrow, Mademoiselle, Accent, The Atlantic, The Yale*

The Best American Short Stories 1944 edited by Martha Foley. Houghton Mifflin.

Review, are represented, there is only one lone specimen from the vast flock of stories in *Collier's* and the other big-circulation weeklies, but this is the verdict of an expert in individuality, and Miss Foley is no faddist.

Well, the exhibits are laid out for us, nearly 500 pages of them, and no one, not even the editors of the big weeklies, can call them uninteresting. The number of stories that put English into a zoot suit has diminished. In one story two men hurry, "their boots sighing softly in the damp earth," and in another, "when afternoon had moulted its light, the nurses would come back, and the doctors, their soles kissing the parquet floors and sealing the compact with the tiny noises of lovers." But this is no longer typical of "best" stories. The war has changed them. The number of corpses has gone down. We have babies instead. The style is more direct and more trusting. Even the conviction that you cannot do people in the round unless you include their bottoms no longer seems imperious. The stories are fascinatingly diverse, sober, sensitive and accomplished. What they lack, and it is the fundamental problem of the "best short story," is some sort of strong emotional resonance.

For the "shock of recognition," to use the phrase Edmund Wilson chose for his anthology, there is nothing like a short story. It can flash on you like a face, and it must be a close-up. The whole figure may be omitted, but the eloquent passport has to be there, the one passport we all carry with us, and the most legible. If there can be a clash of expressions, a criss-cross of motives, a duel of glances, an intrigue—so much the better; that intensifies the shock and grandly heightens the recognition. But it is a new face we must see on life—quick, shocking, recognizable. And for this there must be established both an emotion and an intimacy.

What handicaps the "best" stories, in this essential respect, is the way graded and packaged America forces its young writers into autobiography, simply because they do not feel confidently at home. In this book, for example, we have several little scared, sensitive, mewing women with new babies and j. g. or GI husbands, but remote and caged in their meticulous self-inspection. We have Saul Bellow revolving on his navel, and a number of other self-referential portraits that never lift into creation. Quite apart are Ruth Portugal's stern tale of a girl whom a tough soldier tries to carry by assault, and Astrid Meighan's perceptive vignette of an alimony tangle. But for the liberation of power, of humor, of wisdom and of salience, there just has to be a community, and here it is that Carson McCullers writes with the amplitude of a person wholly at home. It hurt me to the quick when she forgot that Marvin Macy had "slow gray eyes." A few pages later she gave him deep-blue eyes. I once knew a cat that had a blue eye and a yellow one, but never a grown human being who started with gray and ended with blue. Apart from this slip, the rich Mc-Cullers story goes far to show that for individuality we do well to go South. It is not so standardized. Perhaps people are more deeply at home there.

September 30, 1944

DUNSANY IN GREECE

MOST readers, even kind-hearted ones, reach a point where they can no longer kneel and take on another load of grief. They feel compassionate enough, but when they have spent sympathy on the Jews, on Poland, on Norway, not to speak of those earlier victims on Musa Dagh and recent victims of the Japanese, it seems impossible to add fresh claimants to the list, especially when the hurricane may wreck one's own beloved trees, or the boats at Little Compton or Martha's Vineyard. The heart becomes trampled like old snow, and what began as a sheer purification ends as a job for street cleaners. Red Cross or no Red Cross, we shrink from a novel about Greeks, even if it is by Lord Dunsany. The Italians may be nearer to us, or the Finns. No day passes without adding to the sum of misery and the inadequacy of the heart to encounter it.

Guerrilla by Lord Dunsany. Bobbs-Merrill.

But it is a peculiar fact that suffering alone becomes bearable when it is borne. The mere attempt to shoulder it constitutes the best part of the act of sympathy, and when a true artist, whether in music or the written word, shows the power to lift the burden (which is proved by form quite as often as it is proved by the contortions of formlessness), something flows from the work of art that is both comprehending and remedial.

It would be no use to recommend *Guerrilla* on the grounds that, of all peoples on earth, the Greeks have been the most undaunted since 1939. Just as many bad books are produced from good causes as bad wine from the good vineyards. But if one happens to respect Dunsany as an artist, it is a deep pleasure to find in *Guerrilla* not only the nobility of its subject but the power to press from it both strength and enchantment.

Lord Dunsany has never been fully at home with the outside, the rough-and-tumble world. He can't help the fact that he is a peer, and he has never had the slightest inclination to help it. "In the family barnyard," he once was heard to say with the arrogance which is three-quarters self-defense, "they have hatched out an eagle, and they don't know what to do with it." He was quite wrong. What families do with an eagle is put it in a cage, especially if it is an Irish peer who is a literary fledgling.

Had he been a painter he might have been a Puvis de Chavannes. He removes his figures from the common world or else sees them as linked to an idea, abstract, sometimes impersonal or fantastic. To the beauty of form he sacrifices those bold, intimate, animal verifications from which an Ernest Hemingway never shrinks. The elements with which he conjures are fire and air, not clay or water. Forced to the earth, he is instantly moved to the mountains.

But in *Guerrilla* the mountain is everything. When the Germans move into a Greek city, about the size of Canterbury in England, the only answer that the affronted Greeks can offer is to withdraw to the mountain. Though they move a little with the measured tread and the studied impersonality of a tragic amphitheatre, and though the gestures may only indicate a bloodstained hand or a face like carved wood ("his face seemed to wear resignation like an ancient national dress"), the artist's object is to achieve with sparse and proud economy the highest contrasts of a calm demeanor and a catastrophic disturbance. The danger, in a modern novel, has always been to produce asphyxia rather than breathlessness, to mount so high that the audience passes out, or to create the austerity but also the soporific of monotone.

Guerrilla is saved from this by the pure and flaming sympathy of an artist who has the dry concreteness of a soldier. He really makes us understand the boy Srebnitz, whose mother hates the occupation and is promptly murdered. He creates tension by forcing us to see the good reasons why Hlaka, the guerrilla chief, is so harsh. We become Srebnitz's partisans until he is initiated, until he draws blood, until he kills several men with the knife and learns to be a sharpshooter.

The fierce pride of Greece is pointed like a lance at the reader, and his heart quivers under this brilliant and unremitting assault. It is a terrible thing for the Germans to have been unjust, terrible for them to be seen as apes, as beasts of prey, as obscene and filthy creatures who are lower than animals. This is what Dunsany does in a few pages, with lemon trees, and orange and peach and wisteria, under the moonlight. He gives Srebnitz to the sharp mountain, to guerrilla life and the war, to the loyalties of manhood and the sacrament of patriotism.

This is a beautiful and persuasive book, sharp, swift and irresistible. Perhaps the Dunsany who once lived in County Meath may have been wooed by the thought of other guerrillas from whom history had separated him. Ernie O'Malley, who wrote *Army without Banners*, is another Srebnitz. Well, for Edward John Moreton Drax Plunkett Lord Dunsany, it was much too long a way to Tipperary and the Galtee Mountains. But it came near him in Greece, and it touched him with divine fire.

October 14, 1944

THE CLASH OF RACE

ONCE Stephen Crane wrote books that were like a flash from a heliograph, and now half a dozen Southern novelists are doing it. There is an alertness about Hodding Carter in his first novel, *The Winds of Fear*, which admits him right off into a brilliant company, but this time on a press ticket.

His novel, that is to say, is right on the heels of the news. The place he writes about is a typical Southern poor-white town of about 4,000, to use his own words, and nearly one-third of the people in it are "race citizens"—Negroes. The central figure is a young editor, home from the Pacific, where he lost his left arm in combat. And the theme, race conflict, is such hot news that a reporter from *PM* is on the spot, literally and figuratively. You can't crowd on the heels of passing events much closer than that, and this makes a novel perishable.

But if a press ticket for the literary Valhalla is issued to Mr. Carter, it won't be on account of his centering his action in a newspaper office. It will be because he hasn't written a novel as such. He has chosen to quicken it with purpose, and to make it the direct vehicle of opinion. Why this should put him in a special category so far as fiction is concerned has no bearing on merit or demerit.

It is a simple classification. Had he triumphed as novelists do who catch the shifting winds of life, we'd lose ourselves in the sense of life itself. But we are soon aware that Mr. Carter propels his story by the auxiliary engine of a purpose, and that purpose is practical and political. Once such a purpose permeates a story, there is a propulsion in it, a rhythmic throb of intention, that borrows sympathy for itself, or forfeits sympathy, on grounds that are outside the literary craft. People may like or dislike *The Winds of Fear* for reasons that have nothing to do with Mr. Carter's remarkable art.

His purpose is magnificent. Instead of building up Carvell City as a city of people, he exhibits it as the battleground of

The Winds of Fear by Hodding Carter. Farrar & Rinehart.

race. On both sides of this conflict he is sharply and intimately informed. He knows everybody, black and white. He makes us see, hear and smell them. He has, in fact, a nose like a hound, so that he can give us not only the smell of a cab or the smell of the depot but actually the smell of a hardware store. Yes, sir, "the metallic smell of the nail bins was clean and cool," and no dog can do better than that. Into this little town, one-third of which is Negro, he brings a simple clash between a bus passenger, on the one hand, and a local marshal, on the other.

The passenger is a young Negro, aggravated in his ego by high wages and whisky. In the ensuing brawl he and the old die-hard marshal are both killed. This mobilizes all the forces in the small community, and it is like watching the behavior of deep-sea life in a tank. The new marshal who whips up latent fears and prejudices is a primitive, pure white trash. He has many exasperated citizens behind him and is in cahoots with a liquor dealer.

But while he is a bad actor, he is up against a Negro doctor full of race hatred and another primitive who is a Negro liquor vendor. These live in the quarter where a Negro school superintendent and a Negro preacher try to temper the winds of fear. The new marshal is a killer, and before the book is finished there is plenty of blood, sweat and tears.

Mr. Carter plays no favorites, and his drama is immensely, brilliantly vivid. We never get the slow-maturing situation. The action is rapid and streamlined. If man is a wedge that comes to a point, Mr. Carter never loses himself in the thickness and spreading background. He gets right to the point, but he makes his point with a precision and heartrending fairness that fill me with admiration. This book is beautiful in its sincerity. The language in it is often revolting but never is it uttered except in that fidelity which, whether the object is a swan or a cancer, elevates by the honesty of intention.

Mr. Carter does not perhaps use his literary gift with a clear grasp of all the advantages that a novel gives him. He has used the brittle method of the moving picture, our attention is shifted too often, and our minds are kept flickering. The

montage, in fact, is quite bad once or twice. But what redeems
the unsparing fidelity to barbarous, drunken, murderous fellow-citizens of ours is Mr. Carter's complete absence of partisanship; and if he handles a Southern marshal without mitts,
he is no more loyally impartial to brute fact than contemporary
decisions of the Supreme Court.

The South in this book is not that sober territory over which
Ellen Glasgow reigns in her massive, commanding creations,
nor is it the bed of roses of which Stark Young caught the
perfume. This is the South of a new self-assertion, crackling,
sharp, immediate. Mr. Carter is a fearless guide to it, in a hard-
hitting novel which is still essentially tender.

October 21, 1944

FRANK O'CONNOR'S ART

THOSE who have already acquired a taste for Frank O'Connor,
no vast army as yet, must turn to *Crab Apple Jelly* with a
pleasant crinkling of whatever the organs of taste are. Is Frank
O'Connor growing, or has he learned to cheat? Is he still the
most accomplished short-story writer in Ireland?

The twelve stories and tales in *Crab Apple Jelly* are reassuring. He is not a lean wolf like Liam O'Flaherty, baying the
moon and causing the pale moon to seem even paler with
alarm. While he has as much temperament as that master of
effect, he does not wreak his vengeance on life through literature. These stories are indescribably tart, indefinably piquant,
but they are singularly understood as a fine art, and completely, or almost completely, disciplined.

Did he learn this from Chekhov, as W. B. Yeats suggested?
He probably learned it, as no doubt the Russian did, from
pursuing a choice that few authors afford themselves. In none
of Frank O'Connor's stories are we induced to accept his people or his themes by reason of our sympathy with the subject.

Crab Apple Jelly by Frank O'Connor. Knopf.

Our hunger for love is not directly placated. Our existing sentiments about politics or economics or theology do not collaborate to make us like his work. All that movable material which might win us first to a Finland and afterward to a Greece, depending on the trend of the news, has no place in his continent approach. There is no one-legged soldier who is to be consoled in love, or, if you think of a story in a college quarterly, who is to lose the other leg in a street accident.

In any popular art, as in typing itself, if Q W E is to be followed by R T Y, even blindfolded girls can hit the right keys. This is the value of a standard keyboard, and great popular story writers like Kipling or O. Henry managed, no matter how they changed the formula, to prepare their readers for such consoling and habitual sequences. But with Frank O'Connor, as with Chekhov, the quest is for finer, truer, less familiar symbols, and this is the distinction of his art. It does not make for lascivious ease in appreciating him, but it makes for a higher delectation.

Higher, because all through this volume we have human beings heard and seen with a verity more strict and secure than any we are accustomed to. Frank O'Connor has his roots in Ireland. He actually clings to his native earth like a crab tree, tenacious, twisted, idiosyncratic, wild. And yet with this tight, this almost savage individuality and localism, he is freed into his art by a spacious wind of the spirit, so that what is earthbound is also liberated, and breaks the "cake of custom."

The stories that best illustrate this liberation are the ones that give us humble and what might seem insignificant people. He wins his tricks without court cards. In "The Long Road to Ummera" Mr. O'Connor portrays "a shapeless lump of an old woman." He does not spare us her ugliness, her squalor. "Her eyes were puffy and screwed up in tight little buds of flesh, and her rosy old face, that might have been carved out of a turnip, was all crumpled with blindness." This old woman, living in a slum in Cork, wants to be buried over the hills at Ummera. Her son does not see why. She saves or secretes the money for it. She is balked, but in the end she has her way. "It was a spring day, full of wandering sunlight," when they

brought her over the long road. And the melancholy Pat, fulfilling her promise, says to the waiting neighbors, "Neighbors,
this is Abby, Batty Heige's daughter, that kept her promise to
ye at the end of all." It is the completion of a fidelity. "Stay
for me there, I will not fail to meet thee in that hollow vale."
"Ah, Michael Driscoll, my friend, my kind comrade, you
didn't forget me after all the long years," she raved. This solace
of reunion is for a sniffing and smeary old woman.

Not in every one of the stories are the frustrated given solace. "The Mad Lomasneys" is a tale of exasperated love in
middle-class Cork.

"The Luceys" is a quarrel between brothers that ends in a
deathbed cleavage. "The Bridal Night" is a lyric of a boy who
goes mad and a girl who goes to bed with him in pity for his
frustration. This is told in matchless English by the mother of
the boy. Another tale, "The Grand Vizier's Daughters," is
related of two young girls ashamed of their worthless father,
who break in on his rambling story to cry that they are not
ashamed.

Passion and loneliness fill these stories of Ireland. Under the
coif of each nun there is a woman, sister to Cait, "the black
shawl drawn tight under her chin, the cowl of it breaking the
curve of her dark hair, her shadow on the gleaming wall behind." If "Ned caught her looking at him with naked eyes,"
her beauty goads Ned. It goads the priest, Ned's brother, who
wakes in disgust next morning. He lights his cigarette "at the
candle flame, his drowsy red face puckered and distraught. 'I
slept rotten.' "

It is a long way from Canon Sheehan and *The New Curate*. But with the clairvoyance that is Frank O'Connor's, the
equanimity and the compassion, we have the dregs of Cork no
less, or even better, possessed than the clever and disconcerted.
He is developing an art that melts incident into character, so
that the stories center on themselves as if perpetuating their
own motion. He knows how passionate these people are, how
much part of that green-lighted landscape, with the bars of
heaven so often bared as the sun sets.

November 18, 1944

HENRY JAMES REVISITED

HERE is good news: an edition of Henry James' notebooks, which run from 1878 to 1914 and contain 150,000 words, is being prepared by F. O. Matthiessen and Kenneth B. Murdock. This fact is mentioned in Mr. Matthiessen's new volume, *Henry James: The Major Phase*.

Why the news is good becomes eminently clear as one winds through the Jamesian territory in Mr. Matthiessen's company. He does not dwell on the tidewater James, the James who wrote in his first fifty-two years. He devotes his book to the major novels, as he deems them: *The Wings of the Dove* (1902), *The Ambassadors* (1903), *The Golden Bowl* (1904). And he adds the unfinished novel, *The Ivory Tower*. His consideration includes *The American Scene* and *The Portrait of a Lady*, but this last, though seductive on its own account, falls outside the argument.

What he argues, of course, is the importance to ourselves of Henry James' superlative achievement, the novels of "his three miraculous years." It was a romantic achievement, and that, in James' own words, stands "for the things that, with all the facilities in the world, all the wealth and all the courage and all the wit and all the adventure, we never can directly know; the things that can reach us only through the beautiful circuit and subterfuge of our thought and our desire."

This is tall talk, but for a tall object, and when you go back to Henry James, either in memory or in fact, you do know what he is tall-talking about. Mr. Matthiessen is a perfect guide to the man as well as the work. Not only is he absorbed in the most subtle of verbal intoxications, but he has a clear head in the midst of it and a fidelity to honest critical standards. His book is one of the happiest adventures in criticism that this

Henry James: The Major Phase by F. O. Matthiessen. Oxford University Press.
The Great Short Novels of Henry James. Edited by Philip Rahv. Dial Press.

tortured world has recently seen. It estimates very coolly and sanely one of those perilous, lonely journeys that an artist has pushed to his last ounce of endeavor. He sees how surefooted Henry James was, how bound to two contraries at the same time—the earth and the stars. You can't talk of this sort of thing easily, but Mr. Matthiessen does make it easy. His book ranks high as criticism.

By seizing on "the related state, to each other, of certain figures and things," Mr. Matthiessen grasps the inwardness of Henry James' preoccupation. His drama was invariably the drama of human dignity—of pride, sensitiveness and integrity—but he restricted it to a society that he could ideally control, and one in which the points of reference were so many and so firm that he could cross his references at will. The groans of his parturition are sometimes like Brahms', but it is a small world in birth, and nothing is so costly. We must sweat with him.

We do it, if we have any sense, because he saw so much, felt so much, was so many people. He was Isabel Archer, for example, and he felt the American girl's romantic plight, quite unsentimentally but with agony, "her meager knowledge, her inflated ideals, her confidence at once innocent and dogmatic, her temper at once exacting and indulgent." Even Woodrow Wilson had many of her traits, but Henry James touched them with the light of pure dawn. He was one of a great Boston constellation. As a young American abroad he was touchy, and rather prim to begin with, feeling a French and Italian threat to his Puritan virginity, yet forever deepening his knowledge of that good and evil which, as Mr. Matthiessen seems to miss, is the kernel of Swedenborg's religion, however the elder James may have softened it. Henry James softened nothing, though he was tender above everything.

It is not necessary, however, to brush off Van Wyck Brooks for suggesting that Sherwood Anderson was tender and sensitive in realms closed to Henry James. Had every artist shirked the plunge into Winesburg, Ohio, into "that splendid, dreadful, funny country" at which James gave so many a shiver and shudder, we'd have a meaner consciousness today. Besides,

Sherwood Anderson never supposed that a "maid servant crying for her young man" was inherently banal. His Plimsoll line wasn't so waist-high as Henry James', which Mr. Matthiessen discerns.

But *The Great Short Novels of Henry James*, with most useful and keenly placed signposts by Philip Rahv, offer us splendors of sheer delectation into which Anderson never sought to liberate us. These are often early novels, but the passage of time, as great art proves, cleans up and clears off a good, true, lovely thing so that it has another novelty. It is renewed from a natural abundance and sufficiency within itself. It is fresh, like a spring. Here we live again in an America crisp and young and romantic. Who did it better?

December 14, 1944

RUSSIA WITHOUT CENSOR

NORBERT GUTERMAN has translated a Soviet novel by Leonid Leonov, called *Road to the Ocean*. It is rather a shock to have Russians come out from behind the samovar to "bawl" each other out, to say, "I've outsmarted them" or "I'm in a tough spot" or "I get you." Mr. Guterman has them "barge in" and "check" the neatness of their locks—everything except chew gum; and his printers strike the right note by printing "its" author as "it's." A cinder in your eye? This is a railroad novel. Leonid Leonov places Molière in the eighteenth century. Why not? That is not the main issue. Taste is minor. So is accuracy.

Leonid Leonov was 15 in 1917. He has had a quarter of a century of Soviet emotions and convulsions. "I place him," said Maxim Gorky, not long before being murdered, "with the greatest figures of our old literature—Pushkin, Turgenev, Dostoievsky and Tolstoy." Why not have added Shakespeare? But even that is a minor point.

This novel is of major importance to us as to Gorky, on the

Road to the Ocean by Leonid Leonov. L. B. Fischer.

level of its content. *Road to the Ocean* is a manifesto. Leonid Leonov has the glint of morning in his eyes. He is a revolutionist. He is on with a new love, and the old love, the Russian old order, he views with detestation. He never knew it, but he loathes it, and he gives us a good chance to look deep into his intense, blinding hatred. In a novel like *Boston Adventure* there is a certain mild animosity, but the Boston vodka is poor stuff compared to the original article. *Road to the Ocean* has bold, cutting ability and the virtue of sharp outspokenness.

The novel's method is that of a film like *Dr. Mabuse*. It is oblique, wilfully dislocated, deliberately incoherent. Scenes are flashed on us from odd angles, and we might be at the Duke of Portland's, so little does anybody introduce anybody. In addition, the author occasionally comes in front of the curtain to ram a long wad of history into us, using "I" as if he and his hero Kurilov were equally authentic. Which, indeed, is the marionette in this dance on strings?

Kurilov is a revolutionist, head of the railroad political bureau, a party cleanser who is juxtaposed against sons and daughters of old Russia, political illegitimates. Leonov thinks of him as very old, all of 52, and can only ascribe his falling in love with Liza, a young actress, to a disease. Liza is linked with him temporarily. Then he goes to the operating table, while she, shaking off bourgeois falsities, moves into regularity. Every time Leonov shakes his clinking kaleidoscope it is to show who is, and who is not, acceptable politically. This Russian is nothing if not graphic.

"The span of the future is boundless," and Russian mastery of it, by means of two world wars, is to enable the Soviet to push its railroad to Shanghai, where Ocean is to be the ideal modern city. The wars tear away "the tattered fig leaf of bourgeois humanism." We must defer to the engineer death. The "call" of mankind is to be "definitely identified with the concept of creativity, that is to say, *mastery*." Hitler has said it, many times, and Leonov reserves his loud diapason for Iron Necessity and the men who obey it. For that he can forget the garbage of the past and exalt his skyscraping enthusiasm for blood sacrifice.

It seems perverse to call non-party railroad men a "human cesspool." And is not murder, after all, a bourgeois prejudice? But *Road to the Ocean*, a manifesto of Russian expansion, shows that a real revolution is such a total and heartfelt transfer of allegiance that it must mingle two moods, the mood of a new religion and of a *crime passionel*. Leonov smears the old Russia with dirt because he has heard "the scraping of Tsarist officials' quill pens and the grating of the iron yoke on the neck of the enslaved people. And so the inkwell was hatred."

Can we blame any Russian for excess, even extended to the Lomonosovs and all the old railroad men, all the old Russians and all the old world? *Road to the Ocean*, should not make us feed its devouring hatred with our own resentment. But neither should we blink the fact that Russia is drunk on that wild young intoxicant, the Future.

December 16, 1944

A JOYCE DISCOVERY

THE actual process of writing a book can be frightfully costly. Everyone is aware that plays have to be pulled apart during rehearsal, and even after production may be reconstructed. The energetic producer spares no one, not the actors, the actresses, the playwright nor himself. But in solitary activity a good author spends himself no less. For every good book that sees print, there may be two, three, four versions, some of them complete books, and relatively dissimilar. For the sake of a satisfactory entity a writer may destroy his original sketch, and even let its freshness, its untouched purity, be wiped out for the sake of a more governed, more deliberated, more drastically intended end.

Seldom has so precious an exhibit of this process been presented than that now made available by Harvard College. In Harvard College Library since 1938 there have been 383 pages

Stephen Hero by James Joyce. New Directions.

of script, bought from a bookshop in Paris. The first page is numbered 519, and the 518 pages that preceded it were probably burned. This bundle of script, about 60,000 words, was part of a book by James Joyce. When he could find no publisher for it—it was already 150,000 words and not completed—he took this portion now preserved at Harvard to make an essence not a quarter of its original size.

The name he gave to the 902 pages was *Stephen Hero*, and that is the name of the published fragment. But Stephen in quintessence he incorporated in *The Portrait of the Artist as a Young Man*.

Students will compare this first with the final draft, because comparisons of a matrix with a finished work of art are full of interest. *Stephen Hero*, however, is a book in and by itself. One odd thing about James Joyce, in spite of the supervisions to which he attached importance, is that the loss of more than half of a manuscript leaves a segment that seems intact. Like a tanker that has been chopped in two, one part going to the bottom, this truncated *Stephen Hero* is navigable. Joyce was supposed to compose works of art that have the subtlest unity, with all kinds of cross-correspondences and counterpoint. But as Joyce's main theme was Joyce, you can enter into his spirit in any subsection, because he enables you, from any page, to watch the eternal flow of ego. The intolerable loss that one feels when a true drama is interrupted, balking one's passionate desire to know what is going to happen, won't be felt by many people who read *Stephen Hero*. Joyce had a consuming interest in himself, and you can absolutely count on this in these pages, all through, no matter where you begin or end. This makes it organic. His comparative indifference to the rest of his characters is annoying, because the parts of them that don't turn a bright face to Joyce are just as forgotten, and nominally just as non-existent, as the hind side of the moon. But Joyce has the gift of multiplying himself, like a plant that grows from slips. Stick a slip of him in print and he grows on you. He is a colossal egoist, colossally interesting.

In Mr. Theodore Spencer's unassuming but admirable introduction, which suggests that Joyce wrote *Stephen Hero* when he was between 22 and 24, the fact that Joyce was still rather soft-shelled, and therefore more easy to see around and see into, is well perceived. Joyce's art of being enigmatic was already in evidence, but he speaks of it candidly, and behind his egoism, brazen as it is, the "sluttish streets" of his native city seem to be peopled by his unhappy wraith, so compelled to walk in a lonely defiance of the ugliness and opposition that crowded on him.

Dublin in 1900 was in between two worlds. The world that had died was still ignominiously unburied. It was stertorous when Joyce was at school at Clongowes, and its death rattle in student Dublin seemed odious to him. The new world about him, young Ireland, he saw as a wrinkled monster, bawling hideously, wet. One of his foils in this book is so reported from life that he is not MacCann but Sheehy-Skeffington, who did indeed die because of obstinacy, as Stephen Hero said he would. His obstinacy was shown in 1916 when he was arrested for rescuing wounded during the Rebellion. Stephen Hero fights off the patriotism that tempts him. He throws off the religion that entangles him. He opens his arms to the sun, and in these days of his own fame, for Joyce's least word absorbs scores of talented writers today, it is instructive to reflect that the sun that dazzled him and enraptured him was Ibsen. Joyce-Hero learned Dano-Norwegian (he calls it Danish) in order to read Ibsen. He had nothing on the late William Ivins, once candidate for the mayoralty of New York, but this power of worship was the other side of his thwarted being. And *Stephen Hero* is a document on the thwarted.

He makes no bones about his sacred egoism, and he narrates with studied callousness and indecency the death of a sister to show that a sobbing Dickens didn't have the patent on death beds. As for his father and mother, he puts teeth through them, sharper than the serpent's. The Jesuits, of course, he devours without salt. But if his youthful gesture is rather like that of Mussolini, clocking God whom he defied to strike him dead as he held a stop-watch, Joyce's impudicity had a fierceness behind it, the fierceness of a soul that demanded manumission, so that he could love, feel, assert, test for himself, create. Up and up, under pressures insupportable, the jet of this violent nature mounted. In *Stephen Hero*, under sodden Dublin skies, he is accumulating this energy. The Jesuits tried to smooth his way and his intransigence by offering him a little job. But no one could sit on that geyser.

January 18, 1945

JOHN GUNTHER, NOVELIST

THE presumption is always against any established man who ventures into an entirely new field. Paderewski was handicapped by his music when he became Premier, just as Winston Churchill started from behind scratch when he took to painting. And even if a good reporter can tell a story as a matter of course—it is his first business—a champion in his field like John Gunther must be stripped of reputation rather than clothed in it when he dares to write a novel. Inside Europe, Asia—that's what we expect of him. Inside John Gunther? Good lord, has he insides? Who ever told him he could write a novel?

Of course he can write a novel, and a living one. *The Troubled Midnight* is inexpert in several serious respects, and naturally refuses to yield the kind of ultimate satisfaction that is secured for a reader by that long, or at any rate deep and faithful, devotion to a medium which alone gives mastery. But emotional affluence can't be faked. *The Troubled Midnight* actually has a strong, provocative theme, and where it jars is on another level.

The theme is modern. When a Victorian girl received a proposal she was supposed to exclaim, "This is so sudden!" In Mr. Gunther's book it is when the young matron wakes up in the tycoon's bed that she exclaims, "I'm the most surprised woman who ever lived." And then she bends her head with a "strange, wild, maidenly look." But we do not meet Leslie until she takes

The Troubled Midnight by John Gunther. Harper & Bros.

a lend-lease job in Constantinople, after four years of strange, wild and not so maidenly intimacy with the tycoon.

Arriving in Istanbul on her own, she has fashionable gear that Mr. Gunther lovingly details in every particular, and he knows her from hairdo to toenails; she is emotionally in the same state as those Africans who, without having malaria themselves, are instantly contagious. Leslie has merely to sit at Taksim's with a British secret agent to inflame the Nazi opposite number sitting at a near table. And the British agent, dry as he is, registers temperature himself. Even a sappy younger Englishman, who is obsessed by a topaz-eyed dancer, wants Leslie for his friend. She is launched on a run into trouble.

The situation is real. Hugo, the Nazi, makes her sharply respond, but this ability to respond leads nowhere. She stirs the Nazi to his depths, but when he tries to reach her—and that evening on the beach "if he had so much as kissed her, she might have been lost"—she protects herself by thinking she is "a very private person, who hated aggressive curiosities." To him, however, she puts it on political grounds.

But she is so sorry for Hugo, she gives him many a rendezvous. And this nasty fellow grows finally so desperate that, rather than throw a child under an Englishman's car as demanded by the Nazi mastermind, he decides to change camps. Leslie, sorry for him as she is, pours it out in Taksim's so that the Greek waiter can hear her. And that is too bad for Hugo.

The topaz-eyed dancer is meanwhile disengaged from the susceptible young Englishman by Leslie's being a lady and showing him tenderness. Once more she salivates but cannot swallow, while the young Englishman takes her down, hook, line and sinker. The jealous Nazi reacts as one might expect, and Leslie is still "the most surprised woman who ever lived," and no one hits her on the head with a candlestick. Everybody, even the girl with the fabulous topaz eyes, loves Leslie, and Leslie is never disturbed in her ego. Sense of sin? "A sense of sin was so vulgar, so cramping and debilitating." And she had "learned the tremendous lesson that in the long run healthy people do what they want most to do."

That tycoon, by the way, once sent her "one hundred dozen

tulips, her favorite flower." Even if she had used milk bottles, how could she house them? She must have given them to hospitals.

With the whole world to choose from, John Gunther shrewdly selected Istanbul, "as of tonight, April 6, 1944." It gave him an international meeting place. Much as the taxpayer's heart may bleed when tots of brandy cost $4 and when love seems to have priority among these privileged war workers, the novel reports it with compensating lust and sparkle and vigor. Mr. Gunther has planted his people close, as amateurs plant tomatoes, but even if they crowd as they develop, and come to us with dossiers that should unfold through the narrative, he still has a narrative that carries on. "With the terrible ruthlessness of one who really loves," the girl is quite an attractive female. It is a pity she talks politics, but to have her play havoc and still stay so surprised is fascinating. And Mr. Gunther has a big final curtain.

February 1, 1945

RIPENESS IN A NOVEL

AT LAST, thank Heaven, a good novel! One could assume that Frank Swinnerton would bring a practiced hand and a clear head to *A Woman in Sunshine* since he has been a long time in the business. But the secret of a good novel is to be looked for further down than the brow. It comes from the regions that absorb and convert sound material into lifeblood. It remains visceral. Mr. Swinnerton has been rather autumnal in some of those recent books that brought his total up to thirty, but in *A Woman in Sunshine* he has a creative buoyancy, a surrender to a principal character that is the most dangerous and most winning of commitments in the whole enterprise of fiction. He has reinforced it with a three-ring plot, but what is so alluring is the conviction he brings to it, governed by an honest

A Woman in Sunshine by Frank Swinnerton. Doubleday.

sense of people in general, and warmed to the right temperature.

For a fastidious writer the easier end is to pick the milieu. London does Mr. Swinnerton well, and so does the class to which writers, actors, actresses, barristers, self-conscious and literate people belong. He can manage Kensington delightfully, and the Ritz in the Thirties, and the young Bloomsbury set, "Stephanie's friends, hangers-on of the arts, who drank and trooped and sniggered at all the decorums." More than that, he has no difficulty with the brasses, with those squalid discordancies so loud and harsh, whether in side streets near Regent's Park or in a villa blinking at the sea. Mr. Swinnerton easily catches "the far, embracing murmur of London," that London now scarred and amputated, but intact in this novel.

It is impregnation with significance that is the bigger difficulty. What theme can the great city frame for him, and what range can he span in it? Is it to be a wet autumn or a resplendent one? He has at times been almost as gray as George Gissing, who really was as dispirited as a November with sinus trouble. But *A Woman in Sunshine* lives up to its title.

Mr. Swinnerton has the courage to center his tale on that creature with whom Balzac so often failed—a good woman. He succeeds by showing her in action. Letitia would have been insipid in repose, or too sweet for words, but this English author has not that passion for jam which once threatened the British Empire with diabetes. He goes back to Milton for his keynote. "He that has light within his own clear breast may sit i' the center and enjoy bright day."

The darkness encroaches on this sunlit woman, as it does on everyone, by reason of her fondnesses and loyalties. Bright in herself, she is plunged in turmoil and confusion for love of others. Mr. Swinnerton summons all his powers to make the battle a real one, each character vividly observed in order to display the civil war within, while Letitia is the one through whom the hosts go tramping and for whom she cares. "She was seriously indifferent to her own importance; a definitely pre-modern type."

The novel is not quite shapely. It begins brilliantly, played up to Letitia as if it were to be exclusively psychological, with sharp, witty dialogue. This gleaming promise is intermittently fulfilled. The amorous son Julian, "outwardly languid, but inwardly as quick, as uncertain as fire," legitimately steals the interest when his mother sees him in London, though he is supposed to be in New York. She discovers him with Stephanie, his brother's wife. Out of the hard conflict, involving her two adored sons, Mr. Swinnerton derives a succession of big scenes, all of which he handles directly, firmly, seriously. So far the shape is pointed and speeding, but Letitia's own family, with a shrieking mother, a sister who squdges in fat feebleness and a wicked schemer of a brother, crashes into the deft social comedy for which *A Woman in Sunshine* begins by exciting our preference.

Perhaps the idiom of the bearded villain suggests bookish romance a little. He cites Sterne, Plato, Dürer, Henry James, when it is his manipulator who has this ingrained habit. But Letitia's brother is bogus even in villainy. The very conception of villainy, in fact, is pointed back to defects in character. Letitia is no villain when she is proud that her husband's best friend, so to speak, comes offering her his love.

The theme of the book, "evil lies in character," probably gains from the gargoyles and grotesques with whom Letitia has to involve herself and for whom she has to drink the lees of publicity and family disgrace. Her promptness of heart, certainly, is the clue to her charm. The muddle in which she lives she feels to be disorderly, and made more so by the young. Still, she gives it order. She is "strong enough to be good," strong enough to love other people better than herself, strong enough to be herself "in a world full of pretentious cures for humanity that don't touch human nature." The total effect is one of sensuousness trodden for its juice and ennobled into wine.

Is it romantic? Well, no Foxy Grandpa could have written it. It sprawls a bit, in the sense that a champion leaps and even overreaches on the tennis court. The neat and nifty are sometimes beaten by these extravagant ones. There is much to be said for a generous, illuminating novel that has emotion and brains and literary conscience commingled.

March 10, 1945

GREECE ON FIRE

THIS war is too big to be grasped, but sometimes a book appears that helps one to bring a little bit of it into focus. *The Price of Liberty* by a young Greek named Mikia Pezas, has the supreme virtue of being clear and easy to read. It is a personal story, and all the better for it, but through the lens that Mikia Pezas has ground and polished, one can look at the Greek resistance to the Axis and see it for what it was. This is one of its values; it is a tangible chapter of history.

Over four years ago Mussolini stuck out his blue jaw and made a noise like a conqueror. He had tackled other enemies in the course of empire, and now he said to Germany, "Leave it to me," and he made the Greeks his target. What happened was almost incomprehensible to a democratic world that was much in need of encouragement. The Greeks seemed to be in a hopeless case. They had few big guns and no wealth to speak of, but they met the Italians head on, and drove the Italians out of Greece. That winter resistance was so unexpected, so spontaneous, so brilliant, that it inflicted a serious body blow on the Axis and gave Italian pride a wound from which it could not recover. It is this fight, a people's fight, which Mikia Pezas tells in English, which he learned when his father was consul general in Chicago. It is straight from the horse's mouth, and the horse was a young war horse.

Mr. Pezas might have been met in a cocktail bar in Athens. He moved in the diplomatic set and even played cards with the Italian Minister the day before hostilities began. From gadding around, practicing law, poking for chromium, playing tennis and admiring the girls, he was suddenly one of the mobilized

The Price of Liberty by Mikia Pezas. Washburn.

youth, traveling in a box car to the front with an acrobat and a sponge diver. He was a surprise to himself, on his way to the mountains. Soon he was hunting Italians in zero weather and hunting lice in the sunlight.

Behind this book, like the music of a flute, is the long, fluent, melancholy line of Greek history. But the cure for Homer's heroes and Greek mythology is gaiety, and *The Price of Liberty* has in it the same gaiety as *The Crock of Gold*. It has gangrene in it, and bitter death, but it has the breath of violets as well. It is as fresh and lively and bubbling as a fountain, and its skillful talk plays on all of Greece, on love, unnecessary poverty, even on religion.

The contrast between *The Price of Liberty* and so memorable a book as Lord Dunsany's *Guerrilla* lies in the native intimacy that Mr. Pezas can impart by his humor. Lord Dunsany, by his own special art, converted the aftermath of this Albanian campaign into a graphic and formalized, impersonal tale, in which the fame of Greece was grave and inescapable. Mr. Pezas carries this like a cloak flung carelessly. His book has no metaphors in it, no weight of responsibility. We live with him day by day. He has the light touch of a young man for whom reality is so terrible that he must ward it off by quickness. "Would I go to a party again? With clean clothes and without lice? Lousy! How many times I had uttered that word without thinking it could ever apply to me." But, as he muses or broods, his life is merged with that of his company, soon reduced from seventy-seven to twenty-seven, and he has acquainted us with so many of them that the killing of the acrobat, the gangrene of the sponge diver, grip us as shocking and personal.

What makes it even more personal is the readiness with which Mr. Pezas makes friends. All through the book runs his friendship for the one-eyed murderer, Christo the Cripple, who helped the Greek Army to win by supplying it with brandy and Turkish Delight. But there is a very, very old woman who gives him her talisman and tells him the story of her life. Not only she, but twenty others, and last of all a leper in whose hut he has to take refuge before he escapes to Turkey.

At times, in the exuberance of his youth, he passes from Colonel Bramble to the Three Musketeers. He is even aware of pathos. But as he shivers before battle, 6,000 feet up, there is no false pathos in his situation, nothing but thorns pressed into living flesh. And when the coward Corned Beef is buried in his own dugout, "Extra Quality Corned Beef" is his flippant epitaph. The Greek in this young Mercury flashes from black cloud to brilliance.

To see a newsreel of Finland in a comfortable cinema in Athens was a diversion. "How could I have known then?" How many thousands of youths must make this reflection. But the reflection is forcible on those icy heights in *The Price of Liberty*. The book is not merely gallant and magnetic, it happens to be intrinsically modest. They are different, these Greeks, with their quick tempers, violent spurts of temperament, moods that charge and discharge like their own sudden rivers. But they come near to us in *The Price of Liberty*. It has beauty in it, fire and clear blue light. At times it has magic, so that we yield to its generosities and share in its suffering.

March 17, 1945

BITTER FRUIT

CRIES of pain are seldom pleasant to overhear, but few kinds of human expression prove more instructive. Anyone who reads *The Power House*, a novel by Alex Comfort, must be prepared for pain. The book is uncompromisingly harsh and by deliberate intention. How much of this harshness is tolerable depends on the reader, but *The Power House* affirms agony in a manner so cool and dry that it has kinship with the poetry of Rimbaud.

To equip himself for the novel Dr. Comfort has gone straight to experience. His whole novel is placed in France, and in the present time, but it is from the inside of the working class, at

The Power House by Alex Comfort. Viking.

least to start with. Having made us acquainted with the textile town and its peculiarly downtrodden inhabitants, the author carries two of them into the French Army. Thereafter the story shifts its axis. Until the invasion is over we have less to do with these two young workers who become soldiers than with their young lieutenant. But when the conquest of France flattens out these combatants, we follow them through the occupation and into the underground. One of them is executed. The other two go back to the original scene, the power house. And the novel ends when the RAF bombs the power house.

It is, to put it mildly, a scream of protest, but what makes the protest so scarifying is the neatness with which it is organized. By a judicious admixture of a small and smelly stockyard, the crowded homes of the workers, the formidable machines of the power house, the technique of engineering and the blinded and impotent personal relations of the men and women, a mood of utter dejection and insignificance is produced in the reader, and liberally promoted by a cumulative series of industrial hazards and accidents. In this story the French are licked from the start, and Dr. Comfort makes his point as if he had France jabbed into a pencil sharpener. The first climax is a murder.

With this murder of a morbid woman to slide down from, we are plunged into a morass of military boredom and incompetence, in the company of a gun crew engaged in coastal defense not far from the textile town. The struggle of all concerned, one begins to gather, was not against the Germans. "The real struggle was against society." If the industrial life was a tanglefoot for flies, army life is blind man's buff in a switchyard. And when the French step into it, with the Germans overhead and advancing on every side, the defeat accelerates, in horror and benightedness and degradation. The picture is keen and slashingly vivid. Dr. Comfort writes in shortwinded sentences, and he makes it more breathless by changing the pivot continually, but this zigzag gashes the reader into strained attention.

The lieutenant soon finds himself wearing a red coat with black frogs on it, playing the piano in a restaurant gypsy orchestra. He and his fellows from the gun crew are up against the occupying Germans. Without patriotism, merely as men, they react to their masters. Some of them conspire. Death is in the air, like brick-dust in a shattered town. The emotions are as brittle as the wrecked houses, the wrecked lives, the wrecked ideas.

The art of this novel is not merely to throw light on a graveled France. It is much more to confound life itself by the device of humanizing the machines and mechanizing the people. "Her neck throbbed like an engine," but "the trucks have morose metal faces, or noses like frogs." Dr. Comfort's imagery is an excitation that never ceases, borrowing not a few new words and metaphors from science. Sand banks, for example, are like the exposed muscles of a leg, a parquet floor like the muscles of a fish, and various other things "crenated" and "particulated." The proofreading turns "blobs" into blebs of grease, and "corral" into coral, thus heightening the general excitement.

Inherent in the excitement, however, is the injury that certain members of the young generation are now sustaining and displaying. "People ask, what is the use of life to a slave? That's bilge—what's the use of freedom to a corpse?" The bitterness is only gently suggested by such sentences. The book reveals a trauma. The author is a soul in travail, hostile and aware of Society's sweeter lies. At times he is as blatantly obstinate as any man who would insist that he should be let drive on the left in New York City. But *The Power House* howls to Heaven, and you have to listen to its howling.

March 22, 1945

O. HENRY

NOT everyone realizes that O. Henry did not come to New York till he was 40 years old, and was dead eight years later, in 1910. In the neat volume that Bennett Cerf and Van H. Cartmell have put together, *Best Stories of O. Henry*, another astonishing fact is recalled; he left more than 600 complete stories. During those eight years a prodigious number were written, and he spun his substance into them. To these *Best Stories* the deft and helpful introduction hides nothing about his flight to Honduras, his return to an ill wife, and the three years at Ohio Federal Penitentiary for bank shortage. Nor do the editors make excited claims for his work. "The bulk of O. Henry's written work, truth to tell, does not measure up too well against the exacting standards of the present day," though this volume, in the editors' opinion, does show that "O. Henry, at his best, however, deserves rank with America's greatest masters of the short story."

"Rank" is an army word. In art, however, definite grades are too rigid, measuring the immeasurable. But anyone who refreshed himself with these stories, so well selected, can hardly fail to be assured again that O. Henry is a master.

He came to his fulfillment in the big city, writing for the big public. Like Maupassant and Chekhov, he set out to capture the readers, not of books, but of newspapers. He was, indeed, a newspaper man. And while he never told his story in the first paragraph but invariably began with patter and palaver, like a conjurer at a fair, it was the art of the anecdote that hooked his public. He planned, first of all, to make his theme straight and clear, as a preacher does who gives the text. Then he established his people with bold, brilliant strokes, like a great cartoonist. But the barb was always a surprise, adroitly prepared, craftily planted, and to catch him at it is an exercise for a detective.

Best Stories of O. Henry. Selected by Bennett Cerf and Van H. Cartmell. Sun Dial Press.

This method is now old-fashioned. Anyone who grows accustomed to any "modern" pose, let us say the jackknife pose in a short bathtub, such as tyranny has imposed in New York, forgets that a round tin put in front of an open fire might also fill the bill quite luxuriously. When O. Henry overworked his method, as "The Marry Month of May" in this volume shows, he could lack taste and inspiration. Having no feeling for the people in this story, he depended on his formula. But when he built back from a surprise that had gallantry and pathos in it—and he could have done it by musing on the fact that a Sarah Bernhardt went on tour after she had a wooden leg—then the formula was a help because of his peculiar endowment.

That endowment he had derived from an imagination grimly educated. O. Henry was at the other pole from the restless analyst Henry James. Only when he held forth, half waggish, half sentimental, did he write atrociously. He could call an unknown destination "the undesignated bourne," and he could call feet "walking arrangements." His was the era in which storytellers were often mock heroic, out of a jaunty, facetious self-consciousness. It was the other side of his glamour, his extraordinary power to go ahead at any risk into the most dangerous and most precious experiments.

O. Henry was a Southerner. "I desire to interpolate here," he says in "A Municipal Report," "that I am a Southerner. But I am not one by profession or trade. I eschew the string tie, the slouch hat, the Prince Albert, the number of bales of cotton destroyed by Sherman and plug chewing." Like this character of his he came from a land of defeat, and there is a note in his many Southern stories which vibrates as in nothing else, even when "a blackjack bargainer" is rather slow motion in its surprise.

He can do tobacco road characters, as in that divorce tale, "The Whirligig of Life"—"a faint protest of cheated youth unconscious of its loss"—which suspends sentimentality with a lifted hand that admits deep pathos. It was the Southerner in him who saw the charm of New York working girls, and saw the awful boardinghouse carpet that "grew in patches on the staircase." It was the Southerner who was so entirely at home outside that prudent vice, the instinct of self-preservation.

New York gave this wayfarer his chance. His life had been shattered into a kaleidoscope, and each bit seems to have been, not so much himself as one of the persons he had musingly, bitingly, lovingly, made part of himself. He was aware of multitudes, many in ironic plights and shabby circumstances. With the fashionable he was gauche. His tenderness, like Ernie Pyle's, dwelt on simpler people, the vulnerable who had a flame in them. He knew the worst, "the hideous veracity of life." He thought that "nearly everybody knows too much—oh, so much too much, of real life." But there was a mysterious elixir in "The Lost Blend." It was just water with a sparkle in it. O. Henry's blend had this simple magic in it: without it the eye cannot weep or even see.

April 21, 1945

THE GOOD GERMANS

GERMAN sentimentality has something special about it, being thicker and richer than any other. All sentimentalists have the same need, to obtain your emotions under false pretenses, but the Germans put their whole ego into their pretenses and fight for them. In this way they make exceptional trouble.

Ludwig Bemelmans, the author of half a dozen playful and whimsical books, gives an example of this in his anti-Nazi book, *The Blue Danube*. He is a disarmingly sympathetic writer and a graphic artist of high order. To bring out the subtle problem of the good German, the anti-Nazi German has chosen the smallest of the small people in the quaint town of Regensburg, which outsiders used to call Ratisbon, to show what it was like for them, as it might be for ourselves, to be up against the Nazis. It is a story to make us feel pity for the Germans, but there seems to be a fallacy in it, and it is a deep one.

The Blue Danube by Ludwig Bemelmans. Viking Press.

There is no fallacy in his showing that old Anton is good or that his sisters are saints or that young Leni is irresistible. With Mr. Bemelmans' lovable touch and his native ebullience, he gives us the idyl of that kind and jovial Germany for which he has imagined a delightful setting. A radish garden in a river is pictorial, but a radish garden in the blue Danube, with its waters overlapping to frill under an old bridge near the toy island, is in itself enchanting. These good people, ruined by the fall of the mark, make a bare pittance on their picturesque island. They belong to the old Germany, the jovial Germany. "It was," said the Bishop, "the place where the good word *Gemütlichkeit* was invented. It was a democracy, solvent, content and happy."

With this particular setting so beautifully indicated, a Regensburg that is not a great airplane factory or the site of a concentration camp, but a historic town, with its cathedral and its clock tower, and its beer garden, we naturally identify ourselves with old Anton when the local Gauleiter, "an animal with a voice," falls foul of him. The old Bavarian is doing no harm as he eats his black bread and radishes, and drinks his beer in what was once his own beer garden. When he is grossly bullied and insulted, he does what anyone might do, he hits the brute and bully. Mr. Bemelmans succeeds in making our blood boil. We, like old Anton, belong to the anti-Nazi world. Like him we listen to the clock striking, we row from the river's edge to the island where the French prisoner comes after Anton has fled, so that we wish to help them, as the prisoner does so sensitively. The Bishop comes too, to eat goose on a great occasion. And later, in spite of all, music and light fill the cathedral.

Where, then, is the fallacy? The small people of Germany, innocent of evil, were caught in a system that gave immunity to scoundrels. Mr. Bemelmans makes these small people a touching symbol of human goodness, one that has validity for millions of Americans, as was seen in *The Song of Bernadette* and in *Going My Way*. These people, like ourselves, were devoured by the disease of nazism.

The fallacy seems to lie, first of all, in suggesting that these good Germans, so jovial and so harmless, were overrun by an "enemy." The truth is, they were harmless when they should have hit hard. Harmlessness is not enough. The Nazis, as Mr. Bemelmans says himself in his last line, did not meet brave opposition. "Those within the walls who had courage and spirit were too few, too old, and much too sentimental." But further than that, it is false to push the identity beween these pious Germans and the church members of all lands. True, the Nazis insult the Bishop by calling him "Pfaff." But *Pfafferei* was attacked a hundred years ago by the best elements in Germany. "We call our society the United Free German Congregation," said a refugee from church persecution who wrote in Wisconsin in 1851, quoted in the current Wisconsin Journal. "Its purpose is to unite the foes of clericalism [*Pfafferei*], official dishonesty and hypocrisy." The church and the state were hand in hand in Germany to suppress that very democracy to which Mr. Bemelmans' Bishop so feelingly refers.

Being good nationals, the good Germans were inevitably part of a national will. It is bleating sweetness to absolve them from their part in it, since they shockingly failed to control the power that came from them. But if *The Blue Danube* makes it clear that a most appalling slavery is possible for too submissive people under national sovereignty, this may serve a good purpose. Over the murder camp at Buchenwald was the motto "My Country Right or Wrong," as was told to Lord Halifax in 1939, because Allied diplomats knew all about Buchenwald as early as 1939 and practiced hush-hush about it to appease Germany. Behind the hateful Gauleiter at Regensburg was more than Hitler—there was an international system based on appeasements, for fear of Russia. "It would have been wrong," said His Majesty's Government, "to do anything to embitter relations between the two countries" by publishing the terrible facts about Buchenwald. (White Paper, Germany, No. 2, 1939.) So, while every country was saying "My Country Right or Wrong," the good Bishop of Ratisbon just cast down his eyes and held his nose when he visited the Nazi concentration camp. Of what use, then, to talk of *Gemütlichkeit?* The "good Germans" did not make good. The only good Germans,

or good Russians or Americans, are those whose goodness
works for a world order. It works against a world order to be
sentimental about these beer-and-sausage nationalists.

April 26, 1945

ENGLISH INTERIOR

FOR the purposes of fiction there is nothing like the institution
of the family. You begin with intimacy and widen out from it.
Family life establishes and accounts for intimacy from the start.

R. C. Hutchinson knows this, and he has the additional sense
to funnel his family through a house. The house in *Interim* is
in the country, somewhere near Grasmere. It is one of those
English houses which live in wedlock with earth and sky, but
Mr. Hutchinson selects it with a disarming admission that it
is relatively shabby and commonplace. The furniture, except
for one or two precious things from China, is a job lot. Refugees, three of them, infiltrate the English family, and the
head of the house is a doctor married to an aristocrat. He is a
bit of a farmer, rather inexperienced, highly communicative
and witty, touched with arthritis, endlessly busy with chores.

Telling his story in the first person, Mr. Hutchinson begins
with a mere casual, unorganized, apparently unsuperintended
group. Their situation etches itself like frost on the window
pane, out of vapors and breath. But from our first acquaintance
with Orchilly, to which a bunch of invading soldiers comes
one midnight uninvited, the essence of the place and the quality of its people are what concern the narrator, so that when
the story begins to get going this visiting soldier is legitimately
the character on whom the relationships are precipitated. He is
a sentient visitor, and very soon the whole thing is in movement and the movement is in depth.

English writers like Kipling were masters of moral situation,
and Galsworthy learned from Turgenev how to deepen the

Interim by R. C. Hutchinson. Farrar & Rinehart.

situations that Kipling hammered out with his iron fingers. But in R. C. Hutchinson the movement and inflection retain Kipling's edge and Galsworthy's awareness of British quality with that degree of privacy, of insideness, which often became mawkish in the Anglo-Indian and Galsworthy alike. One does not like to be present when the strong, silent Englishman rolls up the asbestos curtain and shows his innards. You either have to avert your eyes or take to your knees and join him in prayer. The art of the English novel broke into the brittle laughter of Waugh and his kind because comedy seemed the only answer to these awkward intensities.

Mr. Hutchinson gets over it by adding sheer brains to edge and sensitivity, while his real drama is the deep old Anglo-Saxon one of personal dilemma. He disentangles it from sobs and theatre and removes it from Shangri-la. He uses a precision instrument, not a pie-knife, to cut under the apparent English eccentricities of his Dr. Quindle, with a wife withering like a flower in an empty vase, a daughter of 34, perchance "vain and selfish," a son who says, after words about "the melody of battle," "there's no music in any battle I've had anything to do with."

By extraordinary awareness of the living scene—the smell of a house, the struggle with chores, the weather of invalidism, the sharp idiom of long talks by the fire—Mr. Hutchinson establishes this family in its abrupt assertions of self and the bondage or harness of its loves. The wealth of emotion that he has to dispense, however, is something we earn from him penny by penny. Mr. Hutchinson can do little or nothing for those who like to climb mountains in a funicular. If you don't want to hear about a "frondose cloud" or "anchylosis," if it worries you to have big-bosomed windows called "papulous bays," if "curtilage" taxes your flittering attention and "flames inside a Matilda" bedazzle you, this is a book to return to the library. Mr. Hutchinson helps you along by cracking many a joke. "Death is the very life of undertakers." But there are no spring seats in this conveyance.

Nor do lovers me-ow and clinch. All the insupportable blows that can possibly land on the adult are here skillfully and implacably arranged for, and no favorites are played. But it says a great deal for *Interim* that the novelist's art has been so employed as to allow irony to disport itself and beauty to grow out of its horror, not the least of which is that meal after church service. "The woman I took to be our hostess gave me pink blancmange in a breakfast cup, and directly afterward I had to take potato broth from a milk-jug, using a gravy spoon."

But the best of *Interim*, among all its sufficiencies and masteries, is the flexibility of its mood, though its ultimate object is not to show flesh and blood but to dramatize the inner faith these English live by. "I wouldn't change it, no," says the doctor. "I swear I wouldn't change it. I'd rather keep the life I've had, the whole dismal procession of failures, than the triumphant life I used to dream of having."

By enabling us to hear and overhear, Mr. Hutchinson secures a self-searching England for us that lives and moves in a superb affluence as a work of art. *Interim* is a treasure. It weds rich perception to richer meaning, and never squanders a word.

May 12, 1945

FIRST NOVEL

THIS is too much. The quick pen of a publishing house says that *The House in Clewe Street* begins with the penny-pinching landlord of "a tiny village." Miss Mary Lavin's Irish novel is a remarkable one, but the most remarkable thing about it is her saturation with this so-called village. She is steeped in it like a baba au rhum. And this "tiny village," going strong since 1173, so far as its mighty buildings testify, housed persons no less famed than John Talbot, who aroused Joan of Arc, and Wellington, the trailer to Napoleon. Small indeed is the shell that held these pearls, but a great moated castle, a ruined abbey,

The House in Clewe Street by Mary Lavin. Little, Brown.

a friary from the thirteenth century, are not to be sneezed at by Boston. "A tiny village." The author herself was born in East Walpole, Mass., which is still in diapers by contrast with the castle rampart of this novel.

But Miss Lavin's counter-emigration to Ireland as a child brought with it the ache of loneliness for Massachusetts, and if she fulfills the great promise of *The House in Clewe Street*, this transplantation to the lap of Meath will long be scrutinized as a most memorable experiment. For the emotional crisscross caused by the re-export of an imported Lavin has a tantalizing richness unusual in the art of the novel.

Most novels are lit by electricity, bright, rational, social, sociological. Miss Lavin's is lighted by candles and lamps and the moon. It is as pre-sociological as a Brontë novel. There is a coldness in it that the Brontës, exiled to the wilds, were wholly incapable of. Miss Lavin does not feed on her own heart for the sustenance of her ravenous romance. But *The House in Clewe Street* achieves the triumph of disclosing the resources of a superb temperament. And a story ostensibly realistic, written to satisfy a dominating imagination, has a quality denied to all rational novels. It takes courage to spread wings and lift with them the weight of reality.

Many Irish novelists have tried to do it. *The Valley of Squinting Windows*, by Brinsley McNamara, was an attempt at it. But the oppression and compression inflicted by an old town on a nature throbbing to expand is usually embittering. The novel then becomes an indictment. In *The House in Clewe Street* Miss Lavin levels her unsparing and at times supercilious gaze on the fat and sloppy Irish matron of a hotel, on the mother of a brood that in East Walpole would be "shanty Irish," on the neat and nipping bank manager's wife, on the go-getter who means to marry the daughter, any daughter, of the local plutocrat, and on the frustrated sisters who become pious. Miss Lavin does not evade the sordidness common to all stagnant communities. Her imaginative demands are too resolute, too independent, too fortified by inner dignity, to permit either evasion or submission.

Humor of a withering detachment is her weapon, and a steely refusal to be enlisted by the community. Even the minor character who prepared her shroud and her mortuary cards is held at arm's length as comic—though it was never comic when a poet like John Donne did it.

But Miss Lavin's Irish heartlessness is not penury. She hoards her emotions to buy dreams with them, and even an unfeelingness that gives Gabriel's mother the insubstantiality of a myth comes from a preoccupation rather than a dearth of nature. What she spends on, with royal profusion and Proustian indulgence, is a succession of incomparable emotional moments for which her novel has come into being. In these moments she is a great writer, as in the twilight magic of the garden that brings together the couple who are to be Gabriel's father and mother, or in the mad race of two funerals for precedence, or in the thunderstorm that reveals to Gabriel in a grimy Kildare Street studio the animal superstition of the Tinker's daughter he has eloped with. Miss Lavin lays it on thick, just as thick as Thomas Hardy, but she does it for the same reason—to give majesty to what would otherwise be base embroilment, and thus she can re-create Stephen's Green in Dublin, that handkerchief of a park which she picks up with the tragic gesture of a Duse.

But in the novel we expect a logic of events, and it is idle to pretend that her experience of people is quite adequate to the situations which she so grandly imagines. Psychologically her makeshifts in *The House in Clewe Street* are tolerable because the texture is so rich and the power is so deep. Only a young Chopin could find music for such a love scene as that in the garden, and it scarcely matters that it is bestowed on a couple flimsily propped into place. But it is serious that no preparation is made for Gabriel's economic helplessness and Onny's moral looseness in Dublin. Gabriel, the heir to a fat property, would have been induced to borrow on it in Dublin. He would never have tried for a literary job at Onny's urging. The compulsions in a novel, as *The Old Wives' Tale* exhibited, have to be underpinned; if Miss Lavin masters this in an art so endowed as hers is, all else will be added unto her. Meanwhile *The House in Clewe Street* offers the rare delight of a proud, spirited, lovely talent coping with a theme of magnitude.

May 26, 1945

A GREAT STORYTELLER

A MOST remarkable example of the storyteller's art is to be found in *The Townsman*, by X, who uses the pen name of John Sedges. What could be more depressing to the soul on a wet day than a lower middle-class English family that lived near Blackpool eighty years ago? The thought that this family moved to Kansas after the Civil War falls on one like a ton of bricks. To make it worse, the hero of *The Townsman* is a dry schoolmaster, tight of lip, prudent in disposition and essentially a moralist. The book, in short, is the epic of a Kansan bluenose. But such is the art of fiction that a great storyteller converts this labored mud into an Odyssey. The legend of a bourgeois town on the plains of Kansas flowers so nobly that you are melted before you end.

The father of the family, a rough and blustering Englishman, has the brazen adventurousness to emigrate. For the rest of the brood it is like the pulling of wisdom teeth. Jonathan, a boy who loves his mother and is jealous of his driving father, dissolves into jelly at the first Kansan thunderstorm, so that his father clouts him to bring him to his senses. The father had preceded them to the tiny hamlet of Median, a community rooted in a sea of mud. Before these gentle English can be backed into pioneer shafts they tremble and balk like agonized animals. Most terrible for Jonathan are the frustration and laceration of his plucky little mother.

While the father's selfish recklessness and incompetence make the boy desperate for the mother he loves, she is at once alive to his yearning and truly mated to her coarse spouse.

The Townsman by John Sedges. John Day.

Their sod house is a fortress against misery, but soon she follows her sanguine man to the Golden West, leaving Jonathan
to turn the sod house into a school.

It could be incomparably dreary. But in the species of novel
that Daniel Defoe created the groundstuff is something against
which an individual, palpitant and tangible, works like the solo
instrument in a concerto. Whether the community is on a ship
or in a township it becomes the foil of the individual. The
facts may be as obdurate as a packing case, as plain as a Robinson, but out of its square, solid resistances Robinson becomes
Robinson Crusoe and a marvel is conjured that is unforgettable.
It is storytelling that moves from milk to milk punch.

So in *The Townsman*, Jonathan, terribly honest, falls in love
with an itinerant preacher's ravishing daughter, but, though he
will not "bundle" with her, she captures him forever. "You'd
say she was a good girl if somehow you could be sure she was."
And, as the author has enticed us to rely on Jonathan, because
of his feeling for his mother, we are engaged when Judy entangles his heart. A Freudian novelist would have written a
Sons and Lovers, but this novelist is in the sound pragmatic
tradition of the English novel from Defoe to Fielding, Fielding
to George Eliot, George Eliot to Pearl Buck. Jonathan strikes
up an instant friendship with a dashing young Southern lawyer,
but the violent attraction between the two men brings Judy
into play between them, and, if the staid schoolmaster wishes
Median to be a county seat, his gay friend has no scruples and
works for it as a cattle town.

By bathing us in the community of Kansas, full of strong
likes and dislikes, and love revealed in all its instinct and variety, the fertile creator of *The Townsman* never needs to ana-
lyze. It is Wordsworth, not Freud, who gives us Jonathan's
sister Ruth, "adolescent and so filled with sensitive feeling that
everything hurt her." It is this timid and hurt immigrant girl
who has to see her mother through her last childbirth when
adversity has sent her back to her honest son. And this on the
night before Jonathan's wedding!

The struggle carries from character to character as if they
were all habitants of one emotional medium in which feeling

has its liberal course like sound underseas. Each ego is self-contained, but drawing to itself the sustenance of approval and the fusion of love. And tension is redeemed by prairie idiom and dry humor. Median sees Jonathan stricken by Judy's suddenly deserting him. When she disappeared the night of the blizzard, Mrs. Drear couldn't think "she'd get to any place of sufferin' without savin' herself before she reached it." " 'Any luck?' she asked Henry. 'Nope.' 'I'll bet she ain't dead,' she retorted. He gave a slow wink with a half-frozen eyelid. 'I ain't bettin' against you.' " It is their angular daughter who worships Jonathan. She pains him when he sees the soles of her bare feet as she says her night prayers. But theirs is a marriage.

This book fearlessly denudes the lives of many people, and yet it respects them. Fresh and fecund in its invention, it gives a nimbus to one star in the Union, with Median at the center. It is American Gothic with a heart.

June 14, 1945

CONQUEST OF FEAR

PEOPLE who enjoy peace cannot imagine the war. Anyone who lives in the country, who can sit in a chair and look at a jug with peonies in it, is a million miles from hell. The red of these flowers has purple in it, and the white has a glow of pink, but the color, the odor, the shape, are less than the life in them. They are not just flowers in a room, these big pompons; they are living, with something in them that makes the heart glad.

And yet, out of a brief novel from the war, *Stronger than Fear*, by Richard Tregaskis, something that gladdens the heart in the same way can be dwelt on and contemplated. Of all the books on the war this little one comes nearest to the core of it. It comes nearest, I think, to making us feel why men back from it cannot talk about it. As a novel it is seemingly artless.

Stronger than Fear by Richard Tregaskis. Random House.

But it has enough art to make you say, "This is it," and to bring the whole thing home to you.

Unterbach is a small German town, and the Krauts have to be driven out of it. If you want to understand Paul's mood about it, get it through your stomach. No committee of loving women figured out K rations for their soldiers. "At platoon headquarters they sat down and munched K ration biscuits and a can of cheese. Of all of the K rations the cheese unit, called the supper unit, was probably the least objectionable. The meat-and-pork loaf was an abortion; the so-called ham and eggs were like a glob of oleomargarine, and the supper unit was the least undesirable. It took a hungry man to eat the orange-colored biscuits. As for the dextrose tablets which were supposed to be a dessert, Paul would have wagered that the European Continent was virtually paved with them." And "there was no hot coffee to go with the meager meal."

But if little Dolores had no hand in it, she and Suzy back in the States were much on Paul's mind, too much so. He had previously got his Purple Heart, and he wasn't tough about it, but danger was danger this cold gray morning in Unterbach; "he didn't want another Silver Star or a Congressional Medal to be sent back to Suzy Kreider, honoring Capt. Paul Kreider posthumously." Silver Star Kreider was "a different, an older and wiser Kreider, now."

Unterbach had to be taken. Colonel Tom didn't wake him up to talk about peonies. He said: "Kreider, just got orders from the boss. The boss wants us to get to Phase Line D today. . . . And listen, Kreider." This hurt. "Keep up with Company A and Company C today. Ride on your platoons. Keep 'em going, even if you have to push them yourself."

"Okay." But how okay? "Another day of ducking, sweat and noise." And right by his side Jerry Bull, the parachuter, his best friend, his hero at school. No, his conscience keeper, the eye that watches Paul and sees what's up. Unterbach is unhealthy. The Krauts are cross-stitching it with shells that come more frequently. "Paul wasn't worried—as long as the streets were quiet."

Here is the material for one of those hard-boiled, laconic

stories in which the author is God. *Stronger than Fear*
achieves no less perfect a bleakness. Unterbach is more than
Paul can bear, and there is no disguising the good reasons he
has for wanting to live and the crashing, unreasonable death all
about him. Jerry Bull sees it. He sees that Paul is afraid. Jerry
Bull "looked into Paul's eyes and saw something there which
was not pleasant." A cornered animal. He said, "You and I are
going to have a talk," and then he led the way into the front
hall of a German house.

What passed between these two in the house, as Bull
"brushed aside the plaster fragments from the top of a table,"
and as Paul sank onto a settee, makes the climax of Richard
Tregaskis' story. The long curve of fear lifts up to a point, and
nothing could have been more convincing than the means by
which Paul Kreider got there. His friend can't change the laws
of war for him. Unterbach is ominous. Suzy and Dolores are
still back home. Death is death. Within these inexorable facts
a young American for whom war was uninvited and unnatural
and distasteful recognizes that there is no escape. Not only
that, but he must not be passive. He must act. He must act
from his own center. And he must discover, that morning,
where his center is.

What is "stronger than fear"? Agree that "democracy was
an outmoded concept. Most of the boys agreed that the world
was swinging to a totalitarian economy." What was the basis
of the war, then? What, "from all this wreck and welter of
blood and misery," could a young man, only 25, discover that
would take in himself and Suzy and Dolores?

Very surely and very delicately this American war correspondent reveals the bare inwardness of a young fighting man.
Only in his own words should it be learned, but no petals of a
flower have in them a purple heart more stained with experience or a whiteness so tinged with light. This is a real book,
grimly honest, but with beauty and consolation in it. Every
trick in the hand is lost, but the game is won.

June 16, 1945

BRIGHT NEW FAITH

WHEN *Ulysses* was taken out of the black market and sold over the counter, numbers of good Catholics shook their heads. But the large process of liberalism that benefited James Joyce has in another fashion benefited Mother Church. Down in the Deep South there may still be mutterings about Romanism, but not in Hollywood, not in the magazines or bookshops. Franz Werfel, A. J. Cronin, the makers of *Going My Way*, have brought Catholicism before the wide open public on their own terms, and the public is eager for it. What used to be the most sinister and unmentionable of institutions, the dubious Lady of Babylon, is being created anew in films and novels, of which the latest is Bruce Marshall's *The World, the Flesh and Father Smith*.

The title seems to be quite brainless, though piquant. Father Smith is one of those priests whose possession of the true faith has consumed in him the substance of the ego while leaving him humble and insignificant in his own eyes, and ambitious only for God. The French have written a number of novels on these lines. For the good reason that among celibate clergy this kind of pastor, ambitious only for God, is to be found in a perfection that leaves the layman under the same spell as when he sees a milk-white hind. The specimen is not rare in literature. The authors of *My New Curate* and of *John Bull's Other Island* have observed him. But Bruce Marshall goes his own way about it, and with bells on—church bells.

Bruce Marshall proves his native hardness of head by being a chartered accountant. He also proves it by being a resounding convert to Catholicism. The ritual and the rubric which so many born Catholics take for granted are for Bruce Marshall a living language, a language of universality, a language of ineffable beauty, and instead of wooing beauty with the diffidence of a Walter Pater, Mr. Marshall comes whirling like the

The World, the Flesh and Father Smith by Bruce Marshall. Houghton Mifflin.

bagpipes and slaps beauty on the back. "Christianity is not a respectable habit of restraint," Father Smith says, "but a loud, vulgar, clamorous heroism." That is Bruce Marshall speaking, as of a Salvation Army. For while his Father Smith is sweet and selfless, no more assertive than the flame of a candle under the stars, Bruce Marshall is using him to vivify the creed he espouses and to show it as heroic.

Blithely and briskly he gives us this gentle pastor in a Scottish setting of the Church of God. This is not the tragic institution of the Grand Inquisitor, the Church of Jesuits, or even the Church of Argentina and Franco. Bruce Marshall has heard all that old stuff, but his is a young, weak, unworldly Church of the Common People, a church in a leaky fish market on which the heathens scrawl, "To hell with the Pope." It has no money to speak of. It has only the power of the word. It is threatened and spat upon. The Bishop works up from penny fares on the tram to owning an Austin Seven. But his good priests succor the weak, harbor the exiled French nuns, see old sailors into eternity after a bit of dry cleaning, take as his successor the son of a car conductor and receive into the church's lap ten thousand pounds from a movie star, the girl who always loved that same car conductor's son.

It was Father Smith who baptized these two, one a Scot and the girl an Italian. Her father runs the local cinema, and it is a pity Mr. Marshall misspells Spencer Tracy. Does he not also misremember the singer Frances White? But against the rising and falling of movie stars, against the ebb and flow of political opinion, pro-German, anti-German, pro-Mussolini, anti-Mussolini, he depicts an unchanging church, whether Father Smith is trotting around the parish or in the trenches with Archie McNab or seeing Archie on to the scaffold after his murder of the slut Annie Rooney. They sin, these Scots, and with the arrival of the Poles "the most popular of the mortal sins had increased in the diocese by 243.75 per cent." But let the people come and go, eat fish and chips in the porch of the church at midnight, and canoodle at the same time, let them come and go, the Church goes on forever. And "the big blowsy Jezebel from the docks" went with "Father Smith when he saved the sacrament from the burning church," "because she said that she would like to chum him."

Bruce Marshall slathers his book with sentimentality, and manages to make concupiscence quite vivid. His object in doing this is to spice his story. He has inserted into it a great deal about the meaning of church symbols, a great deal about the current ration points that are exacted from human nature, and a lot about limbo, unbaptized babies, the fate of the malicious sinner and the existence of hell. The book is a high-spirited one, easy to read, and calling Seraphim and Cherubim by their pet names. But as a novel *The World, the Flesh and Father Smith* is utterly synthetic. Everybody talks by the book. All the characters obey their lively prompter. Bruce Marshall invents comic cards and plays them artfully, but they are all marked cards.

June 30, 1945

REBEL GERMANS

EVEN in a land of abundance there can be shortages. It is now over a year since Mr. Alfred Neumann finished his novel, *Six of Them*, and only the paper shortage could have kept it from being printed. In one way the delay appears most unfortunate, because it seems late in the day for anyone to conjure up the horrors of Nazi domination. The immovable SS men, the sardonic examiner at police headquarters, the laconic president of the inhuman People's Court, all now have the tang that comes after the fireworks. But familiar as stale brimstone is, thanks to surfeiting news and fiction and film and radio, Mr. Neumann's novel bears on the present situation of the Germans much more than on the terror staged by the Nazis. His book is about the inner workings of the German spirit, its powers of revolt against its desecration by the Nazis, and the hard road it must travel after its vile submission. This has not suffered by delay.

Six of Them by Alfred Neumann. Macmillan.

Mr. Neumann has been audacious in this novel. He seems to have begun it after receiving the handbill "distributed by the students of the University of Munich in the spring of 1943." That handbill, written "in the manner of the liberation pyrotechnics of 1813 which so extraordinarily irritated the Olympian Goethe," was a historic act of defiance. It was "absorbed by the student body, soaked up like rain by arid earth." The principals were arrested, tried, condemned, executed. And of course they were definite persons.

What Mr. Neumann has done is to create his own persons, so far as one can see. He has kept the historic fact and then founded on it a group of Germans, the most telling and vivid possible, through whom he could show the spiritual forces alive in the German people. In the actual handbill issued after Stalingrad these rebels spoke as Europeans. "The people of Germany," they said, "are ready to end Europe's enslavement by nazism and to fight for a true and rejuvenated faith in freedom and honor." Mr. Neumann, living in Los Angeles, conceived from his own lifestuff and his own intuition the kind of Germans these men and women were.

To ask of his novel the sharp and quivering intimacy of Koestler's *Darkness at Noon* would be too much. Koestler did not have to imagine the impersonality his man was up against. The claws of that beast had been buried in his own flesh. And he could put voltage into the man he was describing, which is what a novel is best fitted to do. The more salient the precipient is, the better. Mr. Neumann could not do that, because for one thing he had chosen to have six percipients, each done from the inside.

But the laws of imagination are not codified, and Mr. Neumann has adapted a concrete event to the needs of his powerful, graphic, subtle talent. By utilizing the court procedure to allow each of the defendants to be outspoken, he has produced a conflict of spirit for which he has prepared by showing us the ironic West Prussian professor, the author of the handbill, in advance, and his devoted wife Dora, who came down at daybreak to her door to await the SS men. The sixth of the conspirators, a dark, wild young man whose father was a

drunkard and epileptic, was he a Judas? That, too, is held in
suspense until the court is in session. All this is masterfully invented, and to admirable purpose.

On the bench of the tribunal is nazidom. Mr. Neumann
shows the judges as careerist and conformist, but of many patterns, brutal or pessimist or fanatic, scarlet as sin, gray as
desperation, black as death. They should, if the professor were
right, be victims of a society. But out of them has been drawn
"intolerance, primitiveness, irresponsibility, want of dignity
and conscience, brutality, avarice, power lust and murder lust,
paganism, Satanism, megalomania, hysteria, psychopathy, sexual pathology—in short, all criminally anti-social tendencies."
And confronting this vicious tribunal, perverted through German ambition and pride, are Germans of Bremen and Ulm and
Marburg, Prussia, Bavaria.

With one voice they say "yes" to Germany's defeat in the
war. The manifesto was distilled out of these rebels, and Mr.
Neumann shows five of them at one, the bonds of love between them tenderly tightened until they vibrate with ever
increasing tension and unison. And across the strings, time and
again, draws the counter-stroke of the only one of them who
will not be beheaded.

If anyone supposes that two Germanys do not exist, this
Bitter One answers that. He deviates from the professor's faith
that "defeat must be Germany's salvation, its liberation from
the curse of having been the container of evil." The bright lad
who had scorned his father, reviled Jews as "the enemy of our
blood," been debauched by his Bannführer, and only come to
himself after mutilation in Russia, is a German saved by defeat. But Sauer's voyage is into a seventh hell, and he is not
sanguine about salvation.

Destroyed under the crass and blinding artificial light of
nazism, the six disclose fidelity to the great society. They
plead for it, not for Germany. Unable to deflect juggernaut,
they are themselves not deflected. Mr. Neumann, in a book
that probes down to German depths, sees in them true compatriots.

July 24, 1945

ACCORDING TO HOYLE

How often a young critic must have said, "Oh that the managing editor would write a book!" The managing editor has done it. It may well have taken W. P. Crozier close on twenty years to complete it. As editor of *The Manchester Guardian* between the wars he had not much time to spare. The very title of his book, *The Fates Are Laughing*, had its irony when he corrected the proofs in April, 1944. Two weeks later he parted from life as well as work, in that wistful period before a child of the imagination goes out into the world.

W. P. Crozier's imagination must have been won at school by what is known as "classical" history. For some quiet and shy boys of active and positive imagination the empire of the past is sovereign. For an English boy, a little Liberal in the Nineties, the Greek and Roman world could have been irresistible. On its outskirts, to satisfy his irony, was a twilight and barbarous Britain, with Christianity as a small, persecuted cult. In the center, a world full of action and peril, there was a drama beyond the reach of chance, sinuous and treacherous in its undercurrents, grand and terrible in its power, capable of the most sudden changes, yet peopled by godlike heroes, by massive statesmen, by pensive slaves. The Trojan horse? "Saw the horse?" as one of Mr. Crozier's characters says. "Why, I slid down the same rope as Ulysses. I saw Troy sacked. I saw Priam butchered at his own altars and Aeneas, another dear friend of mine, escaping with his old father on his shoulders." Greece lived for him. Rome captured him.

It was, one supposes, to possess again this rapture of the imagination that Mr. Crozier went back to the age of Tiberius and Caligula. He, like Anatole France before him, had seen the irony of a Pontius Pilate juxtaposed with a rebel, but he could also echo his own Publius, "Books have been the saving of me. They've been a sure refuge from the men of action who go round making a mess of the world. Yes, I know; I would have

The Fates Are Laughing by W. P. Crozier. Harcourt, Brace.

liked to be a big man of action myself—a political reformer, a
general, an orator, but I wasn't made for it." But books,
"They're always alive, always with you, so that you have
friendships that are never broken, that have no fault in them.
I couldn't tell you how many, strong and delightful have been
my friendships with famous men and women whom most people foolishly think to be dead, some of them hundreds of years
ago."

Such was Mr. Crozier's matrix, and one may be assured that
he hasn't vamped up a historical novel by filching and bluffing;
he knows all there is to know and he has savored it as fine
literature. But to bring the flush of life to a period without
falsifying it calls for true creative power. Bad as it would be
to have Tiberius smoke cigarettes and drink China tea, it is
equally bad to have him the Tiberius of the chronicles. Those
chronicles reported knaves and monsters, with a depravity of
private life and a violence in public life which affect us like
leaden loaves that have not been kneaded. Luckily we know
from our own times that the psychopaths of Rome in A.D. 33
were little different from the psychopaths of Rome and Berlin
in 1933. Gangsters cornered in the Chancellery died as Romans died. So did Mussolini. Sejanus was murdered like Hitler's
buddy in the purge. One look at Goering enables us to take
the measure of any Roman scoundrel in his length, breadth
and thickness. Hindenburg and Ludendorff sprang from legionnaires. And the legionnaires sought to murder Hitler. Any
historical novel of Rome must leave the armchair of Gibbon
and leap into the era of Dachau and Berchtesgaden.

Mr. Crozier does not do this. He adheres to the canon. That
is, to the surfaces made dear to us by schoolmasters. And for
those who have formed the habit of simulacra, with mob action
to speed the narrative, there will be pleasure in this orthodoxy.
Orthodoxy is an armchair, an excellent thing so long as there
isn't a time-bomb under it.

As for the humanizers, Mr. Crozier gives us an English miss,
impetuous and charming, a lover faithful as a Newfoundland,
"of humble birth, modest means and lack of powerful friends,"
and a cold and selfish patrician youth who endlessly pursues

the girl. The family life is Victorian in idiom. "How tiresome you are!" "Silly boy!" "I like your frock, Lollia." "Don't be ridiculous." "Hallo, what does he want here? Some mischief, I'll be bound." "Don't try my patience too far." "You've got some scurvy trick in your head." "Too late. Thyrsus has killed me."

Being feeble in invention, Mr. Crozier violates the simplest common sense. He makes the heroine personally perfidious in order to win a Jewish slave's release. Having put herself in the wrong with the villain, she then repeatedly gives him rendez-vous, while her husband has no function except to stick to her like a stamp to an envelope. Such people never were on land or sea but they throng historical novels. And yet, so pleasant is the sense that Mr. Crozier conveys of an English Liberal, to whom wisdom, moral candor, dignity and pity seem native, that one has to go on through *The Fates Are Laughing*. The English muse may be bunched in curtain hangings and still, out of those awkward draperies, the voice is sweet to the ear. Her heart hasn't been plucked along with her eyebrows.

July 26, 1945

DANISH CLASSIC

It is sad to speak of Hanna Astrup Larsen in the past tense, with her name fresh on a title page. Her translation of Blicher, coming with its striking and massive introduction by Sigrid Undset, is as good work as she ever did, and a touching final proof of her unsparing consecration to the most precious of Northern values. Miss Larsen used her life to a purpose. As an editor and writer, resolute in critical integrity, she was aware of the impregnable place that the North has secured for itself by its culture, but only devotion can carry Scandinavian cul-

Twelve Stories by Steen Steensen Blicher translated from the Danish by Hanna Astrup Larsen, with an introduction by Sigrid Undset. Princeton University Press for the American-Scandinavian Foundation.

ture into world society, and the debt that is owed to Miss Larsen is immeasurable. That her sense of values, her inner flame and her steady loyalty should have led her to communicate this culture in a Danish expression of it is, at the end, both characteristic and admirable. Blicher is worth it, but he needed her.

Blicher had genius, and how keen and bright it is, across an ocean and a century, this book reveals. National piety will revive his reputation when the centenary demands it in a couple of years—he lived from 1782 to 1848, but his edge does not require the soft and deceptive surface of a centenary. It calls for the attention to which this labor of Miss Larsen's entitles it.

Blicher happened to be a Jutland clergyman. He was no more fitted to be a clergyman than a bank president. The fact of his unsuitability, as Sigrid Undset shows in her incorrigibly honest introduction, did not rescue him from the parsonage, any more than such unsuitability rescues writers today from the newspaper office. Steen Steensen Blicher was as much caught in a class system as Jörgen in the fatal quicksand in his story "Marie," and if he were not to sink back "into the ranks of the common people" he had to wear the cloth, to serve two parishes, have a swarm of children, and a round of duties. He was so tied down that it was wholly natural for him to house his old blind father, and only once did he break so much away as to make a short trip to Sweden.

But literature is a yield from pain as well as pleasure. So warmly did Blicher love life, so eagerly did he rush to enjoy it, and so sensitively and tenderly did he respond, that the very fact of his maladjustment, his "frustration," together with his love of hunting and companionship and rum, extracted the amber that few men exude under perfect conditions in garden suburbs.

When a country parson begins to write, he is usually a slavish imitator. Blicher was slavish in one respect, he wanted every picture to tell a heartbreaking story, and he sought for bold, vivid and romantic contrasts. His native heath was as good a place for gypsies, murders, abductions and reprobates as ever was seen, and the lovelorn loom against its skies. But

Blicher, whatever his obligation to be violent in action and passion, instinctively redeemed himself by inherent fidelity to his comic spirit and his recognition of tragic reality.

Hence the tangible world with warm-blooded people in it. This is a world in which people's hearts break, but they are like people one has known. Blicher's men and women are driven by love and lust, but he never forgets the inexorable pawnbroker who holds their pledges, and when time demands the forfeit no one could be more aware of the whole transaction than Blicher. He regards it as tragically familiar, and he participates in it with an utter lack of sentimentality. This makes him as concrete as Crabbe, to whom Edmund Gosse compares him. But Blicher's colors have sun in them, and yet a fetidity. The voluptuous, the headstrong, the unfaithful—he gives them full sway, but, "Lord, how inscrutable are Thy ways!", he at once brightens the contrast, sharpens the surprise and deepens the tragedy. He is never solemn and never flippant.

Besides this, Blicher moves lightly and quickly. Out of the squalor that Sigrid Undset so rightly recalls, and a wisdom that ran ahead of conservatism, this Dane composes a succession of little masterpieces with an air of diffidence and simplicity. So he has disarmingly become a household word, and stirred many an imagination, giving poetry a local accent and homespun stockings.

Spring, 1946

LIAM O'FLAHERTY AS NOVELIST

LIAM O'FLAHERTY is now a man of 50. For over twenty years he has been an ardent and prolific writer, with a reputation in France and Russia, and with his name billed on *The Informer*, a film of the first order. His Ireland is not the sort of Ireland about which people are melting when they read *Lovely Is the Lee.* "Loathly Is the Liffey" would be much more in O'Fla-

Land by Liam O'Flaherty. Random House.

herty's style, which has been deliberately rasping from the start.

He set out, in fact, to make the bourgeois tremble in their beds, the ugly trembling for one reason and the pretty ones trembling for another. "I am a bold, bad man, I am a desperado"—that made them shiver. But, unfortunately for a man of great hallucinatory powers, the bourgeois are no longer in the state of innocence on which Edgar Allan Poe operated. Horror, torture and murder, commodities that once commanded attention because of the economy of scarcity, have in O'Flaherty's time been produced in abundance. Children learn of sadism at the knee and sup on gore as if it were milk.

In a literary situation like this, an old hand like Somerset Maugham knows what to do. If he wants to write of cannibalism he begins with something calm and reassuring, like a ham sandwich. O'Flaherty has never had such craft or such patience. His is the whirlwind approach. He is driven by his nature to shock tactics. And while his new novel, *Land*, marks a departure in theme, as *Famine* did, his old romantic philosophy of violence is beneath it. That makes him understand the Irish as part of a terrific world movement in a way that bourgeois novels, like those of Daphne du Maurier, E. Arnot-Robinson and others, entirely miss. But what makes him a literary "case" is that this very philosophy, while giving him the grim, naturalistic low-down, bars him from a full development as a novelist.

The black, passionate glower that Liam O'Flaherty reserves for civilization is no mere pose. Neither is his necessity to use novels for the purpose of exculpating or inculpating himself. He may have been shell-shocked in the First World War. He was certainly soul-shocked. But *Land* transfers that shock to the Land War in Mayo in 1879, a historic event with the obduracy of fact in it. And O'Flaherty has to distort it because he is still throwing shadows on the wall in order to terrify the timid, though in doing this, even in *Land*, he is often astonishingly powerful, having a wild force of imagination in him.

He was born, to use his own words, in extreme poverty, and

he left "the naked rocks of the Aran Islands" to battle for himself in creative literature, but also to battle with himself for breaking with tradition. That costly procedure was a preliminary to his writing at all, but it came high. "It is terrible to have lost faith," says a character in *Land*. "It is really terrible to be an educated man in our age of transition." But more terrible to be an undereducated man, pitting himself against brute conservatism.

His striking talent was seen from the first by a great connoisseur, Edward Garnett, the London critic. Garnett was a complete contrast to O'Flaherty. He was the son of a librarian, reared in the thick of books. Books twined into him like ivy into an oak, and literally bowed him. As he stood in his long overcoat his pockets bulged with manuscripts and volumes, while his weary eyes were heavy with reading. He did it for a living, but also for a generation; he and Constance Garnett injected Russian novels into the stream of English consciousness, and because O'Flaherty had a deep folk quality akin to the Russian, Garnett took hold of him. "Like a father," O'Flaherty has acknowledged touchingly, "he took me under his protection, handling me with the delicacy with which one handles a high-strung colt, which the least mistake might make unfit for racing." He was a "proud and saucy" colt, and the devil to saddle.

Short stories, however, suited his gift admirably. Charged as he was with nervous force and the life of his people, he steeped these stories in their speech and gave them the tang of personalities that he knew in and out. He loved these people, but without an atom of polite sentiment. He delightedly quivered in his sense of them. "When the fiery ecstasy was young in me," he has said in a florid phrase, "I felt I could storm the highest heavens." He did it often. His short stories include masterpieces that time will not corrode, and Aran is alive in them.

In his new novel he frequently displays the gifts exhibited in these stories. Scathing humor plays around a shopkeeper, for instance. "Too long have I been a toe-rag," he cries. "I can't help being a shopkeeper. God made me one." The rabble in a small Mayo town is harshly seen—bullied by the priest, wheedled by the sexton, bled by the shopkeepers, shoved around by the police, wooed by demagogues. He allows that if they were "free," however, they might have the poetry of religion, "the dark ecstasy by means of which the most lowly confront suffering and death with dignity."

But meanwhile, as the jilted daughter of the shopkeeper has a holy apparition, the business of freeing them falls politically to the Fenian leader, Michael O'Dwyer; to Raoul St. George, a returned Anglo-Irish aristocrat back from Paris, and to Father Kelly, an unfrocked priest. Nationalism is not the them; it is much more Nietzscheism. "The soldier, the poet and the monk must be ruthless with their own emotions and indifferent to those of others when in pursuit of their ideal." This is the philosophy of violence put into frieze. And the aristocrat has a budding daughter, Lettice, who gazes on young O'Dwyer with awe. It is not any surprise when we hear "the first tender throbbing of a young girl's heart," though the sound is unusual in O'Flaherty's fiction. Sex generally stirs in him either the infant prodigy or the juvenile delinquent.

We begin with our hero hunted by Captain Butcher and his Cuban bloodhound. Butcher is the villain, and his bloodhound is the only animal that O'Flaherty, who loves all creatures of instinct, has ever given over to be assassinated. But Michael O'Dwyer, son of Mayo shipbuilders and a man of the sea, is ready to match torture with torture and murder with murder. He stops at nothing, and O'Flaherty makes him a monolith, worshiped by Lettice with the simplicity of a girl in soap opera. Her father is equally out of the theatrical warehouse. "You know," he exclaims, "how cruel and uncompromising men of our family can be, when they feel that their authority is being flouted." Flouted it is by the icy parish priest, who dubs him Anti-Christ. As for the villain, Butcher, Raoul is final about him. "I intensely dislike that man. He has grossly insulted me. Very well! I am going to destroy him." Even in 1879 this was stilted talk. But O'Flaherty, whether contemptuous or inept, makes no effort to realize these figures as human, the central ones in conflict against the empire.

As a matter of fact, he goes far in the direction of a scenario.
All the background of Raoul's life is put into impossibly long
speeches. The focus of the novel is shifted at will, no matter
what emotion or curiosity has been incited, and little is spared
to get action.

The action is vigorous. When it comes to conspiracy, the
author of *The Informer* is violently good. He never supposes
that the land war was between sullen peasants on one side and
benign London bobbies on the other. The voluptuous girl that
O'Dwyer jilts when he falls in love with Lettice is just as
ready to betray O'Dwyer as to have visions. And O'Dwyer has
one man lashed with a cat-o'-nine-tails and another beaten to
death with a club, on the principle that a revolutionary leader
must be ruthless and indifferent. The British respond in kind.
They torture the man who wishes to decoy them, and in the
end only Lettice is saved to give birth to O'Dwyer's heir, heir
to the beauty of danger, the duty of revolution.

Land is no accident in Liam O'Flaherty's evolution as a novelist. In some ways it has a more impersonal theme and a more
concrete purpose than any of the previous ones. The germ of
O'Dwyer and Lettice is in *The Martyr*, where Tracy is a hard-
bitten soldier of class war and Kate a warm-blooded wench
swimmingly in love with him. Mad Skerrett is no less ready to
say, "I never apologized to anyone in my life, and I never
will." But when O'Dwyer utters this phrase as a young bull
might lower his head and charge, he has the civilized after-
thought that he must come to terms with Lettice's father.

Equally striking is it to recognize the most spirited passage in
O'Dwyer's fatal career, when he takes Lettice into a hurricane
out of love of danger, his frail boat leaping "the rising waves
like a hare going through the long grass." This has been trans-
ferred from *The Assassin*, where it was the intelligible day-
dream of an immature and divided personality.

Land, a national epic in fact and a revolutionary epic in intention, might have served Liam O'Flaherty to reconcile the
division that has so long dominated him. It fails to do so, not
because "the fall of feudalism" in 1879 is a meager theme. The
thinness is in O'Flaherty's philosophy. He gives a high hat and

a long cloak to heroics, in order to project a monument. But heroes who are "ruthless in their own emotions and indifferent to those of others" are tough material for a novel. They are good for a ballad, and good for a psychological novel when seen analytically. To reach the inwardness of a society in travail, however, Liam O'Flaherty is too "indifferent to the emotions of others." That makes for rant and melodrama.

May 12, 1946